PHILIP MASON

KIPLING

The Glass, The Shadow and The Fire

'And he went to a lockfast place, and took out a round-bellied bottle with a long neck; the glass of it was white like milk with changing rainbow colours in the grain. Withinsides, something obscurely moved, like a shadow and a fire.'

ROBERT LOUIS STEVENSON: *The Bottle Imp*

JONATHAN CAPE
THIRTY BEDFORD SQUARE LONDON

FIRST PUBLISHED 1975
© 1975 BY PHILIP MASON
JONATHAN CAPE LTD, 30 BEDFORD SQUARE, LONDON WC1

ISBN 0 224 01128 6

SET IN 11 PT GARAMOND 1 PT LEADED
PRINTED IN GREAT BRITAIN
BY EBENEZER BAYLIS AND SON LTD
THE TRINITY PRESS, WORCESTER, AND LONDON

Contents

PART THREE Retribution and Compassion

EPILOGUE

For

Kevin Fitzgerald

whose conversation over the years has convinced me
of the superiority of
poetic truth
to all other kinds

Foreword

The title of this book needs explanation. I had been trying for some time to find a title to distinguish it from other books about Kipling and express the essence of what I wanted to say. I wanted a phrase or series of images that would suggest something constraining or moulding the man into a shape not his own—as the social system of his day, and particularly his school and India, moulded Kipling—binding him within a surface that reflected back his immediate surroundings but beneath which something far more important was astir. I tried many phrases about masks and moulds, craters of volcanoes, crusts above glowing lava, and the like, none of which pleased me. Then I remembered this, from a tale of Robert Louis Stevenson's, *The Bottle Imp*: 'And he opened a lockfast place, and took out a round-bellied bottle with a long neck; the glass of it was white like milk, with changing rainbow colours in the grain. Withinsides, something obscurely moved, like a shadow and a fire.' If you took that bottle to the window and looked at that shining surface, you would see, coloured and distorted, the image of the window behind you and the room in which you stood and yet beneath the surface there would be the shadow and the fire. The metaphor must not be taken any further, because in Stevenson's story the imp in the bottle is very terrible indeed, while in Kipling it is what is below the surface that is best. There is a memory too in this title of George Herbert:

> A man that looks on glass
> On it may stay his eye
> Or if he pleaseth through it pass
> And then the Heaven espy.

But is another book about Kipling needed? Charles Carrington's biography (see 'Some books about Kipling', p. 328) sets out the physical facts of his life and links the events with his writings. I have hardly any information about Kipling's life which does not come from Carrington and my debt to him is enormous—not only

1*

to his book but to his letters and conversation. He has been to Burwash and Brattleboro to collect memories from whoever knew the Kiplings, he has been through the private papers, the letters and the diaries. I have quoted from him constantly and thank him warmly for all his help. Unless a previously unknown mass of correspondence becomes available, I cannot see that there is anything new to say about the physical facts of Kipling's life that is of importance. On the other hand, I often disagree with Carrington's judgment about the writings and there is always room for a fresh interpretation.

Miss J. M. S. Tompkins' book *The Art of Rudyard Kipling* is as complete for the writings as Carrington's book is for the life. It is perceptive, scholarly and thorough and my debt to her is less only than my debt to him. But she says very little about the events of Kipling's life, piously observing his own request in the verses he called 'The Appeal'.

> Seek not to question other than
> The books I leave behind.

But it is surely unreasonable to write all one's life for a wide public and still hope to remain an unknown person. And really to understand and appreciate Kipling, some knowledge of his life is necessary. There are extraordinary contradictions in him which need to be explained and resolved.

We have, then, Carrington's *Life and Work* and Tompkins' *Art*, besides quite a host of other books, of which almost all throw light on some facet of a very complex and puzzling character. Each of the two masterly books I have mentioned supplements the other, but each also needs the other, and in a sense is incomplete without it. My book, much shorter than either, assumes that the reader knows neither Carrington nor Tompkins. It tries to tell him what he needs to know about the life if he is to understand the stories, while it chooses only those stories needed to illustrate the main line of development. If, however, it should find a reader who knows both, he will find some new interpretations of some stories and a fresh account of the continuous thread which runs right through Kipling's life and leads to the last phase of his work, which I think includes his best. It is my view that these last stories show a deeper and more consistent body of belief than most people have recognized.

There is one other justification for a book of this kind. Both

Mr Carrington and Miss Tompkins assume that their readers are familiar with most of Kipling's writings. But a generation has grown up which does not know Kipling and which has a picture of him which I think is misleading. There is therefore room for a book which tries to re-awaken a lost interest, to correct ideas of him which are true of only one part of him, and to answer some of the questions which hang over his life and work. Such a book should as far as possible be self-contained. I have assumed that few readers will know, or at any rate remember, much except the two Jungle Books, *Kim*, and perhaps the stories about Puck. I have therefore usually attempted to give some idea of what the story I am looking at is about. I hope this will make the discussion more readable to the kind of reader I am aiming at and not prove too tedious to members of the Kipling Society, for whom this book is not really meant. To me, the method has proved extraordinarily valuable; whenever I have tried to summarize a story, some unexpected point has come to light. What I hope is that any reader I may find will turn to Kipling and read the best of his stories with a new interest. Some, I hope, may want to go further and will read Carrington and Tompkins as well.

My qualifications for attempting such a book are two. The less important is that for nearly twenty years I lived in India as part of the system of British rule there, and I think that I understand some aspects of it which some of the critics have missed. India, however, was only a part of Kipling's life, a formative influence certainly and a source of material. But he left India when he was twenty-four and went back for only one short visit two years later. Indeed, it is a main part of my argument that in some ways his life among the British in India retarded his development as an artist, and his best work was done when he had put it behind him.

It is therefore more to the point that I can see why people dislike him. I am not sure that either Mr Carrington or Miss Tompkins do. Both, of course, recognize that the dislike exists, but they have lived so close to him that they cannot share it. Myself, I gave Kipling unquestioning adoration as a boy, disliked him as a young man, for many years ignored him and only recently came back to re-read the stories I had known as a boy and to read for the first time the late stories, which were written after I had grown up. So the book is a personal rediscovery which takes account of the irritation which one side of him still causes me.

This, then, is not a new biography, rather an attempt to find the man through his writing, but with as much knowledge of his life as is needed to understand his work. I did not know the facts of Kipling's life when I read him so eagerly, and often uncomprehendingly, as a boy. Now that I do, I ask the reader to accompany me on a journey through his writings and life together. I have tried to display the variety of Kipling's work and its development, and to interpret both in the light of his life and the social background of his day. It is not comprehensive, but deals mainly, though not exclusively, with the stories. Verse really needs different treatment; you must see a poem as a whole, and comment therefore requires to be accompanied by an anthology. T. S. Eliot has made *A Choice of Kipling's Verse* and accompanied it by an essay; more recently, Miss Marghanita Laski has made a collection of verses for reading aloud on radio. This is surely the best method, because verse ought to be spoken aloud. The verse cannot be excluded altogether from my book, but to deal with it satisfactorily would mean another volume and would also involve questions connected with copyright. Of the stories, I have chosen those I find most interesting from the point of view of Kipling's development as a man and an artist and the questions which have to be asked about him.

There are three such questions. Why has Kipling aroused such antagonism, as well as having been so much loved, all over the world? Why is he identified almost entirely in so many people's minds with his early work, while his more mature writings are neglected? Why did he allow, side by side with his most developed work, writing to appear which — though the style proclaims them from the same pen — seem to come from a different and still immature personality? It is not merely a question of uneven quality but of different people in the same skin. Perhaps these three questions are really one. At any rate, I have found it of absorbing interest to embark on the adventure of trying to answer them. My admiration for the best has grown, while my dislike for some of the rest has not diminished.

A result I did not expect has been the growth of a missionary spirit. I find that I want to persuade people to distinguish between the stories which merely reflect back the more superficial aspects of his time and class and the deeper stories, in which there is a stirring of the spirit, something that moves obscurely, like a shadow and a fire. I find I want to convince readers that this is the real man. But I had no such intention when I started.

PART ONE
'A Strangely Clever Youth...'

I

Admiration and Dislike

1. HOW OTHERS SAW HIM

No writer has aroused such varied and contradictory opinions as Rudyard Kipling. He came to England from India in 1890 as a journalist of twenty-four who had published in India a collection of light verse and another of short stories, both of which had previously appeared in Indian papers. Two more collections were published in London and, almost overnight, his name was on everyone's lips. Some of the most exalted men in English letters hailed him as a new star; he was compared to Balzac and Dickens. But from the first there were others who found him disgusting and brutal; his was the voice of the hooligan. He was brash, brassy, cocky; he shouted too loud.

In the eighty years that followed, his books, both in verse and prose, continued to sell, not only in Britain but in the United States, in France, and more recently in the Soviet Union. And British, French and American critics have never left him alone for long. His reputation, among serious critics, fell to a low ebb in the period between the two world wars; many dismissed him as of little account and others actively disliked him. His name was associated with the least attractive aspects of a discredited cause, and in the period between the wars was usually good for a titter if it was mentioned in literary or academic circles. But he continued to write until 1932, his books still sold and there were still supporters to be reckoned with. It was in the middle of this period, in 1929, that Bonamy Dobrée wrote a perceptive critical essay which marks the beginning of a turn in the tide. In 1941 T. S. Eliot published *A Choice of Kipling's Verse* with an introductory essay in which he hailed Kipling as a bard, a ballad-maker of superb skill, making songs which express deep and often unconscious impulses. He was a 'writer impossible wholly to understand and quite impossible to belittle'. Eliot's praise provoked several replies of weight, mostly on the other side. From then on, the flow has continued; hardly a year has gone by without an article, a lecture, an inaugural address or a collection of essays on Kipling, his art or his craftsmanship, or his place in the history of ideas. But opinion is still deeply divided.

Edmund Wilson was perhaps the most formidable of those who entered the lists after Eliot. He put forward the broad proposition that Kipling's life and work fell into three periods. In the first, he was lively and enquiring, cocky no doubt, but cosmopolitan, interested in every human situation, irrespective of rank, race or nationality. In the second period, his mind closed, he reacted with hatred to whole classes of people whom he labelled with show-room tickets; he displayed his inner weakness in bluster that was often hysterical or sentimental. It was only in the third period, after the death of his son, that he emerged into compassionate understanding. This essay, though by no means favourable and sometimes positively hostile, was a step towards a more balanced appreciation of the extraordinary contradictions in Kipling's work, and I am sure Wilson was right in attaching importance to certain main crises of his life — the sense of desertion and despair to which he was exposed in early childhood; the disaster with which his attempt to settle in America ended, closely followed by the death of his elder daughter; finally his son's death in France. But his schooling, his experience in India and his marriage were also formative. And his work does not fall neatly into these periods; there is a story in *Limits and Renewals*, the last volume before his death, which is puerile and silly, perhaps the worst thing he ever did, and it is really not possible to write off everything in the middle period; *Mrs Bathurst*, technically a late story, appeared in 1904. And, considering Kipling's life and work as a whole, it seems to me that Wilson has sometimes misunderstood because he looks at Victorian England as well as at Kipling with a strong social and political bias.

Some of Kipling's defenders ignore the worst of him. They write of the compassion and wisdom he can show and forget the hysterical vindictiveness of which he was also capable, the lapses into vulgar showmanship, the mockingly demure under-statement, the knowing wink which hints at secrets he is not going to let his readers share. Those who attack him sometimes appear equally oblivious of his best work and they frequently condemn him for views which he did not hold consistently. But the problem to be explained is not that men who are writers like himself do not agree as to how he is to be rated, nor as to what was his central message, nor even as to what is his best and his worst work. The reckoning must also take account of a parallel disagreement among people who read books but are not particularly skilled at self-expression. Thousands upon thousands of children have found a pleasure in the Jungle Books and *Puck of Pook's Hill* that is deep and elemental, entirely absorbing and lasts a lifetime. Thousands of doctors, army officers, engineers, merchants, have found something to which they respond, not perhaps with such complete identification as the children, but with a fascination that makes them read and re-read. It is useless to tell them that here the characters are flat, that there the strokes of the brush are too heavy; they want these books to keep and to read again. And it is equally useless to point out his merits to those who dislike him. They cannot put their finger on what offends them, but it is there. An appraisal, if it is to be honest, must fairly take into account the faults as well as the virtues and try to explain why such strong emotions are aroused. But let us look at some of the things eminent people have said about him, for the moment with no other purpose than to show how widely they differ.

London, in 1890, was astonished. 'Towards the end of the last century,' wrote a French observer, André Chevrillon, 'the most notable event in literary history across the Channel was, undoubtedly, the sudden ascent of Rudyard Kipling. "He shot up like a rocket," an English writer told me in 1891 ... All originality achieved by laborious scholarship, all aesthetic refinements, paled before the brilliance of this art as clear and bright as the jacket of an English soldier.' Sidney Low, editor of the *St James's Gazette*, wrote:

> 'I spent an afternoon reading *Soldiers Three* and when I went out to a dinner party that evening I could talk of nothing but this marvellous youth who had dawned upon the eastern horizon. My host ... laughed at my enthusiasm which he said would hardly be justified by the appearance of another Dickens. "It may be" I answered hotly "that a greater than Dickens is here." '

Andrew Lang, in 1891, wrote: 'It is one of the surprises of literature that these tiny masterpieces in prose and verse were poured ... into the columns of Anglo-Indian journals.' Oscar Wilde thought that reading 'Plain Tales from the Hills' was like being 'seated under a palm-tree reading life by superb flashes of vulgarity ... Mr Kipling ... has seen marvellous things through key-holes and his backgrounds are real works of art.' Henry James, still in 1891, is more penetrating and more involved and it is not easy to quote from him with equal brevity. He writes of Kipling's 'freshness', because of which

> our enjoyment of him ... has both the charm of confidence and the charm of suspense. And then there is the further

charm ... that this same freshness is such a very strange affair
of its kind — so mixed and various and cynical and in certain
lights so contradictory of itself ... On the whole, he presents
himself as a strangely clever youth who has stolen the
formidable mask of maturity and rushes about making people
jump with the deep sounds, the sportive exaggerations of
tone, that issue from its painted lips. He has this mark of a
real vocation, that different spectators may like him — must
like him, I should almost say — for different things ... It is the
blessing of the art he practises that it is made up of experience
... the sum of the feeling of life as reproduced by innumerable
natures ... these elements and many more constitute a
singularly robust little literary character (our use of the
diminutive is altogether a note of endearment and enjoyment).

The affection persisted; Henry James was best man at Kipling's
wedding, and was always a personal friend. His literary judgment
became less favourable later, but that remains one of the most
perceptive comments on the young Kipling.

A different note was heard before long. Max Beerbohm was
invariably hostile; Carrington attributes to him nine caricatures,
two critical articles and 'a ferociously malevolent parody'; it was
the parody and the caricatures that did lasting harm. The best-
known of the cartoons bears the caption: 'Mr Rudyard Kipling
takes a bloomin' day aht on the blasted 'eath, along with
Britannia, 'is girl.' They have changed hats, the graceful figure of
Britannia wearing stylishly over one eye a brown billycock hat,
while Kipling, half her size, has put on her helmet and is capering
in distasteful vulgarity, a tin trumpet to his lips. The parody in
'A Christmas Garland' has an extract from *Police Station Ditties*:

> Then it's collar 'im tight
> In the name o' the Lawd
> 'Ustle 'im, shake 'im till 'e's sick
> Wot, 'e would, would 'e? Well,
> Then yer've got ter give 'im 'Ell,
> An' it's trunch, trunch, truncheon does the trick.

Equally savage was the attack by Robert Buchanan in *The Voice of
the Hooligan*. He finds in Kipling's verse: 'no glimpse anywhere of
sober and self-respecting human beings — only a wild carnival

of drunken, bragging, boasting Hooligans in red coats and sea-
men's jackets shrieking to the sound of the banjo and applauding
the English flag.' 'Of Mr Kipling, it may be said, so far at least as
his verses are concerned, that he has scarcely on any single
occasion uttered anything that does not suggest moral baseness or
hover dangerously near it.' Detestable as Buchanan found
Barrack-Room Ballads, *Stalky* was even worse.

> Only the spoiled child of an utterly brutalized public
> could possibly have written *Stalky and Co*. ... The heroes of
> this deplorable book ... join in no honest play or manly
> sports, they lounge about, they drink, they smoke, they curse
> and swear, not like boys at all but like hideous little men ...
> The vulgarity, the brutality, the savagery, reeks on every
> page.

Set against this Bonamy Dobrée's appreciative essay.

> It is really only the high finish of his art which makes him
> seem to lack subtlety ... He drives his thought to a con-
> clusion and it is only when it has reached the force of an
> intuition, of an assent in Newman's meaning of the word,
> that he clothes it in appropriate symbols. He is, one may
> perhaps claim, romantic by impulse; but then he tries his
> romance seven times in the fire of actuality, and brings it to
> the clearness of crystal.

As to his central message, Dobrée compares him with Jeremy
Taylor and quotes from Taylor a passage of which Kipling would
certainly have approved: 'Softness is for slaves and beasts ... but
the man that designs his son for noble employments ... loves to
see him pale with study, or panting with labour, hardened with
sufferance or eminent by dangers. And so God dresses us for
Heaven.' And finally, after considering those stories which are
concerned with the breaking strain, with healing and compassion,
Dobrée concludes: 'Surely these are not the words of a man who
symbolizes the literature of hate and malignity, but of one who,
for all his rough scorns and his sometimes infuriating blindness to
the other side of the question, symbolizes, rather, a profound
understanding compassion.'

In 1948, Boris Ford wrote of Kipling: 'his mind was a very
crude instrument, seldom if ever in touch with finer spiritual
issues, and in consequence his grasp on anything at all delicate has
about it the virtuosity of a Chinese juggler.' *Kim*, says the same

writer, is 'so disarmingly superficial that even its less pleasant elements ... fail to give any sharp offence.' George Orwell in 1946 begins his discussion of Kipling with the remark that: 'During five literary generations every enlightened person has despised him and at the end of that time nine-tenths of those enlightened persons are forgotten and Kipling is in some sense still there.' Orwell does not like Kipling – and particularly his political side – but he pays tribute to a clear-sightedness which the 'pansy-left' cannot claim. Kipling, he says, is *responsible* in the sense that he sees the need for administration; it does no good merely to pass laws and to suppose they will make mankind virtuous. 'It would be difficult', writes Orwell, 'to hit off the one-eyed pacifism of the English in fewer words than in (Kipling's) phrase, "making mock of uniforms that guard you while you sleep." ' And he brilliantly contrasts Tennyson's view of war with Kipling's. Which do you prefer? This:

> Forward the Light Brigade
> Was there a man dismayed?
> Not though the soldier knew
> Someone had blundered.

or this:

> And now the ugly bullets come pecking through the dust,
> And no one wants to face 'em, but every beggar must;
> So like a man in irons, which isn't glad to go,
> They moves 'em off by companies, uncommon stiff and slow. *

But in spite of his recognition of Kipling's realism, Orwell feels that 'even with his best passages, one has the sense of being seduced by something spurious'.

About the same time, Lionel Trilling recorded his early delight in the Jungle Books and 'the blessed relief' from the 'offensive pieties' of a large New York High School which he found as a boy in the 'scornful individualism' of *Stalky and Co*. But from then on his disenchantment grew and Kipling 'ceased to be the hero of life and literature and became the villain.' 'Kipling', he wrote, 'is unloved and unlovable not by reason of his beliefs but by reasons of the temperament that gave them literary expression.' But the fact remains that he *was* loved by many unenlightened persons all over the world. C. S. Lewis in 1948 wrote that he had never 'been

---

* I have slightly de-cockneyfied this verse. It is George Orwell's point that the verses are often improved by de-cockneyfication.

able to understand how a man of taste could doubt that Kipling is a very great artist.' But to read much of him produced a sense of weariness, because of 'vagueness at the centre'. Kipling, he thought, was the poet of work; he had reclaimed for literature the enormous area in men's minds taken up by the earning of daily bread. It is his creed that the job must be done well — and this is worth sacrifice. But what, asks Lewis, is the purpose of the job? And to this Kipling really provides no answer — there is 'a bleak misgiving, almost a nothingness, in the background.' He goes on to suggest that his real passion is for 'intimacy in a closed circle'. 'In the last resort, I do not think he loves professional brotherhood for the sake of work; I think he loves work for the sake of professional brotherhood.' 'But he was a very great writer.'

To many of these points we shall come back, but two in particular I must mention here. I question whether Kipling really 'drove his thought to a point'; he perceived emotional truths by intuition and expressed them vividly, but it is an essential part of my view that he did not really think things out. On the other hand, the emptiness at the centre — which was perhaps fair comment on the early Kipling — filled up as he grew older.

It is time to bring to an end this quick first glance at the diversity of some opinions. I cannot however resist contrasting with Buchanan's a quotation about *Stalky* from Stephen Marcus:

> we come to ... the secret which Kipling, like all distinguished writers about boyhood, has grasped. It is that boys live a life which is passionately moral. Half of the intensity, difficulty and refractoriness of boys may be traced to the fact that their passionate moral demands on life seem in the sad course of things bound to be frustrated and betrayed ... boys are ... religious fanatics for justice and the last true believers in the divinity of law. Boys slavishly worship tradition, blindly reverence ritual ... every liberal or radical has within him a boy who once found out that 'they' were telling him lies, who discovered hypocrisy, sloth and double-dealing in his elders and superiors ...

Let us, for a moment, end with T. S. Eliot, who, after setting off these fireworks by his championship of Kipling's verse in 1941, returned impenitent to the theme in 1959. He was proposing the toast of 'The Unfading Genius of Rudyard Kipling'. 'What is one to say, in a few minutes,' he said, 'about the amazing man of genius, every single piece of writing of whom, taken in isolation, can look like a brilliant *tour de force*, but whose work has nevertheless an undeniable unity?' He goes on to select, from half a dozen lines of thought he might develop, Kipling the Seer and Kipling the Moralist. And he makes the point, which surely no one will question, that Kipling was an intuitive, not an intellectual, and for that reason underrated by intellectuals who are not intuitives.

2. A PERSONAL REDISCOVERY

That brief selection is in no way complete, and in particular stops short of some important studies of the last ten years. Except perhaps in Buchanan's case, the quotations do not do justice to the depth of the criticism, but they do illustrate the range of opinion. It is time to state my own position. My copy of the *Just-So Stories* bears the date of my fourth birthday; *The Jungle Book* came for the Christmas of the same year, before I was five. They must have been read aloud to me at first, but I was soon reading them to myself and, on one of those long, long summer mornings before the grown-ups would let one get up, I remember vividly the sensation of pure delight at starting to read 'Mowgli's Brothers' for the fourth or fifth time. It was like coming home to a world in which one was sure of complete escape and complete enjoyment. By the time I was fourteen, I was an idolatrous Kipling fan and had read, often without understanding it, practically everything he had then written; I had identified myself in turn with Mowgli, Kim and Beetle. But by the time I left school for a university, I disliked what I thought Kipling stood for and found many of his mannerisms irritating. Something remained — fragments of verse, odd scenes, glimpses and scents of the bazaars and the Grand Trunk Road from Kim — and it was these which sent me to India. But I did not read Kipling when I was in India. I hardly looked at him again until I began to read the Jungle Books to my own children. I found they had much of their old spell. The child playing with pebbles in the moonlight while the wolves come one by one to sniff at him; Bagheera the black panther lying on the string bed in Messua's hut and yawning in the faces of the terrified villagers — these are unforgettable. When I began to re-explore the stories meant for grown people, I became aware of something rather curious. There was a good deal more than I had supposed in stories I had always liked but had taken simply at their face value; the mere force of the narrative had carried me through the tale and I had hardly been aware of deeper implications. But there were others in which I was repelled by some stroke that seemed self-conscious and misplaced, sometimes cruel, sometimes vindictive or callous, but most often merely tasteless because it seemed to be intrusive, trying to make a point, or simply, in his own phrase, showing off. Coming back to Conrad or Hardy, contemporaries of Kipling, whom I had read when a little older, I found neither the entirely new dimension nor the repulsion.

Take, as an example of the gain, an early story, 'Without Benefit of Clergy', written in June 1890. It seems, at first, a simple love story. Holden, a young English civil servant, has a bungalow in the 'civil lines' — that is, at some distance from the Indian city. Here he lives a bachelor's life with his own establishment of Indian servants — a chilly impersonal existence, varied only by visits to the club to play snooker or pool, a place where men call him by his surname and would hardly know he had gone if he died in the night. But, in the city, he has taken a house where he has placed a Muslim girl, Ameera, with her disagreeable and mercenary old mother and an old manservant Pir Khan to protect them. 'When the big wooden gate was bolted behind him he was king in his own territory, with Ameera for queen.' 'She was all but all the world in his eyes' and in her eyes he *was* all the world without that qualification. The story is simple enough; when it opens, a child is coming and Holden is inclined to resent the intrusion on their happiness, while Ameera is delighted because his love 'will be held fast by a baby's hands'. When the child is born, it comes about as she had hoped and they are drawn still closer in wondering adoration. But Tota dies; 'the life was shaken out of him by fever — the seasonal autumn fever. It seemed altogether impossible that he could die and neither Ameera nor Holden at first believed the evidence of the little body on the bedstead.' The numbness begins to go and they begin to learn to live again and Holden tells Ameera: 'I love more because a new bond has come out of the sorrow we have eaten together.' But famine comes and cholera; Holden is officially ordered 'to keep himself in readiness to move' to replace the next man who should fall. 'There were twelve hours in each day when he could not see Ameera and she might die in three ... He was absolutely certain that her death would be demanded — so certain that when he looked up from the telegram and saw Pir Khan breathless in the doorway, he laughed aloud.' Ameera's last words, breathed into his ear, are: 'I bear witness that there is no God but — thee, beloved!' The furniture is disposed of and the house begins to crumble in the monsoon rain as though it had been 'untenanted for thirty years instead of three days'. And then it is decided to pull it down and sell the timber and build a road across the site, 'so that no man may say where this house stood'.

I did not read this story between the ages of 14 and 40. The loss of a child and of a dearly loved woman cannot mean the same to a boy and to a man, but it would be quite wrong to suppose that an adolescent as old as Romeo's Juliet cannot be moved by this kind of sorrow. I understood too that the secrecy added to the poignancy; Holden could not speak to his own kind of what had happened. The joy when Tota was born, the sorrow when he died, had to be harshly repressed. I did not identify with Holden, but I did think I knew how Holden felt when he left Ameera and went back to the club, full of men who made fun of his work. The contrast between a world of love and an unloving world of work was something that hit me three times a year when I went back to boarding-school. The atmosphere of doom — of death from cholera or 'fever' always waiting to strike — pervades many of these early Kipling stories, and this I had almost come to take for granted. What I did not pay much attention to was the attitude with which these star-crossed lovers faced the universe. Ameera prayed for a man-child and sent gifts to Sheikh Badl's shrine, and she knew God would give them a son. But Holden, sent away on duty at the critical time, was so sure she would die in childbirth that he wrote out the telegram to himself announcing her death, and gave it to Pir Khan to send him if it should befall. He left her 'with the sensations of a man who has attended his own funeral'. When he came back to find the boy born — and the helpless little hand had closed feebly on his finger and the clutch had 'run through his body till it settled about his heart' — Pir Khan suggested that he should sacrifice two goats, because life must be given when life comes into the world.* Holden, 'hardly

---

* Pir Khan instructs him to kill the goats by beheading. This is the method of slaughter used by Sikhs and Gurkhas; a good Muslim, like a Jew, should cut the throat and let the life run out with the blood. In the United Provinces, Muslims insisted that their meat must be *halāl*; perhaps they were more careless in the Punjab. But I think Kipling simply chose the method that was more dramatic.

knowing what he did', muttered a Muslim prayer as he killed the goats: 'Almighty! In place of this my son, I offer life for life, blood for blood, head for head, bone for bone, skin for skin.' Later on, after the child's death, when 'they touched happiness again, but this time with caution', Ameera is sure that it was because they had loved Tota too much that he had died. They must now 'go softly underneath the stars, lest God find us out.' But the Powers were busy on other things and the cholera came. Holden tried to send Ameera to the hills but she would not go. She stayed and again they were happy, with a special happiness 'snatched under the shadow of the sword'. Now they called each other openly 'by every pet name that could move the wrath of the gods'.

Nor did I as a boy perceive the irony of the title. If I thought of it at all, I took it to mean that Holden and Ameera were not married. Probably that is what Kipling supposed most of his readers would think at first reading. But he must also have hoped for a more perceptive audience who would remember that 'benefit of clergy' meant the exemption of ecclesiastics from the King's courts of justice—the question on which Thomas à Beckett and Henry II finally split. And here in this story it means, surely, that no one can claim exemption from the apparently arbitrary strokes which crush human happiness. 'The President of the Immortals ... ' another was to write, 'had ended his sport with Tess'; while that phrase might be said to summarize Hardy's view of life, Kipling, less concentrated and integrated a character, came back to that note only occasionally. But he did return to it, notably and with greater maturity, in 'The Wish House' and the poem that accompanies it, 'Late Came the God'.

'Without Benefit' was written when Kipling was twenty-five. It seems to me artistically of a very high order. Somehow, with extraordinary skill, Kipling can wring the heart by a simple touch describing something of almost universal human experience. Ameera is telling Holden of how Tota had 'swayed on both feet for the space of three breaths'. 'And they were long breaths, for my heart stood still with delight,' said Ameera. Ameera herself is drawn with firm delicate strokes; the relation between the lovers develops; Tota, in the brief space allowed him, asserts his dawning personality. The story is complete in itself and stands against a metaphysical background that is complete. Nothing moves the Powers, neither Ameera's gifts nor Holden's despairing certainty of disaster; nor does anything avail in that impersonal world of the Club and the English who build canals and try to check famine. It is only dirt playing with dirt, as one of the Hindu gods says in 'The Bridge Builders', and as Mrs Mallowe, Mrs Hauksbee's wise mentor, also says. This is not at all the doctrine of Empire usually attributed to Kipling. Certainly at fourteen I did not perceive that, at the back of all this admiration for hard work and self-sacrifice and the team spirit, there was another more shadowy figure, laying her skinny finger on her choppy lips — pointing out that it was all in vain, India would go on unchanged. But it was right, none the less, to endure stoically and carry out honestly the appointed task. And perhaps work might dull the pain.

One critic, Dr Elliott Gilbert, has written at length, and often perceptively, about this story, but he is profoundly wrong in describing it as 'a farewell to ritual'. What he means is that neither Ameera's offerings at the shrine nor Holden's due observance of the routine of the Club, of the European life of the station, nor even his crop reports and census returns, were of any avail to deter the gods. But there is a distinction between ritual and magic. Kipling did not believe that 'the gods' — a term he used ironically and often varied by 'Allah' — could be moved, still less compelled, by magic formulas. But he did profoundly believe in ritual — the performance as a discipline of certain acts which are socially acceptable and which have also a symbolic significance. Masonic ritual appealed to him; keeping things clean and bright; the craftsman's care of his tools; what he called 'soul-cleansing routine'. And the value of ritual or routine at a time of loss is a point to which he often returns.

That tale is one example of the rewarding second look. In some of the stories the longer you look and the deeper you ponder, the more there is. But — still on this voyage of rediscovery — there are the other occasions where I am conscious of a faint nausea. This happens most often when Kipling himself intrudes in the first person. Sometimes he seems to be trying to push his way into an inner circle to which he does not really belong, or hinting that he *does* belong to an inner circle to which the reader cannot hope for admission. And to that doubt may be added a suspicion that he probably does not really belong to it himself. I began to feel, as I read these tales again after long abstinence, that in Kipling there were a number of elements that had never been reconciled with each other nor even held in healthy tension within a mature personality.

André Maurois said of Kipling that his real significance lay in the fact that 'he has a permanent natural contact with the oldest and deepest layers of human consciousness'. This deep archetypal element welled—I suggest—intermittently to the surface; it provided and helped to mould the material for much of his best work. The contrast between the world of love and the world of work comes surely from such a level, the love in the story we have just looked at, the joy in the child, also the contrast between traditional man who tries to propitiate the gods, modern man who is certain of disaster, and the dark impersonal Powers who disregard both and strike, apparently at random. But there were other moulding forces and material from other levels too. Think of any other writer of this period—Hardy, Conrad, Wells, Shaw, George Moore, Stevenson—and one is aware of a background—that of Polish sea-captain, Dorset countryman, son of the manse, or whatever it may be—and a consistent outlook on the English social scene. Henry James looked at London high society as an American, Wilde from within it—if only just. But Kipling alone has a peculiar ambivalence to a special product of the age, the imperial administrative class which developed to meet the needs of the Empire and to provide which the public schools evolved. Kipling did not belong to this class by family tradition but he went to a school which existed solely to train boys for this purpose. He was himself never a candidate for the imperial class—partly because of his extremely short sight, partly from temperament and family tradition—yet he could never reconcile himself to his exclusion. Side by side with emotions from André Maurois' 'deep levels' there presented themselves to his mind yarns told him by subalterns in the army, memories of his schooldays, incidents of the training and achievements of the imperial class. And on material from these two quite different levels, the craftsman was constantly at work.

He looked always and everywhere for material, and consciously stored it until he could put it to dramatic use. He played the sedulous jackdaw, picking up here one brightly coloured pebble, there another, storing them away and eventually bringing two or three together into one story. Material on that level might be no more than a phrase heard in a bar describing a woman six thousand miles away; it might be the picture of a sentry, 'the night dew gemming his moustache, leaning on his rifle at picket, lonely as Prometheus on his rock, with I know not what vultures tearing at his liver'. It might be a few lines of verse carved on a monument a hundred years ago. The craftsman's mind was always at work on these fragments, turning them over, polishing and selecting. But behind the craftsman, jostling for control, stood a strange group of figures, as odd as any ever assembled in fiction, archetypes of the collective unconscious plucking at the sleeve of a variety of Kiplings, each of whom has put on a special mask for the occasion. There is Kipling the confidant of soldiers and sailors; Kipling the tramp of the seven seas, delightedly observing and admiring but never praising or blaming; Kipling the national prophet thundering out biblical anapaests in the manner of his two Methodist grandfathers; Kipling the literary man who wants you to know that he has read strange books about herbs and astronomy; Kipling the inquisitive boy who had always got into trouble for showing off and could never quite get out of the habit. He had been a journalist, and to get his stories he had been used to listen, to agree, to lead the speaker on, to shape himself for the moment to the other man's mood. It was an essential technique for assembling material—but its effect often lingered on when he came to write his story. His biographer Charles Carrington notes: 'he had a strange tendency, when writing an intimate letter to a dear friend, to vary his handwriting and to imitate the script of the person he was writing to.' And when he came to tell the story he had heard in the mess or the smoking-room, he would not only, and quite justifiably, use that tone when speaking in the voice of the narrator, but in his own voice too when speaking to the reader. So we hear a variety of voices, not only of Mowgli or Mulvaney or the Lama, but of Kipling himself speaking from many different strata of the conscious and the subconscious man. Sometimes he is tender and compassionate; sometimes he is strident and vulgar; sometimes he is brutal; sometimes he probes the sources of pain with fascinated horror; sometimes he sounds a sudden trumpet. He writes of the people of India sometimes with a rare understanding, sometimes with a crusty, stereotyped contempt. Some of the reasons for this varied ambivalence will become clearer if set against the background of his life.

PART ONE
'A Strangely Clever Youth...'

2

The First Years

I. THE HOUSE OF DESOLATION

Kipling was born at Bombay on December 30th, 1865; his parents
had been married in London on March 18th of the same year. He
has sketched, very slightly, what he remembers of his own early
days, and in several stories has said something of the life of British
children in Victorian India. And, of course, there are plenty of
memoirs to supplement his pictures; indeed, in essentials, there
had not been much change by the 1930s when I was in India
myself.

It all seems very strange to their descendants in the 1970s, who
are accustomed to a far closer and more personal contact between
parents and children than was usual in Victorian or Edwardian
times, at least among the professional classes. The difference a
hundred years ago between Britain and India was much less than
this difference between generations, which has arisen in the course
of my lifetime. In Victorian Britain and India the treatment of
children was based on reliable servants and on the principle that
parents should be rather remote figures. The father was a pro-
tector against the unknown and a court of appeal rather than
policeman and immediate dispenser of justice; the mother might
be a source of love but was not usually the close companion of
today; more often a beautiful vision, dressed for a dinner or a ball,
pausing as she floated out to a carriage. Parents did not need to
scold or nag, or even, very often, to say no. The scolding and nag-
ging were done for them. Children would sometimes feel that they
shared with the servants a secret life from which the parents were
excluded. Sometimes on the other hand they realized that they and
their parents were part of a community to which the servants
could never belong. And again there were times when the children
saw a world of children and over against it a quite alien world of
grown-ups. But for most of the time it was children and servants
who made the reality, with parents in the distance.

This was common to Britain and India. The difference was that,
in India, the servants were much more indulgent. The *ayah* was
usually gentle and affectionate; the strictness of the English nanny
was unknown and no *ayah* dominated the child's life as the nanny
so often did. There were men-servants with very little to do who
delighted in playing with children; they would turn themselves
into slaves, patient, obedient, ironic, and watchful. Kipling
describes the relationship several times and comes back to it in

'The Debt', a tale in the last collection he published. Here there is an added twist; six-year-old William has been left in charge of convict One Three Two, judged guilty of murder because he had made the mistake of killing a kinsman on the wrong side of the British frontier. William gave orders and the grizzled old soldier would obey, using only a gentle but inexhaustible tact to keep the tyrant away from the deep brick-lined well and safe from snakes. In such a world the child's will would not be directly crossed; it was in such a world that Kipling lived until he was five. When he went into the drawing-room, the servants used to remind him to speak English to Papa and Mamma.

By English standards, Kipling was a spoilt child when he was left in England just before he was six years old. He was talkative and untidy, incessantly asking questions and expressing his opinions without hesitation. His mother was by all accounts a charming, witty and beautiful woman; she was the eldest of five sisters of whom two married the painters Burne-Jones and Poynter, while a third was the mother of Stanley Baldwin, who was later to be Prime Minister. The painters both belonged to the group called the Pre-Raphaelite Brotherhood, whose clear colours and meticulous detail were to dominate the artistic world in Britain for a generation. Both were beginning to be successful. Alice Kipling had made what at the time must have seemed the worst match of the four. Perhaps it was because the Kiplings did not want to be beholden to their more prosperous relations, perhaps something had been hinted about Rudyard's undisciplined behaviour; whatever the reason, he and his sister, aged only three, instead of being trusted to aunts, were left in a lodging-house at Southsea with a couple who advertised their readiness to look after the children of parents in India. The parents slipped away secretly. The children had not been warned. Rudyard and his sister were there five years before they saw their father and mother again.

Twenty years later Kipling wrote a story, 'Baa Baa, Black Sheep' (1888), which was based on these years. The opening of his unsuccessful novel, *The Light that Failed* (1890), clearly refers to the same experience; in his last years, he returned to it and wrote a brief account in *Something of Myself* (1937). And his sister has also described it. 'Baa Baa, Black Sheep' is fiction and one would expect the colours to be heightened for dramatic effect; in *The Light that Failed*, several changes have been made; the girl who

shares the experience is not a sister, because for the purpose of
that story she has to be the hero's first and only love. Men's
memories often play them false and Carrington has shown that
Something of Myself is inaccurate in several respects. But when all
that has been said, I do not doubt that 'Baa Baa, Black Sheep'
represents substantially what Kipling thought happened to him at
Southsea. Perhaps every incident was not police-court truth that
can be sworn to, but the whole is poetic truth and represents what
he came later to feel had happened.

As a child I found this story almost unbearable, yet was drawn
back to it with fascinated horror. The husband was a naval
pensioner who had been wounded at Navarino; he was a quiet,
retiring man, and it was his wife, Aunty Rosa in the story, who
ruled the household. She was a narrow Evangelical with a strong
sense of hell-fire. She made a favourite of Judy, the little girl — she
had one son, but no daughter of her own; Punch, the little boy,
she seems from the first to have regarded with dislike. He
sprawled on sofas and asked questions and she snubbed and dis-
couraged him. Deserted by his parents, he felt lost and of no
account. She taught him to read, in a meaningless mechanical way.
'Why does AB mean ab?' 'Because I tell you it does.' But suddenly
he found he *could* read and that the written word meant something;
reading gave him the one pleasure earth could still afford. There
was a rain of questions she could not answer and he was accused of
showing off. She hated him to find pleasure in reading because she
was incapable of it herself; to her it was always showing off. A
new weapon was added to her armament; she forbade him to read
and ordered him instead to 'play'. He devised a way of rocking a
table on three bricks so that it sounded like 'playing' and left him
free to read; she caught him and beat him for 'acting a lie'.

The misery mounts. Aunty Rosa's husband had liked Punch
and tried to protect him, at least against his son; he died. Now
there was nothing to check the rule of the Woman, as Kipling
came later to call her, and she encouraged her son to despise and
torture Punch. They would cross-question him about some trivial
act until he was trapped into an inconsistency and then he would
be beaten for lying. He was sent through the streets to school with
the placard 'LIAR' on his back. He was called Black Sheep,
isolated from his sister, lectured, prayed over, suspected, driven to
more deception, found out and punished again in a terrible spiral.
He begins to go blind, is frightened of strange flapping things he

can only half see, blunders into things and breaks them and is punished again for that. Salvation comes after five years; his mother comes to carry him away, loving, understanding and indulgent. But when she came to kiss him good night, Punch flung up his arm to ward off a blow. She would have heard how wicked he had become. She too would be against him now. She could only have come to beat him.

Perhaps Rudyard did not do that; he said he did, in *Something of Myself*, but perhaps he added it to the story to sharpen the dreadful expectation that Punch's mother would have gone over to Aunty Rosa's side. He certainly came to believe in old age that it was what he had actually done himself. Perhaps he did not really try to kill Aunty Rosa, as Punch did. Perhaps he was not really sent through the streets with a placard on his back but borrowed the idea from *David Copperfield*. But he thought these things had happened to him and they influenced him. Whatever the truth about that gesture, it may stand for a defensiveness that constantly recurs in Kipling's early work. And in that bitter and vivid story, there are two key passages which must be taken into account in any reckoning of his life. The first occurs after Punch and Judy realize that they have been left at 'The House of Desolation', as Kipling came later to call it.

'When a matured man finds that he has been deserted by Providence, deprived of his God, and cast without help, comfort, or sympathy, upon a world which is new and strange to him, his despair, which may find expression in evil living, the writing of his experiences or the more satisfactory diversion of suicide, is generally supposed to be impressive. A child, under exactly similar circumstances as far as its knowledge goes, cannot very well curse God and die. It howls till its nose is red, its eyes are sore and its head aches ...'

That is the impact of desertion. And at the end, Punch says to Judy: 'We are just as much Mother's as if she had never gone.' 'Not altogether, O Punch,' is the comment of the writer, 'for when young lips have drunk deep of the bitter waters of Hate, Suspicion and Despair, all the Love in the world will not wholly take away that knowledge ... '

There is also a comment on the experience in *Something of Myself*. 'These things ... ,' Kipling wrote, 'drained me of any capacity for real personal hate for the rest of my days.' On this

Edmund Wilson wrote one sentence in a paragraph all to itself: 'And actually the whole work of Kipling's life is to be shot through with hatred.'

Both judgments are over-stated. 'Real personal hate' is not of course the same thing as 'hatred'. Of the fact of hatred, Kipling was certainly always aware; indeed, that awareness *is* like a secondary colour in shot silk in much of his work. Hatred is strong, for instance, in the Mowgli stories – hate for Shere Khan the tiger, hate for the villagers who cast Mowgli out, hate for the wolf-pack who rejected the old grey wolf who had been the leader. Sometimes Kipling himself gave way to hate which seems far beyond anything the occasion demands, as in 'The Rhyme of the Three Captains'. The creator of Mary Postgate understood hate in a very unusual degree. But Edmund Wilson does not quote the sentences which follow immediately on Kipling's assertion. 'So close must any life-filling passion lie to its opposite,' he goes on. ' "Who, having known the Diamond, will concern himself with glass?" ' That relationship of love and hate is all-important to consideration of the later stories. Here it is enough to say that some of them, notably 'The Gardener' and 'The Wish House', *are* drained clean of hate and filled with compassion.

There are mysteries about this stay in Southsea. The children went once a year to stay with their Burne-Jones aunt – 'The Beloved Aunt'. How is it that she had no inkling of what was going on? Still more significant, how was it that, after the rescue, Alice Kipling allowed her daughter to go back to the House of Desolation for two more years? Children do find it difficult to express what concerns them most deeply; they avoid talking of wounds and humiliation and of so deep a shock as desertion. And to that instinctive dislike of exploring a hurt may be added a very reasonable calculation – hardly explicit but made in the computer-like recesses of the personality – that during a temporary interlude it is dangerous to complain against the permanent rulers of one's life. In the story, it is not suggested that Punch told even his mother all that had happened. Indeed, she was clearly puzzled. And Punch is represented as being outwardly a very resilient little boy. Charles Carrington thinks that the account in 'Baa Baa, Black Sheep' is greatly exaggerated and that Kipling's extreme horror at the place is due mainly to what happened in his last months there when he was getting more and more blind. But very little – much less than occurs in the tale – is enough to make a child feel slighted and unloved. What is important from the point of view of Kipling's development is tolerably certain. Whatever may actually have happened, the boy felt that he had been deserted by his parents and that he had been humiliated and ill-treated by a woman he despised and whom he came to hate.

Those holidays were bliss. Everyone was kind; no one pelted him with sharp words and made him feel that he was despised. Famous people came to the house—Robert Browning, William Morris—men happy in their work as artists and writers, successful and confident, laughing easily. They did not talk about hell-fire and punishment and wickedness but about beautiful pictures and Norse sagas. 'But on a certain day—one tried to fend off the thought of it—the delicious dream would end'—so he wrote in *Something of Myself*—'and one would return to the House of Desolation, and for the next two or three mornings there cry on waking up. Hence more punishments and cross-examinations.'

2. FLAGRANT INJUSTICE

In 1878, when he was twelve, Kipling went to school at the United Service College at Westward Ho! in Devon. This was a deeply formative stage of his life. The school had been founded only four years before by a group of army officers, who had recently been confronted by the fact that their sons would have to pass a competitive examination if they were to get into the service. The existing public schools were not only themselves expensive but often could not get a boy through the examination without a year at a crammer, which was more expensive still. Fees at Haileybury in 1874 (says Janet Adam Smith) were £24.10.0 a term, but a London crammer might charge £300 a year. The headmaster—Cormell Price—had been at Haileybury, where he had been unusually successful at getting boys through examinations in modern-side subjects. He had to start from scratch; it had to be a cheap school and it had to be successful. The masters were, therefore, as Carrington says, rather a job lot, and there was also the problem of getting some older boys and establishing a flow. Price brought with him some boys from Haileybury, accepted some difficult cases from other schools and some 'crammers' pups'—that is, boys who had left school and gone to a crammer and were now moved to Westward Ho! He could not afford to pick and choose and the senior boys too must have been a job lot.

There are three accounts of Kipling's schooldays at Westward
Ho! which purport to be fact. One is his own, in *Something of
Myself*, and there are two by his school friends, 'Stalky' and
'M'Turk'. They differ from each other and also from the avowed
fiction of *Stalky and Co.* (1899). Stalky—his real name was
Dunsterville—points out that the memories of 'old gentlemen'
over sixty are unreliable and says that Beresford's book—
Beresford was M'Turk—contains perhaps as much imagina-
tion as Kipling's: 'what he gives us is what Beresford thinks
Kipling would have thought if he had thought as Beresford
thought.' But there is a good deal in common between all four
sources.

Cormell Price was not at all what might have been expected as
headmaster of a glorified cramming shop for the army. He was a
close friend of several of the Pre-Raphaelite brotherhood, including Burne-Jones, Morris and Poynter, and his friends included
Swinburne and Browning. He had tried several means of earning
his living before discovering his *métier* of getting boys through
exams; he had been a medical student and later a tutor in a
Russian noble family. He admired French and Russian literature.
He was something of a radical and, just before Kipling's first
term, he had helped to organize a 'Workmen's Neutrality Demon-
stration' which was aimed at Disraeli's policy of intervention in
the Russo-Turkish war—the war when Government supporters
were singing: We don't want to fight But By jingo! if we do ... '
In the holidays, he was 'Uncle Crom' to Kipling and his sister and
their Burne-Jones cousins.

Kipling was therefore on firmer ground at Westward Ho! than
he had been at Southsea. He wrote miserable tear-stained letters
to his mother in his first term, but a good many small boys have
done that. Beresford remembers him as a 'a cheery, capering
podgy little fellow' or as 'a smile with a small boy behind it'. But
Beresford's whole account is milder than we should have supposed from *Stalky and Co.* He says the worst bullying was over
before he and Kipling arrived, though Stalky, who was there two
years earlier, had come in for a good deal of it. Beresford describes
a school in which, by the time they left, Kipling's moral influence
was strong; boys by this time admired the 'knightly type' who
would simply be bored by doing anything so stupid as bullying,
and they had come to esteem brains as no less important than
games. This is hard to swallow. It is not only unlike all one has

heard of other Victorian schools but it does not sound at all like what either Kipling or Dunsterville describe.

Dunsterville writes of his own early days:

> In addition to the blows and kicks that inevitably accompanied the bullying, I suffered a good deal from the canes of the masters or the ground-ash sticks of the prefects. I must have been perpetually black and blue ... Kicks and blows I minded little but the moral effect was depressing. Like a hunted animal I had to keep all my senses perpetually on the alert ... good training in a way but likely to injure permanently a not very robust temperament. I was robust enough, I am glad to say, and possibly benefited by the treatment.

That was the standard Victorian view. Cormell Price—who appears from the accounts of the other two much less in control than the far-sighted demi-god of *Stalky and Co.*—must to some extent have shared it, and he usually left things alone unless he saw very strong grounds for interfering. He is represented in one story as pointing out the 'flagrant injustice' of the punishment he is inflicting—but it is training for life. A little injustice is what we must learn to accept. But even he would surely have objected to one practice mentioned by Dunsterville. 'One amusement for elder boys was to hold the little ones out of top-storey windows by their ankles. As the buildings were five stories high, this was rather a terrifying performance.' Kipling in *Something of Myself* says that he was bullied in his first year and a half, but that it stopped when he grew stronger and had friends.

This is the background to one story, 'The Moral Reformers', which is important for the light it throws on Kipling, but which also suggests that Beresford had idealized a good deal. The chaplain of their later days was a broad-minded easy-going man who had the boys' confidence more than anyone else except the Head. In 'The Moral Reformers' he suggests that the Three, Stalky, M'Turk and Beetle, have a good deal more influence than they know and that they might be able to help him in something which is worrying him. He has noticed that a certain small boy is miserable and suspects he is being systematically bullied. But he can't prove anything and there is nothing he can do—will they help? The Three had not noticed, but they will do what they can. They find out that the culprits are not, as they had expected, a mob of slightly larger boys, but two 'crammer's pups'—older than

themselves—who are systematically torturing the victim in their
study. Stalky devises a characteristic plan; he pretends that he has
quarrelled with Beetle and has him 'trussed for cockfighting'—
that is, hands tied below the knees. M'Turk is similarly tied, but
won't 'go for Beetle properly', so Stalky has to hit them both with
a cricket stump. Beetle pretends to weep; they make a good deal
of noise; the 'bleating of the kid attracts the tiger' and the two
crammer's pups come to see what is going on. They allow themselves to be tied so that they can 'go for' the other two—and then
the mask comes off, M'Turk and Beetle are released and the
crammer's pups are tortured in their turn. A long succession of
varied torments succeed each other with question and answer in
between.

'Between each torture came the pitiless dazing rain of questions ... ' At last came tears '—scalding tears; appeals for mercy
and abject promises of peace.' But the questions began again 'to
the accompaniment of keen persuasions'. When Stalky and
M'Turk thought the job was done and both the bullies shattered,
Beetle would not be stopped. He goes on relentlessly with the
cricket-stump; they weep and beg for mercy.

> 'We never really bullied him—like you've done us.'
> 'Yah!' said Beetle. 'They never really bully ... Only knock
> 'em about a little bit. That's what they say. Only kick the
> souls out of 'em and they go and blub in the box-rooms.
> Shove their heads into ulsters and blub. Write home three
> times a day—yes, you brute, I've done that—asking to be
> taken away.'

It was hard for the other two to make him stop.

The story is told as an example of how boys can educate each
other. The chaplain looks in a few days later to say he is pleased
with the Three; young Clewer is getting above himself and has
had to be given fifty lines for showing high spirits in class. As for
the 'other people'—and it becomes clear that the chaplain had
always known who they were—they too are much improved.
' "If I had used one half of the moral suasion you may or may not
have employed ... , I suppose I should now be languishing in
Bideford jail, shouldn't I?" ' the chaplain concludes.

It was the kind of moral suasion that Kipling believed in till the
end of his life; it recurs, with one or two verbal echoes, in 'The

Tie', written in 1915 but published in 1932, in which a partner in a large catering firm falls into the hands of a group of officers of a territorial battalion. The food in their mess is appalling and when they realize that they have in their hands the man responsible *and* that he is wearing an old school tie which one of them can match, they take him into the guardroom, smack his head and talk to him as a group of boys half-way up the school might talk to a fag in his second term who is letting down the house.

That was an odd immature streak in Kipling which did not altogether die even when other aspects of his personality matured. But *The Moral Reformers* also throws light on Beresford's reminiscences. It is impossible, after reading that story, to believe that Kipling was not bullied—as he says he was—in his early days at Westward Ho! He hated bullying but was obsessed by it. Perhaps there was something in him that responded to such treatment by a sick fascination with pain. In *Something of Myself*, he mentions casually that during the happy interlude after he left the House of Desolation, his mother drew the line at his 'return to meals red-booted from assisting at the slaughter of swine'. Not all little boys have such tastes. And if Beetle's revenge on bullies is fantasy—as it probably is—it is told with gusto. Beetle really wanted to repay something of what he had had; he dwells on it with pleasure. When it was over, all three were 'dripping with excitement and exertion'. 'This moral suasion biznai takes it out of a chap,' one of them adds. And here perhaps is a faint foretaste of the terrible close to 'Mary Postgate', when a spinster in middle age, having satisfied her hate, by watching a German airman die, achieves a satisfaction which is sensual, luxurious and by implication as near sexuality as she can get.

Kipling had written of his experience at Southsea that it was a suitable preparation for his future because it demanded 'constant wariness, the habit of observation, and attendance on moods and tempers; the noting of discrepancies between speech and action; a certain reserve of demeanour; and automatic suspicion of sudden favours.' Westward Ho! was a happier experience, because he had friends and because the Head was a wise man whom he admired. But it must have rubbed in those lessons from Southsea; it was a place where colts had to be trained. This was a constant metaphor with Kipling, and he was later to write at the head of one of his stories:

But, once in a way, there will come a day
When the colt must be taught to feel
The lash that falls and the curb that galls,
And the sting of the rowelled steel.

Something was learnt in school hours too. King, a principal
figure in *Stalky and Co.* is, says Carrington, a composite picture of
one Haslam, who left for an appointment in New Zealand, and
Crofts, the second master. But from a photographic group of
Westward Ho! masters, Crofts is immediately recognizable as
King; the challenging expression, the poise of the head, identify
him at once. Kipling owed far more to Crofts than one would suppose from *Stalky*; Crofts gave him a present when he left and they
continued to correspond after Kipling went to India. Crofts
seems to have had a real love for the classics and a sense of
language. 'One learns more from a good scholar in a rage than
from a score of lucid and laborious drudges; and to be made the
butt of one's companions in full form is no bad preparation for
later experiences,' Kipling wrote. Crofts was often in a rage; it
was he who threw *Fifty Men and Women* at Kipling's head, meaning him to keep it. It was a book that had a profound influence. It
was Crofts who taught Kipling 'to loathe Horace for two years; to
forget him for twenty, and then to love him for the rest of my
days and through many sleepless nights.' It was Haslam who said
Kipling would end up as a 'scurrilous journalist in a garret'. This
was part of a long, stinging public harangue, which was meant to
be brutal — 'brutal as the necessary wrench on the curb that
fetches up a too-flippant colt.' On one occasion Crofts poured
public scorn on Walt Whitman, whom he castigated as an undisciplined barbarian. It was easy, of course, to make fun of someone whose verse was so different from Milton's and Tennyson's
and he soon had the form sniggering with him, and Beetle alone
hot in stammering defence of a poet he had already made a hero.
But whether this was spontaneous, or a feigned attack intended to
stimulate the victim's critical sense as well as his tendency to hero-
worship, who can say?

Not every influence at Westward Ho! was on the side of discipline. In *Stalky*, much is made of the privilege given Beetle in his
last year of browsing in the Head's library. But Crofts too
encouraged him in this way, and the chaplain. Cormell Price
admired French literature as well as Russian and he discreetly

guided Kipling into this field. He made up his mind, while at school, that he would be deeply and thoroughly versed in English literature and have a sufficient knowledge of French to be equipped as he thought a writer should be.

There is another matter on which I do not think Beresford is to be trusted against *Stalky and Co.* In the stories, Beetle is always something of a butt. Spectacled and inky—and years later in Lahore he was still usually covered with ink—King made mock of him in class, accused him of showing off, tried to curb his inordinate conceit. His spectacles were frequently broken and mended with string; in the pantomime they cast him for the Widow Twankey. Stalky rends him almost as fiercely as King: 'You *are* so dam' inaccurate!' he says.* Perhaps the picture was a little overdrawn, but I suspect that this was how Kipling thought he was regarded at school, and that it was nearer the general view than Beresford's haloed figure, whose moral influence kept at bay the philistine values of the Victorians and transformed the spirit of the school. Kipling was excused games because of his short sight and this made him odd man out from the start. He was the only boy in the school who wore spectacles. In a school where everyone else was going into the army or one of the Indian services, he intended to live by his pen. He was not even good at the only classwork that counted—mathematics and Latin. He was a freak. Perhaps he came to be regarded with tolerant amusement and even affection as the school poet, and a kind of regimental mascot, but he was always an oddity.

Beresford writes of his despising games, but Dunsterville, always more of a realist, thinks this was a pose to cover his inability to play them. It would be difficult to exaggerate the importance which games were beginning to assume at this period in English boarding schools. It was not so much brilliance at games that was admired; indeed, brilliance might be slightly suspect, although, rather inconsistently, it was also felt that no one should practise *too* hard. It was the 'useful all-rounder' who was the ideal, not only among the boys, but among masters. Masters were often schoolboys who had never grown up, and sometimes the boys themselves laughed at their single-minded enthusiasm.

* Janet Adam Smith has said that no school story was ever so full of literary allusions. This remark occurs when Beetle has come back laden with information about Johnson which the others think may be useful. 'Sammivel not Binjimin? You *are* so dam' inaccurate' says Stalky, contriving in three words to link Jonson, Johnson, Dickens and Surtees.

2*

Army officers too were still often boys, and at least until he was twenty-five, Kipling was to be continually in contact with people to whom games were not merely recreation but a kind of index to moral worth. Kipling never whole-heartedly rejected these values. As the Stalky stories develop, it becomes steadily clearer that beneath all the mockery of conventional schoolboys – the 'Yes Sir and No Sir and Oh Sir brigade' – lies some degree of envy. Kipling would like to have played for the school, 'magnificent in black jersey, white knickers, and black stockings'. He would like to have been Pot Mullins, Captain of Games – but since he was not and never could be, he must take refuge in pretending he didn't care for all that. Thus was born one of the deep contradictions of which he never rid himself.

While the Three are in revolt against school rules about bounds and smoking, while they regard assistant masters in general as natural enemies, they are not in revolt against the idea of school; it is useful for the limited purpose of getting employment but also as a training ground for the world. 'To rear a boy under what parents call "the sheltered life system" is, if the boy must go into the world and fend for himself, not wise.' That is the beginning of a story in *Plain Tales* (1888) about a boy who was reared under such a system and committed suicide, because he took some minor follies too seriously. If only he had been through the mill of a little early brutality, he would have learnt more sense! The phrase 'scornful individualism' used by Lionel Trilling of the Three is exactly right at one level; they are extreme individualists, proclaiming their contempt for a weak and silly housemaster and for the creed of the honour of the house when he proclaims it. But they respect the Head and something which Kipling came to call the Law, though that phrase is not used in *Stalky*.

Here then is a deeper aspect of the contradiction within Kipling about games. He was finally on the side of order as against chaos, and this meant that he admired the prosaic virtues of those who supported order and administered the law. He envied the simple extrovert who was good at games and 'a born leader of men'. There was an element in him that wanted to be loyal to a cause or a leader, to cheer for the house and the school. But another side of him was in revolt against the system in operation, the actual masters and prefects. He admired a sturdy individualism; it was worth anything to be one's own master. He saw the poetry and pathos of being alone in the world, a waif in the streets like the young Lippo Lippi, in Browning's poem in *Fifty Men and Women*, living on the melon-rinds the fortunate threw, learning a wary habit of observation. Yet everyone must find his place in a whole and settle down as a disciplined part of the machine. And much as he admired a stoic silence about a man's inner feelings, he *knew* that he was different from the others and had to show it. He was a committed artist who could not keep quiet; he had to tell the world how he saw it—or how he thought he saw it, because the craftsman was always at work on the raw material submitted by experience.

Patriotism is another matter on which there is a discrepancy in the sources, and something of a paradox in the stories. In 1882, an assassin made an attempt on Queen Victoria's life and Kipling wrote some verses congratulating her on her escape. They were published in the school magazine, of which he was the editor, and are headed 'Ave Imperatrix'—the first of those unofficial odes on national occasions for which he became famous. In form, this ode is an imitation of Oscar Wilde, but the question is what Kipling felt when he wrote it. It dutifully lays at the Queen's feet the homage of a school composed of soldiers' sons:

> Such greeting as should come from those
> Whose fathers faced the Sepoy hordes
> Or served you in the Russian snows
> And, dying, left their sons their swords.

Beresford says they mocked him for this; in his case, the last word should have been, not 'swords', but 'nibs'. It was written, Beresford thought, to get a rise out of Crofts, who like Price was a Liberal and a Little Englander. Dunsterville disagrees; he does not think Kipling wrote it with his tongue in his cheek and, once again, it seems likely that Dunsterville is right. It was quite in keeping that Kipling should pretend he was merely trying to annoy Crofts. That was part of the inverted hypocrisy of school life; the one thing that must never be acknowledged was anything that might be thought virtue.

That discrepancy is matched by the paradox in one of the *Stalky* tales, 'The Flag of Their Country'. A generously built, pink and white Member of Parliament volunteers to address the boys and harangues them on patriotism, finally unfurling a Union Jack and draping it over the rostrum. Most of them were the sons of officers and meant to enter the army—but to talk about patriotism or to wave the symbol of what was really their central faith was *taboo*. It was simply not done; they were acutely embarrassed. The M.P. had cheerfully assumed that they had never previously considered something to which their lives were dedicated. Next day everyone resigned from the embryonic cadet corps which the boys had recently formed.

This is understandable. What is more difficult to understand is why Kipling felt that *he* could talk about what the 'jelly-bellied flag-flapper' could not, why he, who had so clearly understood the discomfort flag-waving caused, should have become associated in so many minds with just that offence. Only ten years after 'Ave Imperatrix', he was to publish a song called 'The English Flag' which in most Englishmen today arouses a feeling rather similar to that with which the schoolboys looked at the Union Jack.

Edmund Wilson condemns *Stalky* as the worst book Kipling wrote, and Henry James regarded it as 'deplorable'. Both, as Americans, have found utterly alien a background not merely British but so peculiarly part of a particular period of British history. Perhaps no one can understand it unless he has been to a boarding school. But apart from the light that it throws on Kipling's life, it cannot be easily brushed aside. No doubt it does not picture schoolboys as all that their parents would like them to be, and it was shocking to Victorians who had forgotten their youth. But a great many schoolboys have felt the pleasure Lionel Trilling describes at a school story which gets away from pretence. At the age of twelve it seemed to me very like the world of school I knew—that outer world of work and competition in which one might at any moment meet hostility and scorn. No other school book gave me that feeling of hostility. They were about boys who felt at home in their schools. Like the Three, I felt just that paradoxical conviction that this was something that had to be gone through, that one might resent every day of it but must somehow consent to the whole process. Again, there is something archetypal about the alliance of the Three against the world; it recurs in almost every school story of the period, and in a host of boys' magazines. The first four stories are structurally the same; a master (or two masters and the school sergeant) lay an ambush for the Three, or oppress them in a way they regard as going beyond the fair limits of civilized warfare, and they contrive a punishment that in some way matches the crime and which cannot be brought home to them—though the godlike Head always knows the truth.

Two aspects of this formula – the aim and the method – remained for his whole life among Kipling's absorbing interests. Call it retribution or revenge, there is a besetting human need to see the equipoise restored, the law maintained, and to this need he constantly reverts. Towards the end, his interest becomes much more complex and in 'Dayspring Mishandled' it is finally drained of malice – but the interest remains.

Retribution or revenge is Stalky's aim. The method is frequently the manipulation of a puppet by a hidden figure who escapes detection. The perfect example occurs when Stalky uses his catapult from the dark on a drunken carrier, who sees as the only possible source of the attack a single lighted window, which is King's, and proceeds to throw stones at it. In the final story Stalky, now in the Indian Army, uses the same strategy to cause fighting between two hostile tribes who are attacking him. Manipulation from behind the scenes is not always directed to revenge; the unknown and unrewarded figure who saves the situation is a variation which constantly recurs.

No doubt the success of Stalky's devices is greatly exaggerated in the tales, and no doubt Edmund Wilson was right in supposing that much of their popularity is due to their supplying schoolboys with fantasies of success in their war with masters and seniors. But there is a basis of fact behind most of them which illustrates Kipling's method of collecting material from observed facts and using it for his own purposes. On a much smaller scale, Dunsterville had developed a technique for drawing masters not unlike his various gambits in the book. He would, for example, excite the attention of a new master by appearing to conceal the book he was studying – but instead of a guilty novel it would be an innocent textbook. Or during an examination he would stealthily consult a piece of blank paper. Or he would embroil one boy with another by 'borrowing' something without permission, leaving it in a conspicuous place and suggesting to an innocent third party that he should return it to the owner, who would immediately assume that he was the borrower. A Puckish delight in mischief created from behind the scenes was common to them all.

After Southsea, Kipling's need to feel that he belonged securely to his background was strong. At Westward Ho! he was plunged into a world that was 'brutal enough' and often 'flagrantly unjust'. 'You've been here six years and you expect fairness,' says Stalky contemptuously. But an inner resilience prevented him from open capitulation; he appeared to rebel against the spirit of the place, read Browning and Ruskin and decorated the study with Japanese fans; he mocked at games. But on another level he persuaded himself that this was a perfect training for life and for many years devoted a good deal of energy to the glorification of the kind of young man that such a system produced.

Thus, from the age of twelve till he was seventeen, Kipling lived in two utterly different worlds. The holidays he spent with his Burne-Jones and Poynter aunts, meeting the Pre-Raphaelite Brotherhood and their friends. He looked at pictures of delicate dream women set against backgrounds of hard bright detail. At school—and it must be repeated that it was a boarding-school with no week-ends away, an interminable thirteen or fourteen weeks at a stretch—he lived among budding subalterns under a headmaster he admired but assistant masters whom he regarded as enemies and in some cases disliked or despised. All his life he was to be divided between his instinct as an artist and his understanding of the administrator; between an emotional sympathy for the waif and the outlaw but a firm belief that, if chaos is to be kept at bay, men must be ruled by laws and the individual may have to suffer. He is usually on the side of the system but often against its manifestations; always on the side of the Head but often against the housemaster.

3. YOUNG MAN IN INDIA

When he came to write *Something of Myself*, Kipling described his seven years in India as 'Seven Years Hard'. They were indeed years of hard work and considerable achievement; they provided a continual store of material to which he would return for the rest of his life. But he did not write fictionalized autobiography about his Indian life, as he did about his childhood and boyhood. It is easier therefore to separate his life from his work and give the bare bones of his time in India, keeping his work for the next chapter.

He left school before he was seventeen and was appointed Assistant to the Editor of *The Civil and Military Gazette* at Lahore on a salary of £100 a year. His headmaster had recognized that he was 'irretrievably committed to the inkpot' and his parents could not afford to send him to a university; they conspired to get him this appointment, but he did hesitate, feeling that he was turning his back on the centre of literary power where his name must be made if it was to be made at all. At last he decided to go and threw himself with gusto into the new world, with only an occasional glance over his shoulder. He wrote to one of his aunts about his cousin Stanley Baldwin: 'I'd give anything to be in the Sixth at Harrow as he is, with a University Education to follow.' And for many years he would display little spurts of animosity directed at those who did have a University education.

He found himself at Bombay moving amid sights, and still more scents, which he had forgotten but suddenly found he remembered; he found himself speaking sentences of which he did not remember the meaning. But he did not pause at Bombay. At Lahore, he was able to stay with his parents; his father was in charge of the Museum and also of the Mayo College of Art. Young Englishmen on first arrival in India often stayed with an older married couple; Rudyard's position in the house was well understood. He had his own room, his own servant, and his own horse and trap. The fact remains that he was, for the cold weather, that is from October till April, under his mother's eye for the first four years.

His father was wise, gentle and kindly, a maker of things. He drew, modelled, carved, designed; everyone knows his illustrations for *Kim* and the description of him as the curator who changed spectacles with the Lama. His son loved and admired him and submitted work for his judgment. Rudyard wrote later that, not having really known his parents since he was five, he might have found that he did not care for them—but his mother was 'more delightful than all my imaginings or memories', while his father was 'a humorous, tolerant and expert fellow-craftsman'. Later his sister joined them and then 'our cup was filled to the brim. Not only were we happy but we knew it.' His life, says Carrington, was firmly based on the Family Square, and that was how it seemed to himself. But his work suggests to me that deep within him there was an incredulous question. *These* delightful Kiplings, whom he liked and loved so much—could they really be the people who had once so cruelly deserted him at Southsea? I do not suggest that he consciously asked this question. But Mowgli, Kim and the story called 'Cold Iron' suggest that it was there. In his most imaginative work, good parents are always foster-parents.

This happy family life was for the cold weather. When the heat began—in April; in May the great heat is in its tyranny—his parents and sister would go away to the hills and he would be left alone in the big house, usually dining at the Club. The Cantonments, where the army was stationed, were at Mian Mir, some miles out of Lahore, and in the days of horse transport Mian Mir was more self-contained than later. The cold weather population of the civil station at Lahore was about seventy persons. In the summer, most of the wives and the Government of the Punjab moved to Simla and the population of the Club dropped to about a dozen. They were all of them much older than seventeen; they talked their own shop and in the hot weather were not always very good-tempered. Kipling was back again in the World of Work as opposed to the World of Love. Of course he was lonely. He was also very hard-worked, since the Editor of *The Civil and Military Gazette* was often sick. Kipling himself had malaria and dysentery; most men did. He was always liable to sleepless nights and sometimes nightmares, and would occasionally spend the night wandering about the Indian city.

North Indian hot weather was not enjoyable, even when there were electric fans; what is hard to endure is a succession of hot nights when the temperature will sometimes not drop below 100° Fahrenheit (38° Centigrade) for a week on end. It must have been far worse when the only means of reducing the temperature was by coolies who pulled the cord of the punkah—a pair of stout laths and a sheet which hung from the ceiling and swung languidly over the bed. When the rains come and the temperature drops, a new plague develops, which must also have been far worse in Kipling's day. The night swarms with winged life; flying ants, moths and beetles flock to any light. If the only lamps are paraffin, it becomes impossible to read.

Kipling seems always to have had a month in the hills, when he joined his parents, usually in Simla, though sometimes in a less expensive hill-station. Later, for his last two years, he had longer spells in Simla as the correspondent of his paper, though he was never there for a whole season.

British society in India was curiously caste-like. There were two great caste-groups, 'officers' and 'other ranks', within each of which marriage was permissible. Marriage between these groups was forbidden, and so was what Indians came later to call interdining. In peacetime, officers and other ranks did not sit down to eat together. All this was very like the great Indian castes. And, again like the Indian castes, the two main groups were sub-divided. True, there was no rule that a man in the Indian Civil Service should not marry the daughter of an army officer or a policeman, and 'interdining' was a positive duty. None the less, these were separate groups arranged in an order of precedence even more rigid than among castes, because it was printed at the end of the *Civil List*, which everyone had on his desk. It showed everyone's pay and his exact place in the hierarchy. But it did not include reporters for *The Civil and Military Gazette*.

In Calcutta and Bombay, no doubt things were different because there were great business houses and men of business who were far richer than officials and were strong enough in numbers to dominate the clubs and social life. But in the Punjab and the United Provinces, the India Kipling knew, the Europeans were officials, except for a few oddities—and Kipling was one of the oddities. The point has to be stressed, because this kind of society is hard to imagine for anyone who has not lived in it. It is true that when Lord Dufferin became Viceroy in 1884, he and his family found the Kiplings agreeable and interesting and used to ask them to small private lunches and dinners. Indeed, Carrington records that Lord Dufferin was so disturbed at his son's interest in 'Trix', Rudyard's sister, that he called on Mrs Kipling to discuss the danger. 'Don't you think, Mrs Kipling, your daughter should be taken to another hill-station?' 'Don't you think, Your Excellency, that your son should be sent home?' And he was. But Rudyard Kipling's share in this intimacy was less than his parents' or sister's; for one thing, he was only in Simla for part of the season. Even for his parents, the favour of one Viceroy would not really make the difference that has sometimes been supposed. Viceroys come and go; the glory of social success in one Simla season was like giving champagne at a party; it bestowed a temporary prestige, establishing in a new dimension a temporary rank which was very important to those who concerned themselves with such things. But the social set were a minority in Simla; most of the white inhabitants were there to work, and for them what counted was the civil list and the official order of precedence.

Picture then a Simla of which the backbone was official and usually ambitious, hard-working, and not very young. There was also a froth of grass widows, a coming and going of younger men on leave. But it was not the sort of leave that colonels of good regiments thought well of. Go to the high hills and shoot ibex or

markhor; go to the Central Provinces and shoot tiger—and the
Colonel will beam. But a young man who goes to Simla for leave
is trying to get into the Political or is after a woman—and the
Colonel will frown. It was inevitable that a young man determined
to make his name by his pen should write about the froth rather
than the backbone of Simla, and no doubt he was right in giving
the impression that within this section of the society there were
women starving for male attention and men anxious for better
jobs and not too scrupulous about how they got them. But the
historian should beware of supposing that what Kipling tells is
the whole truth.

Anglo-Indian society was not only predominantly official; it
was also biased against the young. The two of course go together;
officials who have won a position of authority by age and experience are not inclined to underestimate such qualifications. And,
from their schooldays onwards, most of the seniors had believed
that colts needed both curb and spur; they had gone through it
themselves and it had done them good. Also, in their daily work,
they had no time for argument or discussion. They were so few,
compared with the millions of India, that the only way to get
through the day's work was to take decisions and give orders
which were meant to be obeyed. A young man who asked questions and argued was a nuisance. Nor were they much more
patient with the young when work was finished. After a long day
listening to pleaders and clerks, and after all the exercise which—
it was firmly believed—was so necessary to keep the liver in order,
most men wanted to relax in the evening, and relaxation usually
took the form of gossip and reminiscence about personalities. The
new arrival could not take part in this kind of conversation. He
knew nothing of the eccentric personalities that people told
stories about; the best thing he could do was keep quiet until he
had acquired some reminiscences of his own. Even among the
women, experience told; not only did 'senior ladies' quarrel over
the right to go into dinner first, but men fought for the favours of
women who were witty and self-possessed. As Kipling noted:

> The incense that is mine by right
> They burn before her shrine
> And that's because I'm seventeen
> And she is forty-nine.

And such women only occasionally allowed a very young man to forget that he was very young. Consider the way Mrs Hauksbee treated the Hawley boy in 'The Education of Otis Yeere'.

In the summer of 1884, Kipling was still only eighteen. He was younger than the youngest subaltern. Subalterns had been through Sandhurst, civilians had been to a university. He was young beyond belief in a society in which youth was snubbed or ignored, and which was built up on official rank which he could never possess. He had learnt at Southsea to walk warily and defend himself. The lesson had been rubbed in again at Westward Ho! But he wanted to make his name as a writer; he *had* to assert himself to get anyone to listen to him. It is not surprising that behind all the energy and brilliance of the earliest stories we should be aware of a defensive self-assertion. 'I *do* know, I *do* know!' he seems to be saying. He must assure us—and himself—that he really does know all that we think a young man can't know—all about women and how jobs are obtained and how viceroys talk and what men are like at work—as well as a great many things we have never dreamed of: about natives and soldiers and Eurasians and all kinds of strange folk. He is so insistent on all he knows that we half expect to hear the shrill pipe of the youth whose voice has recently broken and suddenly rises an octave.

Here again, then, there was tension and a basic contradiction. Except in his mother's house, he must still be on the alert, watching carefully who would throw him

> The bit of half-stripped grape-bunch he desires
> And who will curse and kick him for his pains—

But while, for a young official, the road to success was to work hard but keep his mouth shut, this would not do for a young man who meant to make his way by his pen. He *had* to be heard. So he had to talk and write with a freedom and confidence quite unsuitable for his years. And he was up against a society which, though it prized the man who was independent and eccentric within certain limits, could easily close into monolithic rigidity. As a tiny oligarchy amid a vast alien population, it had to be wary; it could never wholly relax. A young man who insisted on being heard was bound to irritate; he must accept that, but on the other hand he must not be too outrageous. These were his readers. And besides, he envied them and wanted to show he was one of themselves—and yet different from them.

All that need be said of Kipling's newspaper career is that he had at first a very hard grind at *The Civil and Military Gazette* under an exacting editor, who worked on the usual Victorian principle that the young needed discipline and hard work before anything. He went on many assignments which gave him material for stories — pebbles to be stored and turned over and polished. Then there came a new, younger, livelier editor and they began to run a 2,000-word turnover article or story. Many of these Kipling wrote and later published as *Plain Tales from the Hills*. His name began to be known; he was promoted from *The Civil and Military*, which had only a Punjab circulation, to *The Pioneer* of Allahabad, which had a much wider public. Here he was given a freer hand, a series of roving commissions. He was no longer limited to 2,000 words, and at the same time he came under a new influence; he had formerly been told to compress; now he was encouraged to expand. The Allahabad stories are more leisurely, less tense, more assured and less sharply edged than the Lahore stories. But health, climate and ambition all urged him the same way. It came over him that he must get back to England, which for him must be the centre of the empire he meant to rule. He sold various copyrights and found he had enough to get back to London. He sailed on March 9th, 1889.

But he did not sail by the shortest route. During his two winter seasons at Allahabad, he had stayed with Professor and Mrs Hill, an American couple. It was much the pleasantest way for a young bachelor to live in India. Mrs Hill — Edmonia was her name but she was generally called Ted — was a lively person of about thirty who was later to provide the physical presence, and perhaps to some extent the character, of 'William', the heroine of 'William the Conqueror'. It is a story about the life of men working in India and their sudden upheaval and dispatch to rescue work because there is a famine in the south. William is a girl with short hair who shares men's work as far as she can, who likes men who *do* things — a new kind of woman in the Victorian scene. When the Hills went to Mussoorie — a hill-station nearer Allahabad than Simla, less expensive and much less official — Kipling went first to Lahore and later to Simla. He wrote Mrs Hill a letter every day, a vigorous running diary; they were the kind of letters he had once written to his aunts and cousins in England, describing his daily doings. It can only be guesswork how the relationship might have developed if she had encouraged him to think of her as unhappily married. As things were, she kept it frank and platonic, but he told her in one of his letters that when he rejoined the family party at Simla his mother and sister were at once aware that he was no longer 'theirs'. When he left India, it was with the Hills; Ted had been ill and they had decided to go to America. Kipling obtained a commission from *The Pioneer* to write a series of letters from America, and decided to go to London the long way round.

There had of course been what Charles Carrington calls drawing-room flirtations in Simla, and Rudyard must have walked a good deal by the side of Mrs Hauksbee's rickshaw. It appears that he never told 'Ted' who was the model from whom he drew that famous lady, but that she, like Ted and his mother, had advised him and criticized his work, particularly on 'women'. Mrs Hauksbee and his mother were on the side of discipline, Ted of free expression. At school, Beresford tells us, Kipling had posed as an authority on women; he had been knowing and secretive, just as he was in his early writings. But he was really quite innocent of any physical knowledge of women, and he looked on those of his own class with the same mixture of fascination and apprehension as any other Victorian schoolboy, brought up in segregation from these magical creatures. He had fallen in love, or so he supposed, at fourteen, with a girl only a little older than himself whose name was Flo Garrard. In appearance, she was very like the Brushwood Girl, with a pale beautiful face and 'abundant black hair, growing in a widow's peak, turned back from the forehead ... ' He had come out to India thinking he was engaged to her, but after eighteen months she wrote putting an end to it. It does not appear that he was deeply hurt at the time; he wrote several stories about young men who came out to India with an understanding – in one case a marriage – to a girl left in England. And it usually breaks up, as the tale demands. There is a story in *Plain Tales*, 'On the Strength of a Likeness', from which Carrington has quoted on this subject. It begins in that light, blasé tone that Kipling so often affects at this period:

Next to a requited attachment, one of the most convenient things that a young man can carry about with him at the beginning of his career, is an unrequited attachment. It makes him feel important and business-like; and blasé and cynical; and whenever he has a touch of liver, or suffers from want of exercise, he can mourn over his lost love, and be very happy in a tender, twilight fashion.

This certainly does not sound as though the blow had been severe, and the references to Flo in letters to his aunt and cousin, the general lively cheerful tone of his letters, tell the same story. On the other hand, it is seldom safe to take Kipling quite at his face value; he would take a good deal of trouble to avoid showing that he was hurt. And it seems to have been more serious when he met Flo again in England.

PART ONE
'A Strangely Clever Youth...'

3

The First Books

1. PLAIN TALES

When he left India in 1890 Kipling had already published in book
form two collections from the considerable body of his verse and
prose that had appeared in newspapers and journals. The verse
collection was *Departmental Ditties*, the prose *Plain Tales from the
Hills*. Some other stories had been published in the Indian Railway
Library for sale on bookstalls; these were collected and published
in London in 1890 as *Soldiers Three* and *Wee Willie Winkie*. In 1892
Barrack-Room Ballads was published, and *Life's Handicap*.
Any division of work into 'Early' or 'Late' is bound to present
difficulties, and this list omits *The Light that Failed*, which appeared
before *Life's Handicap* but is connected with events that took place
after Kipling left India. Some later books, *Many Inventions* (1893),
The Jungle Books (1894–5), *The Day's Work* (1898) and *Kim*
(1901), look back to the Indian period of his life, but these I
regard as 'Early-Middle'; they have a different flavour from the
earliest work, something which begins to appear in *Life's Handicap*; in this chapter I touch only on one or two stories from that
collection and from *Many Inventions*.

The verses of *Departmental Ditties* are as light as those meringues
which Indian cooks would agree to make only when there were
no clouds in the sky. They are highly polished, witty, trivial —
Austin Dobson with an added seasoning of malice and cynicism:

> Jenny and Me were engaged, you see,
>   On the eve of the Fancy Ball;
> So a kiss or two was nothing to you
>   Or anyone else at all.

They arranged to sit out the fourth dance in the dusk, and as
soon as a girl arrived in a pink domino, he greeted her as Jenny:

> That is to say, in a casual way,
>   I slipped my arm around her;
> With a kiss or two (which is nothing to you)
>   And ready to kiss I found her.

But it suddenly dawns on each that the other is a stranger and the
first pink domino runs away. He finds out that there are two pink
dominoes and that this one:

Had cloaked the spouse of Sir Julian Vouse
    Our big political gun.

Sir J. was old, and her hair was gold,
    And her eyes were a blue cerulean;
And the name she said when she turned her head
    Was not in the least like 'Julian.'

And what should happen but that old Sir Julian, 'in the kindest way', made the narrator of the verses his secretary, which gave him the means to marry his Jenny? That is one vein. Another is this:

And One, long since a pillar of the Court,
    As mud between the beams thereof is wrought;
    And One who wrote on phosphates for the crops
Is subject-matter of his own Report.

Some, like that just quoted, were frankly parodies; most were derivative. They fall into line with one mood in the stories, and need not be discussed separately.

Plain Tales from the Hills present a much more varied picture, and in embryo display most of the moods of this early period. The stories were written when Kipling was dealing with the grinding slog of journalism and editorial work on a daily paper that was very much under-staffed. The energy and versatility are as startling as the technical achievement: these tales are finished products; the sentences cannot be easily changed or omitted, and the narrative force carries the reader along. They were read over the breakfast-table from one end of India to the other, and they have always had an audience. They seem to translate well into French, and have been read in France and admired by French critics even when in England Kipling was in the doldrums. It would be unfair to judge them without remembering that they were written for daily bread, and that most of them had to be finished by an exact moment and to fill an exact space. The usual allotment was enough for 2,200 words, and the average of the whole collection is well under 2,500. They were written to entertain in the first place a particular audience – the few thousands of English men and women of the professional middle classes who administered India – judges and district magistrates, army officers, canal engineers, policemen, doctors, and their wives. These people had to be entertained, just as Shakespeare had to fill the

Globe Theatre. But both writers had in mind a more exacting
critic and ultimately a wider audience.

No one, I think, would claim that this collection includes the best
of Kipling. Even T. S. Eliot, coming into the lists as a champion,
speaks of 'those rather cocky and acid tales of Simla and Delhi'.
'Delhi' is here a slip for 'Lahore', but that apart, the judgment,
though widely held until lately in the English-speaking world, is not
altogether justified. It was not shared in France, and it does what
criticisms of Kipling have so often done. It condemns the whole
forty stories on grounds which apply to some of them but not to all.

Many of the stories *are* cocky, some are acid, some are trivial.
But there are some of which one can make none of those judgments. They are extremely varied, and it is not easy to put them
into categories. Most people, I suppose, would say from memory
that they were about official English society in Simla, about the
feminine manipulations of Mrs Hauksbee, about flirtations, and
intrigues connected with getting jobs. But in fact less than a third
can be described in those terms; on my count there are thirteen.
Three of these are farces,* accounts of either practical jokes or
successions of farcical misadventures, a kind of story to which
Kipling came back all his life and which will be discussed later;
you may judge them crude and immature, but they are not at all
acid. Of the remaining ten, which, without being farces, do deal
with Anglo-Indian society in Simla, one at least is far from trivial.

'The Other Man' centres on one vivid and unforgettable scene.
Her parents had forced Mrs Schreiderling to marry a man much
older than herself. She was not yet twenty and had given 'all her
poor little heart' to an Other Man who had neither money nor
prospects and who was 'not even good-looking'. She herself had
never been 'more than ordinarily pretty at the best of times' and
even that came to an end as she came to realize how far from
happy she was. Her looks faded, her husband was increasingly
contemptuous and indifferent; he was a hard man, with neither
affection nor courtesy. No one called on her. Schreiderling left her
alone in Simla one August, when the rains are at their worst, and
she heard that the Other Man was coming up to Simla, very sick,

---

* By my reckoning the three Simla farces are 'The Germ Destroyer', 'The arrest of
Lieutenant Golightly' and 'A Friend's Friend'. The ten concerning Simla which do fall
into the category everyone remembers are: 'Three – and an Extra', 'The Rescue of
Pluffles', 'Cupid's Arrows', 'Consequences', 'Kidnapped', 'In Error', 'Venus
Annodomini', 'On the Strength of a Likeness', 'The Other Man' and 'Wressley of
the Foreign Office'.

with a bad heart made worse by malaria. She went to meet him. There was no rail to Simla in those days and the sixty-mile journey up from railhead was made in a *tonga*, which is a kind of low pony-trap, with a seat facing forward for the driver and, back to back with it, a seat facing the other way for two passengers. There were relays of ponies, changed at each stage. Mrs Schreiderling found the tonga in which the Other Man had come up and began to scream. 'Sitting in the back seat, very square and firm, with one hand on the awning-stanchion and the wet pouring off his hat and moustache, was the Other Man – dead.' The driver had tied him in place when he died. The rest of the story is concerned with the narrator's efforts to prevent anyone else from knowing that she had come to meet the dead man. No one found out and she continued to trot up and down the Mall on 'a shocking bad saddle, looking as if she expected to meet someone round the corner every minute'.

That is an impressive story, and there is nothing acid – and only the faintest touch of cockiness – in the telling. It is full of compassion. Some of the others are certainly so slight as to seem trivial – 'The Rescue of Pluffles', for example. This is about a very young and callow subaltern who has been enslaved by Mrs Reiver, whom everyone knows to be *bad*, and is rescued by Mrs Hauksbee, who, though avid of male admiration, is *kind*, and who marries him off to a nice girl; he ends up 'raising speckled cattle inside green painted fences somewhere in England'. But is even this story entirely trivial? Pluffles was saved for a virtuous if mediocre life; without Mrs Hauksbee's intervention, he would have come to 'extreme grief'. The tale is told to entertain; it is not to be taken too seriously. But there is a hint of the moral tract beneath the surface, though the moral is administered with a sustained light irony. The writer is saying to his breakfast-table audience: 'You and I are experienced and intelligent people. *We* know how silly and conceited a boy straight from England can be. *We* know what a cropper such a boy might come – in debt, disgraced, desperately unhappy, perhaps a suicide. But we can laugh at this tale, because he was saved – and the joke is that he was saved by a lady who was generally thought of as a man-eater – and who saved him by just the arts and wiles in the managing of men which had earned her that reputation.' And readers addressed in this tone of voice feel that they are sophisticated and understanding. But there is a deeper irony. The writer knows very well that most of those he is addressing are not really very sophisticated; many of them are the 'fat Captains and tubby Majors' that boys like Pluffles grow up into. He is laughing at them, but they also smile to think how young and callow the Kipling boy is. He is saying to himself: 'Lord, what fools these mortals be!'

And again, 'Wressley of the Foreign Office' is about something serious. It is full of faults; nearly a page is wasted before the story begins, and even when Wressley appears there is too much parade of inside knowledge—which incidentally does not ring very true—about the Foreign Office and how it works. But the essence of the story is that Wressley, a shy, serious scholarly man, the greatest authority in the world on the Central Indian States, falls in love with a 'frivolous, golden-haired girl who used to tear about Simla Mall on a high rough waler* with a blue velvet jockey cap crammed over her eyes.' He decides that he must bring her a gift fit for her acceptance, takes a year's leave, and writes a masterpiece, bringing to his already prodigious know-ledge 'sympathy, insight, humour and style'—fire and life which he had never known he possessed—and making the dry bones of history something to weep or laugh over. He brought her his masterpiece, blushing and stammering. She read a little and said: 'Oh, your book? It's about those howwid Wajahs. I didn't understand it.' And the fire disappeared; he became 'a compiling, gazetteering, report-writing hack'.

The influence of women on men's work runs through all these stories. Kipling was dedicated to the craft of writing; that was *his* work. Where he was unusual was that he saw other men's work— building roads or bridges, administering a district—as also a kind of art. If a man was in love it might inspire him to work of a kind he had never been capable of, but marriage, if it was what the world calls successful, might lead to a softening of the impulse to create, a self-indulgent breakdown of the discipline art demands, a loss of nerve, a refusal to take risks. This was the creed pro-claimed in the club and the mess, often brutally and facetiously; 'another good man gone', they would say when an engagement was announced and the bridegroom on the eve of his wedding would be referred to as 'the condemned man'. Kipling often expressed this as vulgarly and brutally as they, for instance in the wholly deplorable verses called 'The Fall of Jock Gillespie'. But he, and probably four-fifths of the unmarried who talked like this,

* A waler is a horse from New South Wales.

secretly longed for the stability and comfort of an assured home.
They were pickled, by the social and economic conventions of the
day, in the uncomfortable brine of enforced sexual restraint at an
age when the physical impulses were at their strongest. Apart
from the physical aspect, the extreme individualism of life for the
Victorian English young man—cut off from family ties in the
harsh world of work—is an odd human phenomenon, rare in
history; it was only tolerable under the compelling drive of
artistic creation or administrative detail, which for Kipling meant
much the same thing. If that failed, loneliness would drive a man
back to a lower level of animal mediocrity, to drugs or drink or
loaferdom. While self-indulgent marriage was one danger, another
was the scorn, or the mere stupidity, of an unworthy woman,
which might banish the demon of inspiration and kill the finer
aspects of a man's work, turning him into a mere hack like Wressley.

Eleven stories of the forty in *Plain Tales* are about Anglo-
Indian society in the plains.* They are generally one degree less
superficially frivolous than the Simla stories, because they are
more often about men at work than men on leave. One—'Thrown
Away'—has been referred to already; it is about a subaltern
reared on the 'sheltered life' system who shoots himself after 'an
ordinary colonel's wigging'. Again, there is a vivid central scene.
The narrator and another are worried about what the Boy may
do when they learn that he has gone shooting by himself. They
hurry after him and as they approach the lonely bungalow they
see a lamp burning at four in the afternoon and hear 'the "brr—
brr—brr" of a multitude of flies'. They know they are too late.
He has left long letters, to the Colonel, to his parents, and to a
girl at home. They are heartbreaking letters, deeply distressing
and, as in 'The Other Man', the narrator goes to great lengths to
suppress evidence of what has happened. He and his companion
think it better that he should have died of cholera. This 'concoc-
tion of a big written lie, bolstered with evidence, to soothe the
Boy's people at Home' is described as 'grimly comic'.

Here again we stumble on something characteristic of Kipling.
There is the vivid scene, the lamp in the afternoon sun, the buzz
of the flies, the Boy on the bed with his head shot to pieces. Many

* The eleven stories about Anglo-Indian life not in Simla are: 'Thrown Away',
'False Dawn', 'Watches of the Night', 'The Conversion of Aurelian McGoggin', 'His
Wedded Wife', 'The Broken Link Handicap', 'A Bank Fraud', 'Yoked to an
Unbeliever', 'In the Pride of His Youth', 'Pig', 'The Rout of the White Hussars'.
I class the last two as farces.

writers would have been content to leave it at that, to record the
picture and no more; others might have set it against a background of eternity and of man as plaything of the gods, or against
the crimson of an Indian sunset and the brooding sense of a
continent that engulfs men's lives. But Kipling—having lifted the
coverlet—must replace it, tidy things up, restore the decent
respectable balance of life. This, I think, is in accordance with
something deep in his unformulated philosophy, the need to keep
chaos at bay. And this may be one reason why he has aroused
animosity; disaster does not make him rail against the gods or
revile the society to which he belongs. He sets his teeth and
endures because he is on the side of things as they are, with all the
pretence and injustice that they involve. He is, as Orwell says, at
heart an administrator who tries as far as he can to tidy up. And
this attitude is offensive to those who see so clearly what they dislike in things-as-they-are that they would rather savagely attack
them than make any attempt at improvement.

Two of these eleven stories are farces—'Pig' and 'The Rout of
the White Hussars'. 'In the Pride of His Youth' is a grim little
tragedy of a young man working himself to death for an unworthy
woman. 'False Dawn' comes as close as any to Oscar Wilde's
witticism about reading life under a palm-tree by flashes of
vulgarity. It is the end of April and hot already; the women are
leaving for the hills in a few days. Saumarez gives a midnight
picnic; the guests ride out by couples to a ruined tomb, two and
two, at quarter-mile intervals, to let the dust settle between each.
Everyone expects Saumarez to propose to one or other of the two
Copleigh sisters. 'The social atmosphere was heavily charged and
wanted clearing ... Then the moon went out and a burning hot
wind began lashing the orange-trees ... ' There is a dust storm
and in the blinding dust and darkness, Saumarez proposes to the
wrong sister. 'We were all huddled together, close to the trembling horses, with the thunder chattering overhead and the lightning spurting like water from a sluice ... ' The one he had meant
to propose to hears him and tries to go home. 'I heard a despairing
little voice close to my ear, saying to itself, quietly and softly, as if
some lost soul were flying about with the wind, "O my God!" '
There is a nightmare interlude of wind, dust, dark and heat, with
sudden flashes of lightning, the faces of the two girls appearing for
a second at a time through the haze, one absurdly happy—though
that happy look had to be wiped away—and the other desperately

trying to get away and be alone with her misery. It is a story that is all pictures. For once there is no moral to it, but in the morning 'the air was cleared; and, little by little, as the sun rose, I felt we were all dropping back again into ordinary men and women ... '

Even in the racing story, 'The Broken-link Handicap', quite trivial in what it purports to be about, there is a central unforgettable picture. The favourite is leading and just coming into the straight, when his jockey hears from the past the voice of a dead comrade. There had once been a terrible pile-up at a jump in a race in Australia; four jockeys had been taken out dead and three had been badly hurt, this man, Brunt, among them. He had heard a comrade say: 'God ha' mercy! I'm done for!' and they were the last words he had ever said. Now Brunt heard them again. It was a trick, of course, played by someone who had heard Brunt tell the story and had discovered an acoustic peculiarity of the course. It made Brunt lose the race, as it was meant to, but that was the least part of it. 'He crept up to the paddock, white as chalk, with blue lips, his knees giving way under him ... He took his stick and went down the road, still shaking with fright, and muttering over and over again — "God ha' mercy, I'm done for!" '

Now that story begins in the most cocky vein of Kipling's callow youth. It is all racing shop, a knowing little sermon about how rotten racing in India usually is, told with the air of an experienced old hand who knows all about it. He had picked it all up in the club, listening to his elders. Of course he knew something of horses; everyone did, because India is a country of great distances and horses provided the only means of getting about. But he was not really a horsey man. All this parade of racing jargon is part of his continual effort to show that he really does belong, that he really does know. But embedded in this tiresome pretence is that vivid scene and the dramatic recognition that the jockey *was* done for. The trick — done to win the race — had virtually killed him.

2. DOORS TO NEW WORLDS

There are sixteen tales remaining in *Plain Tales* which in various ways open, for professional middle-class British readers, a door to new worlds. Four are about the three private soldiers, Mulvaney, Learoyd and Ortheris, who, more than any other part of Kipling's repertoire, made his name. Two introduce Strickland, the police officer who could pass as an Indian and who 'held the extra-ordinary theory that a Policeman in India should try to know as much about the natives as they know themselves.' He reappears in *Kim* and in various other stories. Three are about Eurasians, that is, people of mixed Indian and European ancestry, or 'loafers', who had dropped out of the European world; two bring in the supernatural, and five are to some extent about Indians. * All these stories, in one way or another, touch on aspects of life which were not usually talked about in the club or the mess. Of course officers in British regiments did know a good deal about the men under their command — but the civilians did not, and in Simla drawing-rooms or the Punjab Club the lives of British soldiers would not be mentioned from one year's end to another. And, in reverse, the British army officer knew nothing of life in the Indian city, and even the civilian knew only certain aspects of it.

Vivid pictures, narrative force, variety, vigour — these are to be found in nearly all these stories, published, let us again remember, before the author was twenty-two. They achieved their purpose of getting the ear of the limited audience for whom they were meant, and more than one in three of them could be expected to break new ground for most of their readers. One overriding impression which they leave is that sudden death is never far away, another that creative work is the best remedy against loneliness, and a third theme is the remorse for lost innocence and lost oppor-tunity that tolls like a bell through much of this early work. Women are a danger; marriage is likely to soften a man and take the edge off his art or work, while a stupid or contemptuous woman may kill his fire and self-confidence. On the other hand, an older woman, with whom there is little danger of anything more physical than a kiss, may be a valuable influence. There is a bias against anyone who sets up to be an intellectual, or who has a formulated philosophy of life; this is a reflection partly of the society in which Kipling found himself, partly of his regret for the

* The four stories about soldiers are 'The Three Musketeers', 'The Taking of Lungtungpen', 'A Daughter of the Regiment', 'The Madness of Private Ortheris'. The Strickland stories are 'Miss Youghal's Sais' and 'The Bronckhorst Divorce-Case'. 'The Bisara of Pooree' and 'By Word of Mouth' are about the supernatural. 'His Chance in Life' and 'The Gate of a Hundred Sorrows' are about Eurasians and 'Filed for Reference' about a 'loafer'. 'Lispeth', 'The House of Suddhoo', 'Beyond the Pale', 'The Story of Mohammad Din' are about Indian life and I have doubtfully included in this group 'Tods' Amendment', because it is one of the few stories in which Kipling does refer to Indian land tenure and its immense importance to the Indian peasantry.

university education he had missed, and partly of a temperamental preference for the concrete and individual as against the theoretical. In spite of this, there is a sense of chaos and breakdown kept at a distance only by the constant effort of man, a feeling of human society as something which in spite of injustice and pretence must be supported, because anarchy is much worse. Mediocrity is better than ruin, and yet there is a fascination in what goes on outside the safe world of ordered society.

That is a good deal to find in the outpourings for the daily press of a 21-year-old. But it does not explain the irritation which the stories have caused many readers. Let me again speak in terms of personal discovery. My copy of *Plain Tales* is dated for my twelfth birthday; all my friends at that time knew that I wanted every Kipling I could get. I read these stories over and over for the following two years, only half understanding but carried along by the skill of telling, the vigour of the story, the use of language. If I looked at them again in the next thirty years, it was usually to verify a quotation or refresh a picture that had stuck in the memory. During that period, I looked on the whole achievement with a touch of derision; Kipling had become a museum piece, not to be taken seriously, and there were not many stories that I did not find in some way irritating. There is often an introduction to a story, sometimes two or three short paragraphs, sometimes a page, consisting usually of generalizations in a patronizing, knowledgable vein. 'After marriage arrives a reaction, sometimes a big, sometimes a little one; but it comes sooner or later, and must be tided over by both parties ... ' This kind of thing is meant to show us how grown-up this brilliant young author really is and it does not grate at thirteen—but it does between sixteen and sixty! Or take the famous passage introducing Strickland: 'He was initiated into the *Sat Bhai* at Allahabad ... he knew the Lizzard Song of the *Sansis* and the Halli-Hukk dance, which is a religious can-can of a startling kind. When a man knows who dance the Halli-Hukk and how and when and where, he knows something to be proud of.' This is almost self-parody. It is meant to impress—but this time with a special esoteric kind of knowledge denied to the rest of us. This too is utterly convincing at thirteen, much less so when one has heard salesmen's patter more often. Anyone who has ever passed an examination must know something of the trick of implying that the knowledge displayed is only the tip of the iceberg—but a reader does not want to be treated as an examiner.

3

All the same, there are sixteen of these stories which, in one way
or another, explore new fields, and these are usually more free
from this kind of self-consciousness. One indeed, 'The Story of
Muhammad Din', is quite free. It is only half the usual length and
is really hardly a story at all. The *khidmatgar** begs for an old polo
ball which his little son would like to play with. He takes it out on
to the verandah and there follows 'a hurricane of joyful squeaks, a
patter of small feet and the *thud-thud-thud* of the ball rolling along
the ground'. That is the first we hear of Muhammad Din; later we
see him, 'a chubby little eccentricity', always alone, 'a tiny plump
figure in a ridiculously inadequate shirt which came half-way down
the tubby stomach'. He trots about the garden, making patterns
in the dust and crooning to himself, and appearing every evening
to exchange greetings with the narrator on his way home from the
office. And then one day he is not to be seen, and a few days later,
though he 'would have given much to have avoided it', on the
road to the burying-ground the narrator meets the *khidmatgar*,
'carrying in his arms, wrapped in a white cloth, all that was left of
little Muhammad Din.'

That seems to me slight but without flaw. 'Beyond the Pale', on
the other hand, is heavily flawed. It is a first sketch, perhaps, for
'Without Benefit of Clergy'. Trejago, wandering at night in the
city, finds a lane that leads nowhere, the back of a house, a
window—and he hears from behind the window a pretty little
laugh. He remembers the *Arabian Nights* and quotes some verses
which the unknown caps them. He gains entry. She was a young
Hindu widow—'fairer than bar-gold in the Mint'—and, while it all
lasted, 'an endless delight to Trejago'. There was of course an old
woman, who slept outside the door and was the link with the outside world. She brought Bisesa word that Trejago had been seen
to pay attention to an Englishwoman. Bisesa made a storm about
it—and it seemed she had also some inkling that there was suspicion in the household that lay beyond her room. Perhaps the
flurry of jealousy was simulated to cover fear for his safety; at any
rate, she made him go and he was not to come again. He stayed
away for three weeks; when he came back, both Bisesa's hands
had been cut off at the wrists and someone struck at Trejago and
wounded him.

---

* The *khidmatgar* waits at table; he does not put out clothes or take them to be
ironed, which is the work of the bearer, nor does he cook nor clean the house,
which is the work of other servants. He is a Muslim.

The beginning of this story is marred by a sententious little sermon about keeping to one's own kind—with a touch of irony so that you cannot be quite sure whether it is to be taken at its face value or is put in to appease those who will read it over the breakfast-table. There is also some parade of familiarity with the *Arabian Nights*—but the verses quoted are Kipling's own. If they had been from the *Nights*, it is not likely that a Hindu girl, later said to be as ignorant as a bird, should have been able to cap them. Then there is a display of knowledge about object letters—which 'no Englishman should be able to translate'. Trejago, it is ironically remarked, 'knew far too much about these things'—but we are meant to infer that the writer knows and in fact is rather pleased with himself for knowing. But when the story does get going it is vivid and carries the reader along. Here are many of the ingredients of 'Without Benefit of Clergy'; Bisesa's attractive gestures, her love, her jealousy, come through, and the fascination of Trejago's double life without the loneliness of Holden. But it is hard and flat compared with the later story; there is no loss, no shared sorrow for a child. The affair is too short and Trejago is only amusing himself. And the whole episode is highly improbable. It is hard to believe that a Hindu widow living in a mother-in-law's house and working in the house by day could have carried on such an intrigue for six weeks. But that thought does not occur at first reading.

What is more important than improbabilities is that within two or three years Kipling could have achieved on a similar theme a story so much more fully and sympathetically developed. What jars on a mature reader of *Plain Tales*, for all their verve and vitality, is the defensive self-consciousness, due perhaps partly to early history and partly to the very fact that he was opening new doors to readers whom he feared might be unresponsive or hostile. The irony often hides his own ambivalence; the reader perceives a note of mockery, but is uncertain how far the writer means to carry it. There is, for instance, an often quoted passage in 'Aurelian McGoggin' which is directed at intellectual atheism.

But in India, where you really see humanity—raw, brown, naked humanity with nothing between it and the blazing sky, and only the used-up, overhandled earth underfoot, the notion somehow dies away, and most folk come back to simpler theories. Life, in India, is not long enough to waste in proving that there is no one in particular at the head of affairs. For this reason. The Deputy is above the Assistant, the Commissioner above the Deputy, the Lieutenant-Governor above the Commissioner, and the Viceroy above all four, under the orders of the Secretary of State, who is responsible to the Empress. If the Empress be not responsible to her Maker—if there is no Maker for her to be responsible to— the entire system of Our administration must be wrong; which is manifestly impossible.

There are two separate points in this passage. The first is quite serious though purely emotional; if you look at things-as-they-are, free from the trappings of conventional life and intellectual theories, you are bound to feel just as I do. But why? Raw brown humanity in such numbers and such poverty might seem to many an argument for the opposite view. It is no argument at all—in terms of the intellect. But Kipling recurs constantly to a deep feeling that to have some experience of humanity that was not street-bred, that was not muffled in Victorian convention, was to have a deeper understanding of life. The point about the official hierarchy is clearly ironic—but it is not so clear who is being mocked. My own suggestion is that Kipling felt about the Indian establishment—and perhaps about the universe—much as he had felt about his school. He was against the housemasters but on the side of the Headmaster. He accepted and indeed approved of the fact of British rule in India—but he was often highly critical of the forms it took. He mocks at men who have 'the right of wearing open-work jam-tart jewels in gold and enamel' on their clothes, at the whole apparatus of the Simla secretariat. He is scornful about the impact of European ideas but he idealizes the personal rule of the man running a district, while at the same time often showing flashes of jealousy for those who do it. They are the school prefects whom he had made fun of, but also envied and secretly admired.

There are various levels, then, to these intrusive little asides which have so often been called 'cocky' or 'knowing'. Some are meant to show that the writer is not a raw youth straight from England but a sophisticated man of the world, others are meant to show that he really does know something about curb-chains and martingales or some other special branch of knowledge; sometimes, that he has the key to worlds the rest of us know nothing about.

A stone's throw out on either hand
From that well-ordered road we tread,
And all the world is wild and strange.

But here he has to be careful; what he is writing will be read over the breakfast-table by prosaic folk who are part of the Establishment, and so he must make it clear that he too really belongs to their world, that he is not going to become a loafer or go native. And this he does by a patronizing, derogatory manner which suggests that the affairs of natives are not to be taken too seriously. But again he has a second thought and adds an ironic hint which implies: 'This isn't really what I think.' That is how we should read the opening sentences of 'Beyond the Pale'. It applies also to Strickland's 'extraordinary theory' that a policeman 'ought to know' about natives — or the comment that no Englishman 'ought to know' about object letters. This was the kind of thing he had heard said in the club or in Simla drawing-rooms. He slips it into his story in a mocking tone of voice so that it can be taken either way and either way no one can pin him down. He makes the point about his audience very clearly in *Something of Myself*. 'It was mine to be told every evening of the faults of that day's issue in very simple language.' And again, 'I was almost nightly responsible to visible and often brutally voluble critics at the Club.'

The implication that the narrator is still one of the ruling group and shares their prejudices is so marked in one of the stories about Indian life that a recent American critic — Dr Elliott Gilbert — has persuaded himself that the narrator of the story is an entirely fictitious character. But without that implication, 'In the House of Suddhoo', like 'Beyond the Pale', might well have suggested to Anglo-Indian breakfast-tables that this young man would soon have gone native altogether. It is about a fraud practised on an old man by a clever conjuror who pretends to have magic means of controlling spirits, and uses it to extort money from Suddhoo. Everyone present at the show put on by the conjuror is Indian except the narrator; two of the spectators are Kashmiri prostitutes. The narrator in his introduction says: 'Suddhoo is a great friend of mine, because his cousin had a son, who secured, thanks to my recommendation, the post of head-messenger to a big firm in the Station. Suddhoo says that God will make me a Lieutenant-Governor one of these days. I daresay his prophecy will come true.' The tone of this explanation is, I agree, patronizing,

derogatory and slightly facetious, but the expression: 'May you
become a Lord'*—that is, a Governor or the Commander-in-
Chief—was constantly used by any uneducated Indian who wanted
a favour from any Englishman, and it carries no implication that
this is likely to come about in the normal course of affairs. It does
not mean that the narrator was a covenanted civilian. The phrase
would be understood by Kipling's readers as a hit at the conventional flattery used by Indians. The whole passage is meant to
reassure them that the narrator really is a white sahib. The story
itself, when the introduction is over and it begins, is gripping and
impressively described. It ends with the narrator in a dilemma,
which he puts in the same mocking ironic style. He has committed an offence, having connived at obtaining money under
false pretences—but he cannot go to the police because no one
would give evidence; the conjuror has a hold on one of the
Kashmiri girls and the other has vanished, having married and
gone into purdah. He knows that the conjuror is continuing to
bleed Suddhoo, and the Kashmiri girl resents this because she
had hoped to get the money herself; he is afraid she will poison
the conjuror before long and then he will be accomplice to a
murder.

   Dr Elliott Gilbert finds the manner of this epilogue so distasteful that he supposes that the tale is put into the mouth of an
imaginary narrator, a self-satisfied and rather pompous young
civilian who was not Kipling at all. This I find quite incredible. It
is an important misunderstanding, because a narrator in the first
person appears in so many Kipling tales. So it must be dealt with.
In the first place, there are four stories of this period—'The
Phantom Rickshaw', 'The Strange Ride of Morrowbie Jukes',
'The Dream of Duncan Parenness' and 'The Gate of a Hundred
Sorrows'—in which Kipling did wish to dissociate himself from
a narrator who is using the first person, and in each he makes
what he is doing perfectly clear. If he had meant the narrator in
'In the House of Suddhoo' to be a wholly fictitious character, he
would have said so. He was after all meeting every day the people
who read his stories, who were bound to identify him to some
extent with the narrator. And the style in which the narrator refers
to himself—'I am only the chorus that comes in at the end to
explain things. So I do not count'—is to my ear just that in which
the narrator refers to himself in 'False Dawn' or 'The Other

* Ap Lāt Sahib ho jāe—or some form of the same wish.

Man' or 'The Three Musketeers'. Finally, if the narrator had been part of the administration he would have known very well what to say to the police. The final dilemma only makes sense if the narrator is *not* part of the administration, but an outsider whose word carries no weight. The implications of the epilogue are that it is really out of place to apply to Indians western ideas about procedure in criminal cases—a point which everyone at the bar of the club would concede—and, secondly, that 'all these people' are out to swindle each other and hold human life very cheap.

As in so many of these stories, we have the central vivid scene—a bowl with a baby's head in it, floating in phosphorescent fire; the lights turned down, only the glow of a brazier, the two frightened girls and the terrified old man; the conjuror on his stomach, naked, his hands behind him, his head raised from the ground like a cobra, writhing like a cobra round the black shrivelled head in the basin. Perhaps Kipling saw this; perhaps someone told him about it. He had to get it into his story and make it seem true, and that he could do only by having a witness—who for his purpose and for his audience had to be white. So he set it in the framework of narrative by a shadowy 'I', who in his usual mocking and ambiguous style indicates that he does not really approve of all these native goings-on.

That is not to say that in any Kipling story it would be justifiable to identify the narrator entirely with the writer. But in many of the stories the narrator is said to be a writer whose experiences and contacts are much the same as Kipling's; in such cases, we are clearly meant to take the narrator as Kipling. When this is his common practice, it would be strange—without giving the reader a clear signal—to use a narrator in the first person who is not to be identified with the writer in some degree. For example, if the narrator says he was told a story by three private soldiers in a railway refreshment-room at the cost of a good deal of beer, we may take it that Kipling himself has at some time been told a story, not perhaps this one, in such circumstances, and further, that he wants it to be known that he is on terms of this kind with private soldiers.

Even the sharpest critics of *Plain Tales* have usually conceded that—published as they were in collected form when Kipling was only twenty-three—they suggested a talent that deserved to be watched. But if there was any doubt that here was someone with quite exceptional imaginative richness at his fingertips, it ought to have disappeared on looking at the fragments of verse that head each story. They vary a good deal in quality, like the stories. They are not all apposite in the same degree. But many of them show a flash of vision, indeed of poetry. There are forty stories, and T. S. Eliot thought twenty-four of these headings worth including in his anthology. Several take the form of a verse or two from a ballad, telling a story which appears to have some parallel with the main story. Sometimes it is a verse from a song, sometimes an Indian proverb. But in almost every case, what is involved for the writer is composing, in addition to his tale, a linked or subsidiary tale or song of which only a fragment is quoted. To me, as a boy, the effect was compelling; it seemed to add conviction to one's belief in the main story, and sometimes to add a facet, making something strange and wild of what might otherwise have seemed to occur in the natural order of things. Sometimes, too, the verse lingers in the memory when the story is forgotten. And, coming back to them, I still find the effect powerful. Let me give as examples three only, chosen mainly because they are the headings to stories I have dealt with at some length:

'The Other Man':

> When the Earth was sick and the Skies were gray
>   And the woods were rotted with rain,
> The Dead Man rode through the autumn day
>   To visit his love again.

'Wressley of the Foreign Office':

> I closed and drew for my Love's sake,
>   That now is false to me,
> And I slew the Riever of Tarrant Moss
>   And set Dumeny free
>
> And ever they give me praise and gold,
>   And ever I moan my loss;
> For I struck the blow for my false Love's sake,
>   And not for the men of the Moss!
>
>   *Tarrant Moss*

And finally, in a rather different vein, the heading to 'False Dawn':

To-night God knows what thing shall tide,
  The Earth is racked and faint —
Expectant, sleepless, open-eyed;
And we, who from the Earth were made,
  Thrill with our Mother's pain.

In Durance

3. SOLDIERS THREE

I have dwelt on *Plain Tales* at greater length than the collection
has often been thought to deserve because of the light these
stories throw on various riddles about Kipling. In the three
collections of stories that followed he was not bound so closely by
considerations of space, and he moved towards the standard
length on which he eventually fixed, of about 8,000–12,000 words.
This gave him the opportunity to develop his characters more, but
it was some time before he shook off the habits acquired under
that early constriction. In 2,000 words, generally with a good deal
of incident, his characters had no room to develop and had usually
been two-dimensional, one aspect of the man or woman being
struck off in a phrase. It was long before he wholly abandoned
that trick, though in later stories these flat people are set against
rounded characters who we feel might walk off the page and do
something different round the corner. Again, with growing self-
confidence and a wider audience, the defensive asides and ambiguous irony of *Plain Tales* become less common.

It was *Soldiers Three* and *Barrack-Room Ballads* that widened
Kipling's appeal more than anything else. Both in subject and
style they were utterly new to the Victorian public; no one had
written about serving private soldiers — though there are plenty of
retired soldiers in English literature, from Corporal Trim to
Matthew Bagnet and George Rouncewell. As to style, it was the
period of Wilde, George Moore, Pater, Yeats, Conrad, Hardy.
Kipling's verses, in the language of the people and with the
rhythm of the music-hall, could hardly be more foreign to their
various manners. On the other hand, British soldiers were not so
remote from the British public, so alien, as Indians were. Here
was something vivid, direct, refreshingly free from pretence; you
liked it or you didn't, and if Max Beerbohm didn't, the editor of
the *St James's Gazette* did. The soldier Mulvaney grows, coming to
express more and more often that nostalgia for lost innocence and

3*

wasted opportunity which was so important for Kipling and
for others of his period, notably R. L. Stevenson. A writer in
the 1890s, if he was not consciously in rebellion against the pre-
vailing spirit, was almost bound to feel guilty that he was not a
man of action, and his characters are tortured by their failures to
be what they might have been. The soldier stories progress from
the four short pieces in *Plain Tales* to the seven longer tales in
Soldiers Three, and on to the three—twice as long again—in *Life's
Handicap*. Two of these last, 'The Courting of Dinah Shadd' and
'On Greenhow Hill', are by some critics reckoned among the best
stories Kipling ever wrote. There are three more in *Many Inventions*, and one of them, 'Love-o'-Women', is of high quality.
'Greenhow Hill' and 'Love-o'-Women' are both examples at its
best of the story-in-a-frame which was to be one of Kipling's
trademarks. In this form of construction, an incident witnessed at
first hand leads to reminiscence; there is an outer story and
another within it. It is the inner story that is important, but the
outer story serves two purposes. It is the occasion which starts
someone—in the soldier stories it is usually Mulvaney—telling his
story to the narrator, but also, when the construction comes off
completely, it illustrates or underlines an aspect of the inner story
or points it up by ending differently.

In 'Love-o'-Women' the outer story begins dramatically. It is a
superb opening, packed with matter and implication, in style as
good as anything Kipling ever wrote.

> The horror, the confusion, and the separation of the mur-
> derer from his comrades were all over before I came. There
> remained only on the barrack-square the blood of man
> calling from the ground. The hot sun had dried it to a dusky
> goldbeater-skin film, cracked lozenge-wise by the heat; and
> as the wind rose, each lozenge, rising a little, curled up at the
> edges as if it were a dumb tongue. Then a heavier gust blew
> all away down wind in grains of dark coloured dust. It was
> too hot to stand in the sunshine before breakfast. The men
> were in barracks talking the matter over. A knot of soldiers'
> wives stood by one of the entrances to the married quarters,
> while inside a woman shrieked and raged with wicked filthy
> words.

Sergeant Raines has deliberately shot a corporal in his own
company. Everyone knows that the corporal had been having an

affair with Mrs Raines and sympathy is with Raines; there is some hard lying to make it appear that he was given sudden and intolerable provocation. This fabricated evidence is successful and the sergeant gets off with only two years. The whole business prompts Mulvaney to say that the corporal was the lucky man — compared with the sergeant but also compared with what he would have become himself if he had lived. And the talk that follows leads him to tell the tale of a gentleman-ranker he had once known as Love-o'-Women and the fate that befell him.

It was not only a slow death from disease but a racking remorse which we are made to feel is far more searing. Of the many women he has deliberately wronged, one is always in his mind, and the memory tears him apart. 'Diamonds and pearls I have thrown away with both hands!' he says, and Mulvaney comes to think of this woman as Diamonds-and-Pearls. They are on the Frontier and Love-o'-Women tries to get killed, recklessly exposing himself to fire—but the bullets will not hit him. His agony of remorse builds up slowly; Mulvaney has been through bad times but never has he dreamed of anything like this. Then the doctor notices something about the way Love-o'-Women moves his legs; what is killing him physically is an after-effect of syphilis and he knows it—but when the doctor knows too, he crumbles. And then, when the regiments come back to Peshawar, he hears a voice from the litter where he lies dying. It is Diamonds-and-Pearls and he tells the litter to follow her. She stops at a house that is clearly a brothel and she has only the bitterest of biting words to throw at him until he says: 'I am dying, Egypt, dying.' 'Here!' she cries and opens her arms to him. He falls dead in her arms. When Mulvaney comes back with the doctor, she too is dead. ' 'T was the first and last time I've iver known woman to use the pistol.' The doctor has been celebrating his safe return to Peshawar, but he sobers up when he sees these two, records two deaths from natural circumstances and orders them to be buried in one grave at his expense. By the time that story has been told, Sergeant Raines has been taken off to the civil jail and it is time for the guard to march away. As they go, they sing: 'And that's what the Girl told the Soldier!'

This is not a pretty story. A woman's suicide in a brothel, a man dying in the final stages of syphilitic disease, the crows already on the verandah, the drunken surgeon—it is a squalid but unforgettable scene. In general, I find Mulvaney's stage Irish hard to bear;

it does not sound like any Irish I have ever heard, and the effect could be achieved with much greater art by an occasional turn of phrase. It is a convention of the period and a bad one. But by the end of this story I have forgotten that irritation. This must be in part because of the skill with which the tale is constructed. In the frame-story is sketched with great economy of line a picture of Raines, the sergeant, a decent, patient, long-suffering man, of Corporal Mackie, an inveterate philanderer, not from weakness but for love of the sport, and Mrs Raines, highly sexed and irritated by the decency of Raines. Then in the main story we have Love-o'-Women and Diamonds-and-Pearls, whose passion we are meant to compare with that of Antony and Cleopatra. Again, we know nothing of their past; they are revealed as it were by a flash of lightning, in a fixed instantaneous gesture at the moment of death. Love-o'-Women is Mackie writ large; Diamonds-and-Pearls something incomparably better than Mrs Raines — but both are contrasted with Terence Mulvaney and Dinah Shadd. Theirs is married love, cemented by the loss of an only child; we know that Dinah has had to forgive Terence a great deal and how tormented he is by remorse, but in this story they stand for the happiness Love-o'-Women might have had. The construction — a story within a story, and contrast between a triangle and two pairs of lovers — could perhaps be described in musical terms; the three groups of people, like different instruments, repeat variations on the two main themes, remorse, and that rare happening, overpowering and reciprocated physical passion.

Here the 'frame' method of construction reaches its early peak. We have the narrator, who has to report the trial of Sergeant Raines for his newspaper, but also knows the witnesses and is aware that the court has been misled. Discussion of all this leads into the main tale, which is thus doubly distilled, or twice 'reduced', in the sense in which soup is reduced by being slowly simmered to gain strength. Inessentials are steamed away, first by Mulvaney's memory, which selects the more vivid incidents, secondly by the narrator, who guides him occasionally so that there is a sense of running speech and an illusion of unstudied revelation which compels belief. In the result, there is none of the incongruity that one feels in the ironic asides of 'Beyond the Pale'. The writer has established, several stories ago, the fact of his unusual relationship with these three soldiers, and he does not intervene in the action. On the whole, the narrator in the soldier stories shows little sense of strain; he is not trying to put across a point about himself. And he can safely leave to Mulvaney any preaching that is needed.

None the less, I am not quite at home with any of the *Soldiers Three* stories. I did not put them among my favourites as a boy, and even now, though I see the craftsmanship and the power of 'Greenhow Hill', 'Dinah Shadd', and this story, I do not quite believe in the independent existence of Mulvaney as I do in Grace Ashcroft's. He will never walk off the page; she might. Perhaps this is the effect of the dialect, which is more than a trick of speech. It means that from the start the three soldiers are pinned down like butterflies in a cabinet, Irishman, Yorkshireman, Cockney.

It helps to consider the three soldiers in the light of *Stalky and Co.*, written eight to ten years later when the author was more assured of his public. The *Stalky* stories are about boys, of whose daily life Kipling really knew a good deal — more certainly than he did of private soldiers — and they tell us more of himself. The formula is the same as in *Soldiers Three*: three bad boys against the world. There is the same conflict between the need for discipline and the pleasures of anarchic individualism; Mulvaney lost his stripes and has never won them back because everyone knows he can't keep off the beer — yet no one else can knock a batch of recruits into shape as he can, and he can take effective command of a company if the officer is too young to know what to do. Two of the *Stalky* themes recur fairly often, punishment or the restoration of balance, and manipulation from behind the scenes. If the figures sometimes move a little jerkily — like people in the early cinematograph when there was too long a pause between one pose and the next — that is due to inexperience, and the progress between 'The Three Musketeers' and 'Love-o'-Women' is enormous. In the later *Soldiers* stories there are flash-light scenes of great power like the one we have just looked at — or Learoyd holding his tiny rival for the love of Liza Roantree over a bottomless drop in the mine till he is cowed by the little man's courage. There are also touches that may go unnoticed at a first hasty reading, such as Mackie's blood crying from the ground till it is dried, curls up like a dumb tongue, and is blown down the wind in dust or Learoyd plucking at the dog violets that remind him of home as he tells *his* tale of pain and loss.

4. ODD MAN OUT

Bound up in the English collection with *Soldiers Three* is 'The Story of the Gadsbys', a series of dialogues about a cavalry officer who falls sentimentally in love with a girl much younger than himself, breaks off in the most clumsy and brutal way possible a previous affair, and after marriage deteriorates as a squadron leader till he is afraid his own men will ride over him on parade. The whole thing is a lengthy exercise on the theme of 'A young man married is a young man marred' and seems to me to have little merit. Also included in this collection are eight stories which had appeared on railway bookstalls in India with the title: *In Black and White*. They are in the same vein as the stories about Indian life in *Plain Tales* except that they are longer and rather more assured; the most substantial is 'On the City Wall'.

There are three other groups from the railway bookstalls, *Under the Deodars*, *The Phantom Rickshaw* and *Wee Willie Winkie*. *Under the Deodars* continues that strain in *Plain Tales* which sketches Anglo-Indian society, and in one story, 'A Wayside Comedy', takes that particular line about as far as it can go. In his last years, Kipling thought this one of the half-dozen best stories he had done. It is the tale of five English people in an isolated place, distant two days by relays of horses from anywhere else where there are English. Two of the five, Major and Mrs Vansuythen, are newcomers; Mrs Vansuythen is devastating in a peculiarly Kiplingish way, quiet and grave, fair, 'with very still grey eyes, the colour of a lake just before the light of the sun touches it'. Before she came, Kurrell had discovered that Mrs Boulte was 'the one woman in the world for him'; she had believed him and felt for him an emotion that was deeper and more lasting. Boulte was in camp for a fortnight in every month and Kurrell and Mrs Boulte had made use of that opportunity. But now each of the two men, Kurrell and Boulte, separately discovers that, after all, it is Mrs Vansuythen who is the one woman in the world. She will have nothing to do with either of them, but, before she has made this very plain indeed, Boulte has been told by his wife what had been going on in his absence, and Mrs Boulte knows that she has been abandoned by both husband and lover. So Kashima is far from being what is called a happy station. Only Major Vansuythen is unconscious of the passions that surround him; his wife is determined that he shall remain in ignorance and he keeps up 'a burdensome geniality', insisting that 'in a little station we must all be friendly'.

It is a story that has been much admired in France and it is much in the vein of Maupassant. But it is cold and loveless. The characters 'love' without affection. Nobody except Mrs Vansuythen emerges as the kind of person one would like to meet; her husband is intolerably insensitive; Boulte — 'a hard heavy man' — is thoroughly disagreeable, and Kurrell, though he must have had a specious attraction, is quite without honour or decency. It is told straight, without a narrator or a frame, and except for the first paragraph, in which the writer prays the Government of India to disperse these five people, it is flawless of its kind. It is, however, a kind which Kipling was now to abandon; there are other women who are fatally attractive without lifting a finger, but this is the last of what might be called the kaleidoscope school: stories in which the brightly coloured, geometrically shaped characters — orange, blue, red triangles and squares — can be shaken and rearranged on one plane surface in the pull of one force.

Other stories in this vein are spoilt by moral ambiguity; 'At the Pit's Mouth', for instance, must be judged inferior to such a story as Maupassant's 'Boule de Suif', because Kipling half pretends that he is not condemning the Tertium Quid and the Man's Wife — though he clearly is. His admiration is for the sterling virtues of the Man, that is, the husband, stewing in the plains and living in discomfort in order to buy his wife luxuries. In Maupassant's story — beautifully constructed in just the way Kipling would have admired — there is no doubt at all where the writer's sympathies lie. In 'A Wayside Comedy', the writer has settled where he stands — and that is outside the story, neither condemning nor pretending not to condemn. But having produced one admirable example of this kind of tale, he did not come back to it. It was a mask he could now abandon. The interest he had felt in the emotional kaleidoscope was partly intellectual; he wanted to see whether an English public would accept an offering from an essentially French *cuisine*. But there was also an interest basically adolescent, a desire for titillation that it would be an exaggeration to call prurient. His real interest was in permanent attachments — the kind of firm base to a man's life from which he could emerge to fight in the cause of work and art.

The collection of four stories about children which appeared on Indian railway bookstalls as *Wee Willie Winkie* contains two stories

which everyone now finds sentimental, and which for modern
taste are spoilt by the convention that all children under seven talk
a distressing baby-talk. 'Tum wiv me,' says His Majesty the King,
and Wee Willie Winkie wails: 'I've bwoken my awwest!' 'Baa
Baa, Black Sheep', as I have said, is bitter, vivid and partly auto-
biographical. 'The Drums of the Fore and Aft' would have
benefited greatly by compression, being marred by an unneces-
sary excursion on the nature of military leadership and the education of the working-classes. But the story itself embodies an
admirable irony; a British regiment—with 'shrewd, clerkly' non-
commissioned officers—panics and runs in the face of the enemy.
Two drummer-boys, knocked down in the stampede, get to their
feet, march towards the enemy, playing 'The British Grenadiers',
and rally the battalion, which comes back to the attack as the
children fall dead. Highly sentimental it sounds, and the final
scene has been painted in that spirit; but the fact is that the two
boys were very far from being little cherubs; they were usually in
trouble for fighting, swearing and smoking, and at the moment
of their heroic death were drunk, having taken possession of a
cast-off water-bottle, which 'naturally was full of canteen rum'.

This is a revealing story, because it is written from different
levels of Kipling's personality and also addressed to different
levels in the reader. The homily in the opening pages shows
Kipling at his worst; it deplores the effect of half-education on the
young soldier on a short-service system. 'He has no inherited
morals' and has not had time to learn 'how holy a thing is his
Regiment'.

> Armed with imperfect knowledge, cursed with the rudi-
> ments of an imagination, hampered by the intense selfishness
> of the lower classes, and unsupported by any regimental
> associations, this young man is suddenly introduced to an
> enemy who in Eastern lands is always ugly, generally tall and
> hairy, and frequently noisy.

This young man is contrasted with officers who 'are as good as
good can be, because their training begins early and God has
arranged that a clean-run youth of the British middle classes shall,
in the matter of backbone, brains, and bowels, surpass all other
youths.' Here, at his most 'awful'—class-conscious, race-con-
scious, judging dolls with labels as though they were people—
Kipling is writing from the most superficial level of his conscious-

ness. But the story is based on observed fact; there have been British regiments who behaved like this — one at least long before the short-service system — and Lew and Jakin are real boys. The bare outline of the story is novelettish, but the realism with which the boys' character is drawn and the rum in the water-bottle give it a new dimension and make it a sharp comment on Victorian sentimentality. Here is light on the riddle of the different reactions Kipling produces; as artist writing from the depth of his consciousness he is quite different from the superficial commentator. There is a glossy surface, like a piece of glass with something opaque beneath it, which reflects its surroundings, or at least their outline; that is the superficial journalist. But the artist is moved by something within himself that corresponds with what he has seen. Something deep inside him stirs; it may be shadow or fire but it is in the light of that that he must write. This is not what Kipling himself means by working on different levels; then the conscious craftsman is making something which will hold a superficial reader but will say much more to a careful reader. When he does this, he is appealing to different levels in the reader; this is not the same as writing from different levels in himself. He does both in 'The Drums of the Fore and Aft'.

The Phantom Rickshaw is also a collection of four stories of very uneven merit. 'The Strange Ride of Morrowbie Jukes' has been classed by Hilton Brown as 'balderdash', but Edmund Gosse included it in his pick of the best, while later writers have admired its 'Kafkaesque' qualities. Almost everyone has put 'The Man who would be King' in his picked list. As a boy, I felt that this story fell into two halves, of which the second was superbly exciting, but the first 'I did not like so much,' which meant that it seemed rather long-drawn out and not altogether comprehensible. But I now see that without the frame the inner story would have been no more than a boy's tale of adventure. Set as it is, against the daily life of a young man on a newspaper, against the office drudgery and the tyranny of the printing machines waiting to be fed, it compels belief — belief even in a far-away kingdom among snow peaks, a crown of raw turquoise and red gold, the red beard and blind sunken eyes of a dried withered head, shaken out on the table in a newspaper office in the pale sunshine of the dawn. That is the essential key scene, the flashlight photo that corresponds to the Other Man dead in the tonga or Diamonds-and-Pearls opening her arms to the dying man.

The story begins on a railway journey in the course of which the narrator—a young man on a newspaper in Lahore—meets Carnehan, a 'loafer', that is to say a poor white, a man who has been a soldier, who has taken his discharge in India, and now lives by his wits in various disreputable ways. One source of funds is to ferret out scandal in an Indian state, pretend to be on the staff of a newspaper, and blackmail the ruler. He is on some such lay now, and he begs the narrator to give a message to a man he will meet at a certain station on his return journey. The narrator obliges him, and for the first time meets Daniel Dravot with his flaming red beard. Later—on a hot night when he is alone in the newspaper office, waiting for news from some distant continent— these two, Dravot and Carnehan, come to see him again. They have made a contract with each other to keep off drink and women till they have carried out their purpose, which is to make themselves kings of Kafiristan, a corner of Central Asia that is still unexplored. They want to look at maps and consult books of reference. They have twenty rifles and are confident that these, with what they know of soldiering, will be enough. Next day, he sees them leave Lahore, disguised as a mad priest and his disciple, with a supply of 'whirligigs' to sell on the way. Two years later Carnehan, a shattered remnant of the man he had met first, comes back and tells him the tale which culminates with Dravot's dried head on the table. They had won their kingdom but it came to an end when Dravot insisted on taking a woman, who, in the face of all his subjects, bit him till the blood ran, to show he was only human. They made Dravot fall from a bridge to his death; Carnehan they crucified but took down alive.

The difficulty that the craftsman had here faced was how to tell a wildly romantic story in such a way as to compel belief. It was one of the literary problems of the day. Conrad and Stevenson also have tales to tell about scenes far from the lives of Victorian Londoners, and both adopted various means of bringing them into relation with their readers. Both use the observer who is only indirectly part of the story and whose part is written in a deliberately low key. The danger of this method is that it may reduce the vivid force of direct impact. But this certainly does not happen as we listen to the tale of how Daniel Dravot built up his kingdom and met his death.

Coming back in later life to this story, which held me as a boy at the level of boy's adventure, I still find it superb entertainment, and a high technical achievement. But I still think the framework too elaborate, and it does not introduce the theme of the main story like the opening bars of a concerto, as in 'Love-o'-Women'. Nor does it explore human character and passion to the same extent as 'Greenhow Hill' or 'Without Benefit', still less the best of the later stories. Daniel Dravot is a figure of stature, a born administrator with the ambition of Cecil Rhodes and with the same knack of making fantasy come true. What destroys him is contempt for the gods and a pig-headed rejection of human advice. He must have a wife and he will not see that this will shatter the aura of divinity that upholds him. Abler, more ambitious and more determined than Carnehan, he is also coarser. Carnehan is convinced that women are always dangerous, and that to get mixed up with women in foreign parts always means trouble, but Dravot brushes such fears aside. He must have a wife to keep him warm in the winter. And these women are white. 'Boil 'em once or twice in hot water and they'll come out like chicken and ham,' he says. He had seen the force of Carnehan's fear of women before they left India, but now he is confident in his hold on the kingdom he has won.

I cannot feel in this story a strong recurring metaphysical theme as in 'Without Benefit'. The story is knit together by the repetition of certain details. Dravot's crown and his red beard reappear in the hymn poor crazed Carnehan sings after his return:

> The Son of God goes forth to war,
> A kingly crown to gain;
> His blood-red banner streams afar!
> Who follows in his train?

The 'whirligigs' which the kings-to-be had taken with them when they set out are remembered when Daniel Dravot falls, 'turning round and round and round, twenty thousand miles, for he took half an hour to fall till he struck the water ... ' But there is implicit in the story an intuitive understanding of European ascendancy in the nineteenth century, which depended on a fantastic bluff and on the aura of something close to divinity which could be destroyed by a trifle.

The story has another interest because it is the first full-dress occasion in which freemasonry plays a part. It is because they are fellow masons that the young journalist who is the narrator first does a favour to Daniel Dravot and his companion; it is for the same reason that they come back to him before they start on their adventure and that the survivor creeps back to him when it is over. And masonry is one reason for the success with which the kingdom begins; the wild people of the remote Himalayan tract had acquired some fragments of masonic ritual—said, absurdly, to have been left by Alexander's armies—and Dravot could go on where their knowledge stopped. Freemasonry, as various people have pointed out, was bound to attract Kipling; he loved to belong to an inner circle, with secret passwords, where he could be safe from the women who fascinated and frightened him, where he could meet odd people who would give him useful copy but not prove a social embarrassment outside the Lodge.

Thus a fairly detailed look at some of Kipling's early work suggests that he is very far indeed from being the self-confident extrovert that he is sometimes labelled. There are many inconsistent aspects of his personality and a good deal of tension between them. He remembered from his early childhood an India of bright lights, colours and scents, an exciting, vivid life, which attracted him deeply. But he never reconciled this attraction with a slick superficial conformity to the views of the Club and the Mess, which looked with suspicion on most 'natives' other than soldiers. Thus there was a sharp contrast between the generalized view he generally expressed about 'natives' and the judgment he might make of individual Indians he had met. There was the same ambivalence about 'the lower classes', whom he could castigate in general as intensely selfish, while he can portray an individual as a human being, loving or hating or making a sacrifice of life for a comrade or a lover. He was on the side of order and discipline as against chaos, and idealized those who enforced order so long as they rode about on horses. But let them venture to sit down at a desk and they at once became objects of derision. He knew himself to be the swot, the short, spectacled figure who read books and could not play games. But he admired 'clean-built careless men in the Army' and hated intellectuals like Aurelian McGoggin, who is almost a parody of himself. He sought hungrily for the security of a close inner circle to which he could belong—but he was outside the official Indian hierarchy, a civilian among soldiers, an oddity among civil officials. And yet if he ventured into the strange worlds of Indian and Eurasian life he was still a white sahib and a member of the Club—odd man out whichever way he turned. Freemasonry gave him occasional moments of the assured security he sought, but it was intermittent. Work was central to his view of life, and art was part of work. But work was loveless, art demanded a ruthless discipline, both were competitive. He needed a more sympathetic world of love to fall back on. He insisted, from the upper layer of his consciousness, that a man must be independent before all things, but at a deeper level he longed for a warm emotional fortress. There was the Family Square, but despite his protestations about the perfection of this relationship I sense, as I have already said, an unease. To the end of his life, he spoke of The Mother and The Father, or sometimes The Pater, preserving into manhood the belief, inculcated no doubt at Westward Ho!, that it was unmanly, if not indecent, to refer to one's parents except in some depersonalized form.* And, even more than most young middle-class Englishmen of the period who had been to a boarding school, he was in a muddle about women. There were cruel women, like Aunty Rosa and Mrs Reiver, who convinced him that the female of the species was more deadly than the male; there were distant ideal visions like Flo Garrard and the Brushwood Girl; there was the ancient dangerous archetypal Woman of 'The Cat that Walked by Himself', sitting by the fire and singing spells. It was the magical danger that lies in women that was the downfall of Daniel Dravot. There were silly little fluffy women who were dangerous to men like Wressley and Gadsby; there were mother-women like Mrs Hauksbee and his own mother; there were brother-women like William and Ted Hill. It is much more difficult to think of real women; Ameera was one—but then she was Indian—and the Rani in *Kim*. Later, of course, there were to be Helen Turrell of 'The Gardener' and Grace Ashcroft of 'The Wish House'. But even they were not young women of his own class, and in any case much had to happen before that.

---

* Even in the present century, small boys were given this treatment. At my prep school, during the First World War, to say 'My Mother' was a solecism almost as embarrassing as it would have been to the inhabitants of Huxley's *Brave New World*. To them it was smut, but to us it was sissy, babyish, 'not done' among boys who were going to public schools. We had to say 'mater' if we referred to her at all.

4
*An End
to
Boyhood*

1. ROMANTIC FRIENDSHIP

When Kipling left India, he was still precocious and innocent, a clever boy, even if he had a startling achievement already behind him. The next two years were packed with events, some of them obscure, though clearly important in his life. Then came the attempt to settle in America, its abrupt termination, and the loss of his daughter. After that, from the end of the century for thirty-six years, there were only two events of primary importance to the understanding of his work, the purchase of Bateman's in Sussex and the death of his son in 1915. Let us look briefly at the course of events in the years after he left India.

He was travelling, you will remember, with Professor Hill and his wife Ted. Kipling was sending articles to *The Pioneer*; they were vigorous, uninhibited articles, and he said a good deal about America which Americans did not like. He also gave interviews in which he said the same kind of thing—and what he said lost nothing in the reporting. He became news in the United States; he was another Englishman who hated their country. But once again, this was an oversimplification. He loved as well as hated; his views on America were mixed because he was a very mixed person. One side of him liked the directness, the quick emotional reactions, the independence, the egalitarianism, on which Americans prided themselves. There were no aristocrats to look down on him. He admired the self-supporting life of a New England farmstead. He rejoiced to think that Americans were 'of one blood' with the English. But then something pulled him up short and he had to express his distaste for people who really did not understand the kind of things he had learnt so painfully at Westward Ho!—who showed off so blatantly, who were so law-less, so brash and so shrill. This ambivalence lasted right through his life. The admiration is strong in *Captains Courageous* (1897), a novel about the Newfoundland Fishing Banks; the irritation spurts out in 'An Error in the Fourth Dimension' (1898), a tale about an American millionaire who tries to settle in England, becomes almost assimilated, and savagely returns to the blatancy and rawness he had once tried to suppress.

Kipling crossed America by himself, met the Hills again, and sailed for England with Ted Hill, her younger sister Caroline Taylor, and their brother. The party arrived in October 1889. Charles Carrington must surely be right in his surmise that Ted

Hill 'discreetly diverted' Kipling's attention towards her younger sister. The manoeuvre almost succeeded; for some months he wrote to Caroline what he referred to as love-letters, talked about his prospects and achievements and even sent her an explicit statement of his religious beliefs in answer to some unease on her father's part. Perhaps his unorthodoxy provided her with the occasion for breaking off the affair; to me it seems likely that the real reason was his meeting, by chance and in the street, with his first love Flo Garrard. This was early in 1890; by February of that year, he was confessing to his sister Trix that he had exaggerated his feelings for Caroline Taylor and had been deeply moved by meeting Flo. But Flo remained the unattainable dream-girl; she told him she was not prepared to give up her art, for which it does not appear that she had much talent.

There is nothing unusual in all this, but it underlines the desire for a secure world of love in this young man who so blatantly proclaimed his virile self-sufficiency. He seems to have been intermittently more lonely and unhappy in London than he had ever been in India. There was a spell when he had money owing to him for work accepted but would not ask that it should be paid, because: 'People who ask for money, however justifiably, have it remembered against them.' His rent—for a small room off the Strand—was paid but he had nothing to pawn; there was a shop below where for tuppence he could buy 'as much sausage and mash as would carry one from breakfast to dinner', and another tuppence would find him a filling supper. But there was an element of make-believe in this. He had two aunts in London married to distinguished men, and in any case it did not last long. His success really came very quickly. He was selling poems and articles within a month of landing at Liverpool, and was almost at once taken by Andrew Lang to the Savile Club, where he met all the literary lions of the day, and soon became a member. In March of 1890 he was the subject of a leader in *The Times*, reviewing all his work. It was *his* year; he was a celebrity in a way that would hardly be possible today for a writer who was not also a television actor. London was taken by storm, shocked and fascinated. The brilliance of vision, the mastery of words, the compact, concentrated impact of his work, were what struck the writers and critics. A wider public, less conscious of how the effect was produced, was startled by the frankness with which he discussed love affairs outside marriage and the brutality of hand-to-hand conflict, cholera, suicide and murder. He wrote in *Something of Myself*: 'That period was all ... a dream, in which it seemed that I could push down walls, walk through ramparts and stride across rivers.'

None the less, even his own account does not sound as though he had been happy. He met many people he did not like. He still lacked an emotional home; no one was ever more in need of a dependable wife. And, even more than had been the case in India, he did not feel that he *belonged*. He had left England when he was sixteen; he came back at twenty-four a foreigner. He was being labelled a literary man and, though a part of him always proclaimed that this was just what he was, another part indignantly rebelled; he wanted to resume his hero-worship of 'men who did things'. He sent *The Pioneer* some verses, in parody of Lewis Carroll (who himself was parodying Wordsworth):

> But I consort with long-haired things
> In velvet collar-rolls
> Who talk about the aims of Art
> And 'theories' and 'goals'
> And moo and coo with womenfolk
> About their blessed souls.

It was a year of intense work, during which he wrote and published most of the verses later collected as *Barrack-Room Ballads*, seven stories in his now standard length of around 8,000–12,000 words, a full-length novel, *The Light that Failed*, and a good deal that was more ephemeral. It was a year of emotional upheaval, of some ill-health, and finally of nervous exhaustion.

It is perhaps not surprising that some of his utterances were querulous and some bad-tempered. The American law of copyright did not then protect writing first published in England, and he suffered much from American publishers who pirated his works; he transferred the anger he felt at this treatment to a reputable American firm who had certainly treated him cavalierly but were not exactly pirates, and he became enraged with three eminent English writers who ventured to say that, whatever they might have done to Kipling, these publishers had treated them well. He turned this quarrel into a long ballad, 'The Rhyme of the Three Captains', in which he outlines the punishment he would have inflicted on 'the pirate' if he had been able:

I had nailed his ears to my capstan-head, and ripped them
    off with a saw,
And soused them in the bilgewater, and served them to
    him raw;
I had flung him blind in a rudderless boat to rot in the
    rocking dark,
I had towed him aft of his own craft, a bait for his brother
    shark ...

And so on for a dozen lines that are not exactly drained of hate.

The Light that Failed is not a good novel, as Kipling knew; he never attempted anything of that length in anything like that vein again. But it must be mentioned here because in part it is disguised autobiography, because its general tone is unhappy and often irritable—sometimes brutal, sometimes hysterical—and because it does throw some light on what followed. Dick Heldar, the central figure, is one side of what Kipling wanted to be. He is a newspaper man, but of a kind extinct since photography became so much easier; he drew the pictures which then took the place that photos take now. He had knocked about the world and drawn all kinds of strange people and places, but his special skill was battle-scenes and soldiers. As a boy, he had been at a place very like the House of Desolation, and his companion there had been Maisie, who is one of Kipling's pale, dark dream-girls, very like Flo Garrard and the Brushwood Girl. They had been boy-and-girl sweethearts. Dick is with the army when a Sudanese force surprises a British battalion, and for a brief interval breaks into the square of bayonets. He gets a cut over the head from a Sudanese sword, but recovers and comes back to London, where his drawings and paintings win startling success. He meets Maisie by chance in the street—much as Kipling had met Flo—and finds that he still adores her. Like Flo, she is still studying art but has little talent. He begs her to marry him but she will not; she must go on with her own pitiful little dabbling. His art seems to her 'to smell of tobacco and blood'. He perseveres; he tries to help her with her drawing; he takes her back to the scene of their childhood. But it is no use; he cannot wake her up. He worries about what might happen to her; she pervades his thoughts. But it is all a little adolescent; he is surprisingly ready to accept her pose of being unattainable. She too is immature; she likes owning him but is too self-centred to respond. Then he begins to go blind; the sword-cut had damaged the optic nerve. He sets about painting a final masterpiece and keeps going with whisky because he can see better when drunk. The painting is finished and now he is totally blind. Maisie is persuaded to come to see him but she is quite incapable of the sacrifice that would be involved in looking after him, and she runs away. He determines to go back to the Sudan, where war has broken out again, exposes himself to the enemy's fire and is killed.

For Maisie read Flo, for painter read writer, and recall that angry resentment of the rejected adolescent, who says to himself: 'She'd be sorry if I were dying!' It was blindness that Kipling feared more than death, and it was eyeless faces he saw in dreams. And so, when he took refuge from Flo's coldness in fantasy, he pictured himself going blind. But he was realist enough to know that Flo would not come to look after him even if he did go blind. Maisie's emotional inadequacy is contrasted with the attitude to Dick of her room-mate — 'the red-haired girl'; she is never named — who is drawn in a few quick strokes, outwardly scornful but clearly ready to give all that Maisie is not. And that too would add a satisfying touch to the fantasy.

There can be no serious doubt that Dick's pursuit of Maisie is based on Rudyard's of Flo Garrard, whom he followed to France, where she was studying. There runs through the book the man's incredulous feeling that a woman could not say no to such selfless devotion just because she did not find him attractive; there must be some *reason*. Maisie said it was her art — as Flo had said — and the man tries to argue her out of it. But of course there is no arguing about such things.

Let us touch on two minor scenes. One concerns a dispute about copyright. Dick has worked for a firm who paid him a regular salary, no doubt as little as they dared. They have published his sketches in journals, but he thinks the originals are his and should be returned to him. The firm maintains that under the contract the sketches are theirs. The head of this firm is an elderly man with a weak heart who comes to talk business. Dick lives at the top of several flights of stairs and the man is exhausted when he arrives. Dick, without actually striking him, walks round him, pawing him and threatening him, and puts him in such bodily fear that he sends for the sketches and surrenders them. The sketches safe, Dick sends him away in a flurry of contemptuous insults with the threat: 'If you worry me when I have settled down to work with any nonsense about actions for assault, believe me, I'll catch you and manhandle you and you'll die.'

No doubt that is how Kipling would sometimes have liked to treat some publisher. It is a scene of brutal fantasy, and it is matched by one of sentimental self-pity. Dick is blind; he is taken into the Park by his friend Torpenhow and they are near a battalion of the Guards.

> The clank of bayonets being unfixed made Dick's nostrils quiver.
> 'Let's get nearer. They're in column, aren't they?'
> 'Yes. How did you know?'
> 'Felt it. Oh, my men! — my beautiful men!' He edged forward as though he could see. 'I could draw those chaps once. Who'll draw 'em now?'

Kipling often compressed a whole novel into a story. Here something that he — but perhaps only he — might have condensed into a story has been expanded into a novel, stuffed with bits of biography. Nobody reading *The Light that Failed* could doubt that its author took his work seriously nor that he had genius, but as a novel, it sprawls, it hangs fire in the middle. Kipling himself said that he did not understand how to construct a story of that length. But he clearly tried to hold it together by repetitive symbolic patterns, as in the best of his shorter stories. There is, for example, a moment when Dick and Maisie are boy and girl and have gone down to the beach with a cheap revolver. She accidentally fires near his face and he is almost blinded; later, he fires the last cartridge over the sea towards the sunset. A gust of wind drives her long black hair over his face and 'he was in the dark — a darkness that stung'. Elements of this scene are repeated — sand, a revolver, a red sunset — in the square in the Sudan, and again he is in 'a darkness that stung'. And again, just before he meets Maisie in London near Westminster Bridge, there is sunset on the river, the black smoke of a river-steamer drives across his face, and he is blinded for a moment.

There is a great deal of discussion in *The Light* about work and art, and the corruption that success may bring. To please an editor, Dick makes one of his realistic battle-scenes into a sentimental mockery of itself, but his friend Torpenhow — all his friends are male war-correspondents — destroys it. Torpenhow starts an affair with a girl Dick is using as a model; Dick has no desire for her himself but stops the affair, for no reason explicitly stated, but by implication because women are dangerous to work. This girl in revenge destroys the masterpiece which he had worked desperately to finish before his blindness became complete. It is Torpenhow who comes back to look after Dick when he is blind, and not only blind but 'done for' — morally bankrupt and finished. Kipling always liked male company, but I can think of no other occasion in his work when there is so strong an impression of physical tenderness between men.

It has been a commonplace to think of the Victorians as hypocritical because they were silent about much of which they were well aware. But, largely because of that silence, they were often not so hypocritical as innocent. Of course, there cannot have been Victorian men unaware that homosexual acts sometimes took place — but they regarded this as a strange and on the whole rare vice. They were unaware of the many half-shades of emotion and behaviour that are commonplace today, and most of them would have indignantly repudiated the suggestion that there was any sexual element in the platonic male affection that played so large a part in their society. But schoolmasters, dons, army officers, who devoted their lives to looking after young men, were at the heart of Victorian greatness; their charges were the loves of their lives. For most of Kipling's life, this was not so with him. He liked being with men, but it was to women he looked for fascination and attraction. Sore from Flo Garrard's rejection, he felt himself thrown back on men for an affection that was safe, warm and intelligible. And into this mood was suddenly projected a young man who carried with him an atmosphere of intellectual excitement and animal magnetism.

Although artistically a failure, *The Light* was published in America in November 1890, and early in 1891 was reprinted five times in magazine form in England before it appeared in book form in March. But the magazine version was quite different from the book, which carries a cryptic 'preface' stating in two lines that this is the story as the author first conceived it. The magazine version has a happy ending. Now Kipling was fastidious about the sacredness of art. There is a great deal about art in *The Light that Failed*, and one of the crimes inveighed against is to sentimentalize the harsh lines of reality. Yet here he does this very thing — and that within a few weeks of writing the passage in which it is condemned. Not only that, but he agreed to collaborate in a novel with another man—something quite unthinkable at any other period of his life.

This man was Wolcott Balestier,* an American, the agent in London of an American publishing firm. A change in the law of publishing had now given him the chance he needed. If an English writer signed a contract with an American firm before publication he would in future be protected against other American firms. It was Wolcott Balestier's task to secure as many British authors as he could, and he was extremely successful. Not only that, but everyone was under his spell. He had a wider circle of friends in London, thought Edmund Gosse, than any other living American. He charmed people by his enthusiasm; he swept difficulties aside; they were made to be overcome. He was determined to add Kipling's scalp to his already distinguished collection; he came to see him one evening at seven o'clock and, finding him out, waited till he came back at midnight and then plunged into a business talk. They became close friends, and it must have been Balestier who persuaded Kipling to go for big sales in the magazine market with the soft end to *The Light*. At about the same time, he persuaded Kipling to collaborate with him in *The Naulahka*.

This carries the sub-title 'A Story of West and East'. It was Balestier's idea that the author of 'The Ballad of East and West' should contribute chapters on India, while he himself wrote chapters dealing with the expanding Western Frontier of the United States. It was a time when many Americans were excited by vision of a new society and a new outlook, by the feeling that in the West there was no such word as impossible, and that people were in touch with 'reality' in a way they never could be in old lands still in the trammels of convention. With such feelings Kipling was in sympathy, and the idea of transporting two Americans from the far West to India seems to have fired him. There is a description of Kipling striding about the room with Balestier sitting at a typewriter, 'each composing, suggesting or criticizing in turn'. Balestier contributed the first chapters, in which he was allowed a free hand. They amply justify his feeling that he had little hope of success as a writer unless he collaborated with someone already established. But the plot had been agreed. It centres on the now familiar figure of the girl who won't marry her childhood friend because she has a purpose of her own, in this case to nurse the unfortunate women of India. The rejected lover

* Pronounced to rhyme with 'callous tier'.

follows her to India and there preposterous adventures befall him; there are priceless jewels, a beautiful but wicked queen — who makes advances to the hero and who with his help could make all India hers — a sacred crocodile, gold mines that suddenly begin to pay when most needed, a noble act of renunciation, a happy ending — everything. The hero can throw a coin in the air and hit it with a revolver, ride a bucking horse and face death without a tremor. He is straight from the Wild West. The later chapters, though inherently absurd, are enlivened by Kipling's memories of dawns and sunsets in Rajputana, which he had visited as a journalist. There are constant tricks of style that we know, but in the subject-matter hardly a trace of the Kipling who was later to write *Kim*; the people of India are idle, feckless, superstitious and corrupt, and the writers give no sign of dissent from the contempt freely expressed for them by the hero, Nick Tarvin, whose gospel is hustle for its own sake. His impatience, his inability to understand the people, his worship of speed, would have infuriated Kipling in any mood but this; they are exactly the American qualities he criticized in *Something of Myself*. That Kipling should have allowed his name to be associated with this dime novel, still more that he should have allowed it to be included in his collected works, can only be because he was obsessed by Balestier's charm and drive and sales talk.

It was, of course, through Wolcott that Kipling met his sister, Caroline Balestier, whom he was to marry. The Kipling parents were now in England, and Alice Kipling no sooner saw Caroline Balestier than she said: 'That woman means to marry our Ruddy.' Lockwood Kipling observed that she was 'a good man spoiled'. And Kate, the heroine of *The Naulahka*, is a determined little person, not unlike Carrie Balestier, and not at all like Maisie or Flo.

* *The Light that Failed* appeared in the original version — with that strange preface — in March 1891. In this form it was, as Charles Carrington remarks, practically an anti-feminist pamphlet. Does the abruptness of those two lines suggest some rift with the man who had proposed the soft end? In February, Wolcott had written that he and Rudyard were making great progress with their collaboration in *The Naulahka*. In June Kipling suddenly went off to see an uncle on the other side of the Atlantic — his mother's elder brother, whom none of the family had visited for thirty years until Rudyard turned up in New York in 1889. But Kipling had not

then discovered any special affinity for him. He died in 1891 while Kipling was at sea and the young man came straight back. He stayed on his return with the Balestiers in their cottage on the Isle of Wight, and in August left by himself on a voyage round the world.

Now why was this? Why did he bolt? It is true that his doctor and parents were advising him to do something of the kind; he had not been well and his output in 1890 had been prodigious. He needed a rest. It is true that in May Edmund Gosse had advised him in a long friendly review to go East and come back in ten years with 'another precious and admirable burden of loot'. But he was not always amenable to advice. Nor was he a solitary. He liked company on a sea voyage and had chosen to come back from India with Mrs Hill and her husband. Taking into account the dates, the extraordinary influence Wolcott had established over him, and Alice Kipling's intuition, I cannot resist the conclusion that it was from the Balestiers, or from one of them, that he ran away. But whether it was because he was frightened by the intensity of his relationship with Wolcott, whether he felt he must escape from Carrie's pursuit, or whether he had half given in to her and—in view of that other Caroline—felt he must have time to think things over, I cannot feel certain. Perhaps, indeed, it was a little of all three. But one fragment of evidence suggests that perhaps it was mainly to think things over. There is an early draft of the set of verses known as 'L'Envoi' or as 'The Long Trail'. In the form in which this appears at the end of *Barrack-Room Ballads* and in a great many anthologies, the second stanza begins:

Ha' done with the Tents of Shem, dear lass

and 'dear lass' recurs in every stanza till the last. But in this early draft, it is 'dear lad' throughout. Carrington suggests that 'the tents of Shem' refers to a partnership which Balestier contemplated with the firm of Heinemann, and that Kipling was urging him to forget this and come with him. Unless 'the Tents of Shem' does specifically mean some Jewish association, it is hard to see what it does mean; the whole tone of the rest of the ballad demands that the 'dear lass' or 'dear lad' should leave towns, not tents—places of luxury or at least comfort for a roving life. If this was really addressed originally to Wolcott and changed after his death, Kipling may have left with a feeling of soreness at his friend's refusal to come with him, coupled with some self-reproach over

4

the happy ending to the novel, which spilled over into irritation.

All we know for certain is that he went alone, that he reached New Zealand, and that he had meant to go on to see R. L. Stevenson in the South Pacific. But it appears that news reached him which made him change his mind and turn back, in a leisurely manner at first. He was with his parents in Lahore when he received a telegram. Wolcott Balestier had been ill, had become suddenly worse, and had died early in December. Kipling left at once, arrived in London on January 10th, 1892, and was married, almost furtively, to Caroline on the 18th. Wolcott's death must have made him bring to a head whatever understanding had existed before. There is a letter from the best man, Henry James, to his brother William, quoted by Carrington:

> I saw the Rudyard Kiplings off ... the other day ... She ... is a hard devoted capable little person whom I don't in the least understand his marrying ... I gave her away at the altar in a dreary little wedding with an attendance simply of four men — her mother and sister prostrate with influenza. Kipling strikes me personally as the most complete man of genius (as distinct from fine intelligence) that I have ever known.

Carrington suggests that the marriage was a kind of death-bed bequest from Wolcott to both partners. And surely this is right. Kipling, when he met the Balestiers, was unhappy at Flo Garrard's refusal. Wolcott stirred and excited him; he fell under his spell. Then he met his sister and she was included in the glow of romantic affection he felt for this young man who so warmly admired his work and entered so eagerly into his plans. Then he fled — but from what exactly we do not know. When he came back Wolcott was dead, and, whatever the circumstances of his flight, it is surely safe to suppose that Kipling reproached himself for things left undone and unsaid, for time lost that might have been spent with his friend. If there had been some difference between them, then the feeling of reproach would be the stronger. It would surely be enough to push him over the brink on which he had hesitated; it had been Wolcott who had brought Rudyard and Carrie together, and shared love for Wolcott had drawn them closer. To marry Wolcott's sister would give some degree of immortality to the relationship that had meant so much to him.

He would hardly ever speak of Wolcott or of his death; there is no mention of Wolcott in *Something of Myself*, just as there is no mention of the deaths of his daughter or his son. But he dedicated *Barrack-Room Ballads* to Wolcott Balestier in verses whose flamboyance is in strange contrast to this stoic silence. Indeed, they are so extravagant as to be embarrassing:

To these who are cleansed of base Desire, Sorrow and Lust and
  Shame—
Gods for they knew the hearts of men, men for they stooped to
  Fame,
Borne on the breath that men call Death, my brother's spirit
  came ...

and, after several more stanzas:

Beyond the loom of the last lone star, through open darkness
  hurled,
Further than rebel comet dared or hiving star-swarm swirled,
Sits he with those that praise our God for that they served His
  world.

In contrast, there is one restrained and moving comment, made to a close friend of Wolcotts: 'He died so suddenly and so far away; we had so much to say to each other and now I have got to wait so long before I can say it.'

From now on, to quote Carrington again, Carrie 'provided him with his creature comforts, shielded him from intruders, watched his health, kept his accounts, took charge of all his affairs — sometimes with an irksome particularity.' It was a satisfying marriage; it gave him a firm emotional base, even though it might at times appear a little humdrum. When he wrote of working a story at several levels, it may be suspected that Carrie did not trouble herself much with those that lay below the surface. It is surely significant that the narrator in such stories as 'They', 'The Dog Hervey', 'The House Surgeon', 'The Bull that Thought'—always a comfortably-off, middle-aged man, living in the Home Counties, with a car, a house, dogs and a chauffeur—is unmistakably a bachelor. He lived in worlds he did not want to share; Carrie was no Brushwood Girl.

2. WRITING FOR A LIVING

Those two years 1890 and 1891 had been packed with life. Kipling had talked about marriage to Caroline Taylor and they had been

near an engagement, but it had come to nothing; he had met Flo
Garrard again, pressed her to marry him and been refused; he
had formed a close friendship with Wolcott Balestier and been
deeply moved by his death; in January 1892 he had married
Caroline Balestier. His output in both prose and verse had been
formidable. We have looked already, because of their biographical
importance, at the two novels which belong to this period; there
are also two collections of stories, *Life's Handicap* (1891), which
includes 'Without Benefit of Clergy', and *Many Inventions* (1893),
which includes 'Love-o'-Women'. These two stories were considered earlier because they made particular points required at that
stage; it remains to consider the two collections as wholes.

Life's Handicap was published as a collection in July 1891; the
stories had appeared separately before that. Almost all of them
look back to India. There are eleven stories, varying in length
between 6,000 and 10,000 words and averaging about 8,000, that
is, about twenty to thirty pages; there are another sixteen much
shorter pieces, of about the length used in *Plain Tales*, that is,
around 2,000 words. These shorter pieces continue the tradition
of *Plain Tales*, except that there are none about the flirtations of
the English. They are of varying quality, and must on the whole
be judged the pot-boilers of a young and still sometimes careless
writer, with a remarkable gift when he is at his best. One of them,
'Little Tobrah', only five pages long, is a masterpiece of compression. Little Tobrah, eight years old, is on trial for the murder of
his sister, but no one actually saw him push her into the well and
he is discharged for lack of evidence. But he has nothing to eat
and nowhere to go. Someone gives him a meal and he tells his
tale; smallpox had blinded his little sister and killed his parents;
the grain-seller oppressed them, their house fell down, they ran
away. But they had nothing to eat. His sister was blind and it was
better to die than to starve. And so, as she sat on the kerb of the
well, he pushed. Like 'The Story of Muhammad Din', it is a grim,
compassionate story, free from self-consciousness, the more
moving for its restraint, on a tiny scale Kipling at his best.

Of the eleven longer stories, three are about Learoyd, Ortheris
and Mulvaney, one, 'On Greenhow Hill', being generally thought
the best of that kind he ever did. None of the others seems to me
quite of the same calibre as 'Greenhow Hill' or 'Without Benefit',
but, just as at this stage even the best of Kipling's work is often
marred by an error in taste, a story of which the content is de-

plorable may contain a moving passage told with superb mastery of detail. Such is the scene in 'The Head of the District', where the Deputy Commissioner lies dying in his litter on the bank of the Indus in flood, while in the first light of dawn a clumsy boat blunders to and fro across the river to bring his wife. 'The river gulped at the banks, brought down a cliff of sand and snarled the more hungrily.' In the cold of early morning, the men with the litter look for fuel; a horse coughs. The dying man hears the horse and says he is cold too. The men gather round for his last words. His wife comes an hour too late. But this is only the beginning, and the story itself—the plot told without adornment —comes from the level of club gossip. This is also true to a lesser extent of two famous stories in this collection, 'At the End of the Passage' and 'The Mark of the Beast'. Both are horror stories, and in one the horror has a particularly gruesome twist; both are unusual, but they were the kind of stories that one used to hear in India, where English people were more ready than in England to believe stories of the occult, being perhaps mildly infected by the beliefs of those around them and perhaps also because they wanted to believe that India and its people were strange and mysterious. Neither of these stories has depth; the action does not depend on character. Both contain unforgettable scenes and both carry the reader eagerly forward.

'At the End of the Passage' begins with a picture of four men playing whist 'crossly', somewhere in Northern India. It is the hot weather; the bungalow is darkened; they are besieged by the heat. They come to meet each other, if they can, every Sunday. One of them, the host, is Assistant Engineer on a stretch of railway; the other three come from considerable distances, over a hundred miles in two cases, simply to speak to another Englishman once a week. They 'were not conscious of any special regard for each other.' The boredom, the snappish ill-humour, the closeness of death, the heat, the loneliness, the dust, are overpowering. But the four men are working sahibs, like dozens of other men in Kipling who, apart from sometimes slightly unusual surnames, are indistinguishable. Working sahibs are labelled; we know their occupations—Survey Officer, Political Officer, Forest Officer—but apart from that, they are wax figures. Though the story may dictate a role, no difference of taste, character, religion, or background is suggested between one working sahib and the next. We may hear them talk shop, and then of course we know which labelled figure is speaking. In this story, if he talks about the Raja, it is Lowndes the Political Officer, but otherwise, Lowndes and Mottram are stage properties; Hummil, the host, has a role as the victim of the horror; Spurstow also has a special part because he is a doctor. But in the opening stages of the story, there is no difference between them. They are simply four men — any four men — set against the dreadful background. And at this stage, their interchangeability is right; it adds to the desired effect. They give up their whist and betake themselves 'to an aimless investigation of all Hummil's possessions — guns, tattered novels, saddlery, spurs and the like'. They had fingered them a score of times before but there was really nothing else to do. Then as the talk developed it came out that Hummil was not sleeping — had not slept for days — and Spurstow, the doctor, decides to stay the night. Suicide was never far from their minds; Hummil's subordinate had only lately made an end of himself. When the others have gone, Hummil admits that he is near breaking-point; he begs for something to make him sleep — but it must be deep sleep, free from dreams. He is terrified of half-sleep; he had fixed a spur in his bed so that if he nodded off it would wake him. There is a blind face that cries and cannot wipe its eyes which chases him along corridors; unless he can get away, he knows he will die. His terror is absolute, quite beyond reason. Spurstow gives him morphia and he has one good night, but next day Spurstow has to leave him; he is looking after a camp full of coolies where there is an epidemic of cholera. When the three come next Sunday, Hummil lies dead in his bed; he has been unable to escape from the blind face; he has been 'scared to death'.

The theme of unspeakable fear coming in dreams, often recurring dreams, is something to which Kipling returned throughout his life, and he must have had personal experience of that horror. But here there is a suggestion that there was something more than a dream; Hummil's eyes are open when he is found dead and Spurstow takes a photograph of the pupils, develops the film and comes out 'very white indeed', refusing to say what he has seen. The idea was absurd, he said, and quite unknown to medical science. And, of course, he was quite right; indeed, there was a double absurdity. If it could be photographed at all, whatever frightened Hummil must have had the kind of reality that will reflect or intercept rays of light. But he had seen it in dreams, when his eyes were closed. And — even if that is overcome — to suppose that the eye retains the image reflected on it when the brain ceases to live is like thinking that a telescope will continue to record the image of what a man saw in it at the moment he was shot dead.

Thrown in as an extra, we are told that Hummil, when awake, saw an apparition of himself, sitting at table, waiting for him when he came in to dinner. Now to see one's own image is something that has been supposed to be a premonition of death.

> Ere Babylon was dust,
> The Magus Zoroaster, my dead child,
> Met his own image walking in the garden.
> That apparition, sole of men, he saw.

Those lines of Shelley's carry that implication, when they are read in their context. They were quoted by Charles Williams when he was trying to describe the 'black panic' felt by a girl who had repeatedly seen her own image walking towards her and knew that if it met her some inconceivable horror would befall. But for Charles Williams the experience is central to that part of his story; he dwells on the girl's terror, building it up slowly— and he has to, because in itself the sight of one's own image need not be frightening. But in 'The End of the Passage' Kipling, with the prodigality of youth, throws in this theme, so tremendous in possibilities, never develops it, and passes straight on, leaving it unconnected with his main story. Think how Henry James would have rolled it round tongue and palate and savoured the bouquet! Here it has nothing to do with the rest of Hummil's experience. This was something Kipling would never have done in the late stories, when every phrase and incident was weighed and calculated. Here is a brilliant idea—to set the terror of recurring nightmare against the squalid boredom of Indian hot weather and to imagine that the nightmare comes true, that the pursuing horror does catch up. And this has been done successfully; the main elements come off and the story is gripping—but it would be more effective if Kipling had treated it with the austerity of his later period, when he set every story aside 'to drain' and then cut it ruthlessly. He could then have cut the *doppelgänger* or self-image and the absurdity with the camera. And he would have wanted to work out for himself, and at least hint to us, some reason why this terrible affliction had befallen Hummil. He comes back to the theme in a late-middle-story, 'In the Same Boat' (1911), and the difference in treatment admirably displays Kipling's development.

Kipling was intuitive; he *felt* the dramatic force of the loneliness
and heat, of panic and nightmare; and at this stage he was writing
for his living and did not think out the implications of all that he
was feeling and seeing; he was thus apt to include absurdities.
This is even more true of an inferior story in this collection, 'The
Return of Imray'. Imray, a young English official of whose
character we hear nothing, had disappeared. There had been a
search, ponds had been dragged and so on, but no clues had been
found and the case had been closed, an unsolved mystery. Strickland, the policeman we have heard of in *Plain Tales*, rents his
bungalow. But his dog will not sleep in the house or enter it after
dark, and the narrator, when he comes to stay with his friend
Strickland, is aware of strange movements and of someone
desperately trying to tell him something. Indian bungalows were
often built with a thatched roof, sharply pitched, the thatch,
beams and rafters being hidden from the room below by nothing
but a cotton sheet stretched tight to look like a ceiling. In this
bungalow, there are snakes above the ceiling-cloth and Strickland
goes up a ladder with a stick to poke them down. He sees something lying on top of the central beam. He pokes it with his stick
and the corpse of Imray, stiff and horrible, its throat cut, comes
down on to the dining-room table through the torn ceiling cloth.
Strickland has taken on Imray's personal servant, as well as the
bungalow; confronted with the corpse, this man confesses that he
had cut his employer's throat as he lay asleep. Imray had praised
his child and put his hand on the boy's head; the next day the
child had sickened and died and therefore he had killed the
wizard who had bewitched his son. But the man is a Punjabi
Muslim of good landowning stock and will not disgrace his
family by going to the gallows; he puts his bare foot on a snake
that has also come down with the cloth, it bites him and he dies,
composedly accounting to Strickland with his last breath for
shirts and a piece of soap.

Now the last scene is something for which most Englishmen
who have lived any time in India could find some parallel, and it is
dramatic and moving. But the tale as a whole — quite apart from
what you may feel about the presence trying to make itself understood — is altogether absurd. Imray had disappeared and ponds
and canals had been dragged; murder was suspected; can it be
supposed that the house was not searched? It would have been

full of police for a week. It was the hot weather and it would not have been long before a corpse became noticeable. In any crime connected with a European, Indian police always suspect the servants, and Imray's bearer would have been closely questioned; Strickland of all men would not have employed a man who had been under such suspicion. It is quite clear that he had not taken the bungalow and the servant in order to solve the mystery. These are glaring absurdities which Kipling would surely have removed if he had not been working under pressure.

3. MANY INVENTIONS

Life's Handicap was put together, and some of it was written, at a time of intense activity and of personal stress, when money was short and publishers were eager for copy. Kipling was now a freelance, writing for a living, with his way to make in the world. Even so, there are stories that show a real development in power and maturity, and even those which are least mature have moments when the detail of sight, sound and smell burst through the limitations of the story itself. The development is continued in *Many Inventions*, when he was less pressed for time and money. Here are fourteen stories, each of about eight or nine thousand words; this from now on was to be the normal shape and size for a collection. The stories are intentionally varied in subject-matter, as the title exactly expresses, and they also vary not only in quality but in depth. Three are about the three famous soldiers, culminating with 'Love-o'-Women'. In one of them, Mulvaney tames an elephant; it is an entertaining story, but it contains several remarks about the mysterious characteristics of elephants which I believe to be mythology. It is true that elephants *look* mysterious; they have an air of having survived from prehistory, from the age of giant reptiles, and, as he dusts a tuft of grass against his knees, an elephant's eye, like a parrot's or a squid's, seems to meditate strange mischief. The best *mahout* I ever knew assured me, however, that in three weeks or a month a new driver could be on terms with any elephant. There is no need for a life-long partnership. But the English in India, romantics at heart, *wanted* elephants, like natives, to have strange powers.

The third soldier tale is the rather odd story called 'His Private Honour', in which Ortheris, an experienced private soldier, is struck on parade by a young officer. He was a very young officer,

4*

and in a moment of tense exasperation had lost control himself. He had not meant to hit Ortheris. None the less, it had happened; he might have been court-martialled, cashiered and his life ruined, if Ortheris had not saved him by lying to a senior officer. From that moment, the matter was between the two of them, on a personal basis. In the end the officer invites Ortheris to come shooting and — once they are where no one can see them — suggests they should fight it out man to man. Thus the balance is restored and atonement is made. It does not matter that the officer wins; Ortheris had had a fair chance. This principle of atonement, which is so deeply embedded in so many primitive systems of law, was important to Kipling till his life's end. The oddity lies in the unwritten ethic of the whole episode. Ortheris was felt by everyone to be right to cover the officer from official action; he would have been wrong to stand on his rights and insist on a formal apology. He is indignant at the idea: 'I ain't a recruity to go whining about my rights,' he says afterwards. The narrator shares his views; earlier, before the shooting expedition, when Ortheris was still very sore, he makes the point even more vigorously, rubbing it in with the remark: 'Ortheris, being neither a menial nor an American, but a free man, had no excuse for yelping.' This is hard to understand, and perhaps it is not to be understood but only to be felt; the nearest I can get to a meaning is that Ortheris had accepted military discipline by a voluntary act and also — by an act even more a matter of personal decision — had accepted a kind of tribal code of conduct, under which officers and men are linked in a league against impersonal official authority. A man is 'free' when he is under a code of discipline that he accepts of his own will — a point on which Kipling agreed with St Paul. The part of him that did not like Americans would have said that they did not accept any discipline and so were not free in this sense. But the reference to Americans here can be looked on only as a spasm of bad temper.

Another story in *Many Inventions* is 'Brugglesmith', which is a farce; the farces run right through Kipling's work and in my view do not develop much except in style. The content comes from a part of him that never grew up. This makes it difficult to deal with them chronologically, and the same is true of the passion for technicalities which became such a trademark of Kipling. Breaking-strain and revenge are also recurring themes — though here there is real development — and they too therefore

demand separate treatment later in this book. It is enough therefore to say of 'The Disturber of Traffic' that it combines two of
these recurring Kipling themes. It is the story of a lighthouse-
keeper who cracks under the strain of loneliness and suffers from
strange delusions, and it is set within a frame, as with 'Love-o'-
Women', but in this case a frame of carefully acquired technicalities about lighthouses and how they work. Here the technicalities
of the framework add to the effect of the main story, though
Kipling has not yet learnt to avoid that air of displaying his
knowledge and showing off to the reader that was one of his
besetting sins. But here is a beginning not only of his obsession
with how things work but also of his concern with ships and the
sea, and especially the navy.

Two stories are set in London of the eighteen-nineties. In both
there is a self-consciousness about class which corresponds to the
attitude about race that was so marked in 'Beyond the Pale'. Just
as Kipling had gone away from his English friends to find stories
among Indians in Lahore, so he left the writers and painters and
the Savile Club to look for copy in bars and music halls off the
Strand. But again — though not so markedly because he was older
now and a success — he felt he must show his readers, who were
bound to be mainly middle-class, that he had not altogether gone
native. Henry James might confine himself to millionaires and the
nobility, to country houses and Belgrave Square; Kipling would
go into the pubs and meet soldiers and prostitutes. But, in a society
that was intensely class-conscious, he must make it clear that this
was a foray across the border and that he came from the respectable side.

This note is more marked in 'Badalia Herodsfoot' than in 'The
Finest Story in the World', which is the more generally admired
tale. But 'Badalia' triumphs over its self-conscious beginning;
'The Finest Story', though it has its moments, in my view does
not stand up to more careful reading. It is about Charlie, a bank-
clerk with literary aspirations; the narrator is patronizing about
him from the start, because he is a bank-clerk, because he lives
with his mother, who bullies him, because he is ill-read and has no
literary gift. He belongs to 'the poor little street-bred people',
who know nothing of England because they know nothing of
anything else. But one day Charlie is on fire about a story he wants
to write. The story won't come, but he keeps seeing the detail of
it. He can't write, but he can talk, and he talks as though he were

remembering. And it slowly comes home to the narrator that he *is* remembering what he has seen in a past incarnation, when he was a slave on the lowest deck in a Greek galley. In yet another life, it seems he has been in a Viking ship that has been to America. He sometimes confuses the two ships and their captains; the vision or memory comes to him intermittently and fades again, but he throws out, off-hand and as a matter of course, detail he could not have found in books. He jots down something that a slave had scratched on an oar with a handcuff. The narrator takes it to the British Museum and finds that it is 'extremely corrupt Greek' – of which neither he nor Charlie has any knowledge – and means: 'I have been many times overcome with weariness in this employment.' 'Here', says the narrator, 'I capered among the dumb gods of Egypt and I laughed in their battered faces', but here, in my view, the story begins to break down. The narrator wants to recover endless detail so that he can make a story of it, but Charlie will not concentrate; he thinks of taking him to a mesmerist but happens to meet a Bengali student, a Hindu, who tells him that of course this remembering of a past incarnation does happen some-times – though it is unexpected in an unclean cow-eating Euro-pean – but usually 'the door is shut'. And this door will shut as soon as Charlie meets a girl. And of course he does – a girl 'with a foolish slack mouth'. 'Now I understand why the Lords of Life and Death shut the doors so carefully behind us. It is that we may not remember our first and most beautiful wooings.'

Now in this story there are flashes of heaven-sent imagination. 'The sea spurts through the oar-holes and the men row sitting up to their knees in water ... ' On the lowest deck, the only light comes from the hatches and the oar-holes. 'Can't you imagine the sunlight just squeezing through between the handle and the hole and wobbling about as the ship moves ... ?' And the food the men ate – rotten figs and black beans and wine in a skin bag – adds to the effect of sunlight and darkness, glitter and water, against a background of smouldering revolt, always ready to break into murderous hate. If an overseer should lose his balance and fall among the slaves, he will be killed. But does the story grip you? Do you really mind whether Charlie remembers the missing pieces? I think I did at first reading but, coming back to it after many years, I do not; I am irritated by the narrator's extravagant desire to suck – like a spider from a fly – the last drop of juice from the unfortunate bank-clerk, by his capering antics in the

British Museum, and by the conversation with the Bengali. '*I know all about reincarnation and about Hindu beliefs and you, poor ignorant reader, can't be expected to,*' he seems to be saying. This conversation, incidentally, slipped naturally into the vernacular, 'the tongue best suited for it,' but what vernacular would that be? Kipling did not know Bengali and his Bengali friend, a student in England, would feel more at home in English than in any north Indian language. The phrase he uses about the door being shut is simple Hindustani, the lingua franca of the army and of most of northern India. It is a phrase known to every memsahib and used by Indian servants as a convention to mean 'Not at home'.* It is all right if slipped into an English conversation about reincarnation, but it does not sound convincing to me in Hindustani and adds to my impression that Kipling was less fluent than he pretends, and that what he spoke was neither Urdu nor Hindi, the literary languages, but kitchen-Hindustani.† I find the whole conversation with the Bengali unreal. There is also a good deal about Norse sagas and Vinland and the first Viking voyage to America which impressed me when I was fourteen but which I now feel is *meant* to impress me.

But 'Badalia'—it is called in full 'The Record of Badalia Herodsfoot'—is a different matter. In a sense, it was a *tour de force*; to write about the life of the slums in 1890 was a line looked on with favour by publishers and the public; Somerset Maugham's *Liza of Lambeth* belongs to the period. 'Badalia' begins, in a key of faintly facetious detachment, about the customs of costermongers and the habits of Gunnison Street, and returns to this note occasionally, but the story as it develops takes on its own life and the self-consciousness fades away. It tells of a world in which for the men the only recreation is to get drunk; when they are drunk, they beat their wives. Badalia had been with Tom Herodsfoot two years when he took up with another woman and walked out over her senseless body. She wouldn't take up with anyone else; Tom would come back one day, she said, and if he

* *Not at home.* When an Indian servant said 'The door is shut', he meant just what an English butler would have meant by saying 'Not at home'. The door was probably open and in full view, but I guess that the phrase came from Mughal times and meant that the inner door of the *zanana* or women's quarter was shut and the master of the house not available.

† There are Hindustani phrases in 'In the House of Suddhoo' and 'The Lost Legion' which confirm this opinion; they are kitchen Hindustani and would not have been used by Indians.

found her with anyone else he'd kill her as like as not. She earns enough to keep herself. But she can't bear to see the curate wasting custards and jellies on the prostitute Lascar Loo, who gets none of them. Lascar Loo is dying, as everyone knows, but as soon as the curate's back is turned, her mother eats the delicacies he has brought and pawns the blankets for drink. The curate recognizes Badalia's honesty and the 'sacred fever of the administrator' which burns in her veins and eventually makes her trustee of a small weekly sum which she uses for beef tea, medicine, cabs to the hospital and the like, writing down the details in an exercise book — ill spelt, sprawling entries but exact as to detail.

Gradually all the church-workers and dispensers of charity come to trust her, in spite of her godless language and irreverent agnosticism. But she has to fight Lascar Loo's mother; sometimes, in some other tenement, she will have to call in a man from outside to save, from a drunken husband, something she has brought for the baby. Tom, of course, gets tired of Jenny, the other woman, when she is pregnant, and one night when he has knocked her about and is very drunk it occurs to him to go and see what he can get from Badalia. He stumbles on the doorstep over Lascar Loo's mother, who tells him that the curate is keeping Badalia and giving her five pounds a week. Badalia gives him all she has of her own but won't tell him where the few poor shillings of her trust money are hidden. When he hits her she falls and he begins to kick her head with his nailed boots. He is interrupted by Jenny, who had followed him, to drag him back if need be or to fight Badalia. She sees at once that Badalia is past fighting; she makes Tom understand that it will be murder and he must get away and for God's sake clean his boots; she will have nothing more to do with him. Before she vanishes, she takes word to the curate to go at once to Badalia. Badalia can just make herself heard and whispers where the trust money and the book are to be found; before she dies, she tells the curate and Sister Eva, his fellow social-worker, to go and make a match of it. No, she had never seen the man before; Tom hadn't been near her for two years.

All Gunnison Street went to her funeral — all but Lascar Loo and her mother, who was now free to go back to her old ways. There was no one but the cat on the doorstep to hear 'the wail of the dying prostitute: "Oh, mother, mother, won't you even let me lick the spoon!" '

That story walks a knife-edge and brings it off. A hair's-breadth to one side or the other would make it novelettish, plunging into piety or sentimentality or melodrama. It avoids all three, mainly by the grim realism which cuts through the ineffectual efforts of the charity workers. There is the blood on Tom's boots and the details of the deathbed, which are far from pretty, the restraint with which Tom and Jenny are allowed to vanish. But in his later style Kipling would have removed the concessions in the opening pages to the view, so dear to *Punch* of that period, that the manners of the slums are necessarily funny. And he would have been clear himself—even if he had left the reader to guess what he meant from hints—about the nature of Badalia's feelings for Tom and for the curate. As the story stands, I don't think he had thought this out. There are indications that in spite of his brutality she still wanted Tom to be her man. 'Come to bed!' she says, when he comes back. But on her deathbed, she makes over the curate to Sister Eva with the clear implication that she had wanted him herself, though she knew that the difference of class made it impossible. Was it only tribal loyalty that made her say she hadn't seen Tom? Or was she a Desdemona, loving with her last breath? 'Nobody, I myself. Farewell!' It was surely impossible that she should have the same kind of feeling about two such different men; was it sexual attraction for one and a motherly affection for the innocence of the other? It has not been worked out; Kipling was still writing for his living and writing too fast.

That is the only story in that vein, though Kipling did come back to it in the song called 'Mary, Pity Women!' That, he tells us, was based on what he heard from a barmaid, and it must have been in bars that he found a good deal of 'Badalia'. But after his marriage he did not spend much time in bars.

4. THE FIRST FABLE

If one considers *Many Inventions* without its last story, it is arguable—though I would not agree with such a judgment—that there is not much advance here on *Life's Handicap*. The earlier collection has 'Greenhow Hill' and 'Without Benefit'; the later 'Love-o'-Women' and 'Badalia'. But I do not think it is even arguable if the last story is included. This is the first of the fables; it is called 'The Children of the Zodiac'. I did not understand it at all as a boy and in those days left it out when I came back to this period to read again 'The Mark of the Beast' or 'At the End of the Passage'. I am not sure that I wholly understand it now. But I do find it a piece of writing that is moving, that has something to say to me on almost every page, that is concerned with the purpose of life and with something that Kipling sincerely believed. The style is slightly different from that of tales about everyday affairs; it was later to be developed into the special style of the *Just So Stories*, and anyone brought up on those tales will at once recognize something familiar in the tone of voice. And one scene, the visit to the House of Cancer the Crab, has several parallels with the visit to 'The Crab that Played with the Sea'. But the scene in 'The Children of the Zodiac' is wholly frightening. You might think the Crab was asleep if you did not see 'the ceaseless play and winnowing motion of the feathery branches round his mouth', which is 'like the eating of smothered fire into rotten timber'.

The fable tells how, long ago, the Children of the Zodiac lived on earth and thought they were immortal gods. Men brought them flowers and offerings, but they did not understand men because they did not know how to laugh or cry. Then Leo and Virgo the Girl came to see each other in a new way. They learnt to love, and once they had made a start with that lesson they found they could cry. They learnt the fear of death. They had not known they could die till they went to see the Crab and learnt that he would come for them in the end. The fear of death taught them to laugh, and now they began to understand people a good deal better. The last lesson was that if they worked for men it would help them to forget the fear of death. The Bull, who was one of the six children, worked by ploughing, and died content that he had ploughed straight furrows; Leo and the Girl sang to make men laugh or cry and to help them at their work; they went from village to village, once they knew they were to die, singing for their living; the rewards were pitiful and the honours—such as peacock's feathers and buttons—were worse, they were silly and shameful. It was Cancer the Crab, who, as they knew he would, came for them both in the end: for the Girl first. Her breast turned hard as stone. Before she died, the Girl told Leo that he must go on singing, telling men not to be afraid of death. None the less, he was afraid when the Crab came for him and took him by the throat.

That is a very simplified form of the fable. The essence of

being a man is to love, laugh, cry and work. And the essence of being an artist is to understand these four activities of man and to please men by showing them their own laughter and love and tears and work in a new light, so that they feel that they have meaning. At this stage of his life, Kipling often spoke of his work as singing, and I am fairly confident about this part of the interpretation. But why Leo and the Girl thought they were gods to begin with is not so clear. Kipling was a religious man at heart, not that he took part regularly in any form of public worship or adhered to any formal creed, but because he thought much about death and eternity and the meaning of life. This first fable is a statement of his religion in that broad sense as he saw it at that moment. His views developed; the humanism of this stage remained, but something more positive added itself to the stoic attitude to death which the fable suggests. Because he was so essentially an intuitive, his religion expressed itself in stories, fables and verses, rather than in a creed or a reasoned philosophy.

If Kipling had died after the publication of *Many Inventions*, there would have been little to add to the verdict already pronounced on him by such friendly critics as Henry James and Edmund Gosse. Here was 'a strangely clever youth', in what he had already achieved extraordinarily precocious, but in his emotional development still often startling in his innocence. His great gift of fluency in words had been matched by a flair for collecting unusual material and for seeing the dramatic value of a moment—like the dead man sitting upright in the back of the tonga with the wet dripping off his moustache. But he was still often publishing work that had been put together too hastily. His characters still do not develop. More important, he was still unsure of himself, terribly in need of a loving personal background but also of a social background, a club or a caste or a regiment that he could belong to—though that is not to say that if he *had* belonged to such a fellowship he would not have hastened to proclaim that he did not really belong to it but was different. Now that he was married, now that he was enough of a success to spend a little more time on each volume, a great question-mark hung over him. Would he go on collecting the brilliant scenes he had found in the bazaars of Lahore and the pubs by the Thames? Or would he go on drawing on memory, a well from which the water tends to get muddy unless there is an active spring at the bottom? Would he, in short, settle down, like the married men of so many of his own early flippancies, dull and respectable, content to repeat his successes? Or would marriage help him to reconcile that deeper self that understood human hopes and fears with the other element that reflected back the superficial judgments of the smoking-room?

PART TWO
The Search for a Home

5
The Flight from Vermont

1. IN A STRANGE LAND

The Kiplings left on a journey round the world immediately after their wedding. He had put much of his savings into Cook's travel coupons; the rest was in a bank which suspended payment when they had crossed Canada and reached Japan. They were almost penniless; they postponed the rest of their journey, cashed what remained of the travel coupons, and went as directly as they could to Caroline Kipling's home country near Brattleboro, Vermont. The Balestiers, a Huguenot family, had been American for a century: Caroline's grandmother, Caroline Starr Wolcott, came of old New England stock. The Balestier grandparents had retired to Vermont in 1868, a mere twenty-four years before this. Kipling suggests, in *Something of Myself*, that they were still looked on as intruders by the people of the surrounding small farms, whom he refers to as 'peasants'. Carrie's grandfather, he says, had built a large house instead of farming, and had 'dined late in special raiment' and 'drunk red wine after the custom of the French'. The old Balestiers had not really belonged to the local community and now his granddaughter had turned up with a penniless Englishman, on whom they were bound to look with even more suspicion. Penniless at first, but not for long, because money soon began to come in, and that too became a cause for talk; New England farming folk looked on money as not lightly come by, nor lightly to be spent.

And of course Kipling himself had mixed feelings about Americans and their way of life, as he had about most things. In *Something of Myself* he characteristically says nothing at all about the dramatic end to his stay in Vermont. He does say a good deal about aspects of American life which he disliked, implying that the decision to leave was the result solely of a slow process of consideration. But this really cannot be reconciled with the facts. He left suddenly, after a chain of events that he had found painful and embarrassing and which constituted a defeat. But it is true that he had hesitated and wavered as to whether he should settle permanently. Permanence was something he needed. But his feelings about America were so mixed! He saw such contradictions in the American spirit. He put some of what he saw into the set of verses called 'An American', which are not always easy to understand, but to which the key may be the lines about 'the cynic devil in his blood ... ' that 'bids him flout the Law he makes, that bids him make the Law he flouts', or the last verse but one, which reads:

> Enslaved, illogical, elate
>   He greets th' embarrassed Gods, nor fears
> To shake the iron hand of Fate
>   Or match with Destiny for beers.

He writes 'enslaved' partly because he could not believe that anyone was free unless he had accepted a discipline which Americans seemed emphatically to have rejected, and partly because he thought they were enslaved to material things.

On a more prosaic level, he admired the independence of the people around him, but could not be reconciled to their disrespect for privacy. And privacy was becoming more and more of a passion. The Kiplings, on arrival and still at the stage when it was their poverty that was remarked on, hired for ten dollars a month a tiny cottage—seventeen feet by twenty-seven over all he said later—in which they faced the first winter in Vermont. His work-room was seven feet by eight, and the snow lay level with its window-sill. 'We were extraordinarily and self-centredly content,' he wrote later, and when winter closed down 'we counted ourselves secure'. Secure—self-centred—these are revealing words and strike an English ear as noticeably un-American. What the Kiplings tried to build up for themselves was an essentially cosy world—and yet he goes on, uneasily, to speak of the mistrust of neighbours who 'saw no humour in our proceedings'. This was how he remembered it in *Something of Myself*, looking back more than thirty years later; at the time, it seems a fair guess that he regarded his meetings with most of his neighbours in the traditional English country way. That is, he would stop and chat about some matter of common concern, but would not expect the relationship to develop; it would be based on two assumptions, almost universal in England, that everyone wants some degree of privacy and that there are different sections of society with different habits, which should be respected. But these assumptions are not widely shared in America.

A daughter was born at Bliss Cottage on December 29th, 1892, and in the spring of 1893 the Kiplings decided to build a larger house. It was a big wooden house which they called Naulakha—not misspelt as the novel had been. This of course was a tribute to Wolcott, who had brought them together. They were now moving into the phase when, to most of their neighbours, the offence was no longer poverty but that money was coming too fast and too easily. They dressed for dinner in the evening as Carrie's grandfather had done and as the English of the professional classes did. They employed an English coachman. Altogether, they seem to have tried to live in rural Vermont much as one of the English whom Kipling had admired in India would have lived on retiring to England. And this was not understood; they were regarded as strange and stand-offish. To Kipling, on his side, a cause of irritation was the press, whose custom it was—so he afterwards wrote—if anyone refused to give an interview, to make one up.

Altogether, the attempt to settle in America was intermittent rather than whole-hearted; the Kiplings visited England to see his cousins and aunts and parents; they talked of becoming naturalized Americans but he could never quite bring himself to the point. The cement that held the United States together had always been 'twisting the tail of the British lion'; hostility to Britain was the one sentiment that a politician knew would appeal to everyone—North and South, East and West, rich and poor. This of course was distasteful, and at one stage the diplomatic tension grew so acute that Kipling felt he had no choice but to go. But feelings cooled as quickly as they had heated and the need seemed less pressing.

So nearly four years passed in alternating moods of exasperation and affection towards the half-adopted country. It was in one of the former, while on a visit to England, that Kipling wrote 'An Error in the Fourth Dimension', in which he reverses the situation, imagining an American, the possessor of many inherited millions, who, finding that Americans thought he ought to go to the office and work, came instead to England to live, in the language of the day, like a gentleman. His pleasure was not in fishing and hunting, but in collecting rare and beautiful things and making no effort to acquire more money; he lived, in short, like a character in Henry James. He learnt to avoid characteristically American turns of speech and manner, which he came to regard as solecisms, gross breaches of good behaviour, the kind of thing his English friends would tactfully try to ignore. He became at last so far acclimatized that—height of praise!—one would hardly know he wasn't English.

But all this came to a sudden end. One day he sent his butler to wave a red flag and stop a train, just because he wanted to catch it;

the railway company, after some exchange of letters, assumed that he must be a lunatic. When they learnt at last that he was not mad but only American, they were appeased—but he found this so insulting that he went back to America by the next sailing. It is an offensive story, heavy with an arrogance about the advantages of being English that is slightly self-mocking, but no less wounding for that. Edmund Wilson apparently supposed that this story was written after Kipling's flight from Vermont and that its hostility to American ways was due to that defeat. But he is wrong; it was written on a visit to England at Rottingdean, while his home was still at Brattleboro. Wilson never allowed enough for Kipling's ability to love and hate at the same time. Right up till the summer of 1896 Kipling had not finally rejected the idea of a permanent American home.

The book for which he has been perhaps most widely loved, *The Jungle Book*, was written at Bliss Cottage; both his daughters were born at Brattleboro; it was the first place at which he had lived as the head of a family and tried to make a permanent home. His building and planning and planting were all on the assumption that it would be permanent. He worked steadily all the time he was in America, publishing while there *Many Inventions*, though most of it had been written earlier, writing and publishing the two Jungle Books and *The Seven Seas*, and writing, though they were published later, most of *Captains Courageous* and *The Day's Work*. Above all, it was while he lived at Naulakha that he spent loving care on collecting material for *Captains Courageous*. These were all reasons for the affection that underlay his irritation. He was a man who wanted to give affection as well as to receive it.

2. CAPTAINS COURAGEOUS

This is the only book of Kipling's which is set entirely in America. All the characters are American. Not only that, but the heart of the book—its moral in a single sentence—is one of Kipling's main beliefs of this period expressed in terms essentially American, or perhaps more particularly New England. He put it later in verse: 'And the Gods of the Copy-book Maxims said: "If you don't work you will die!" ' It is a saga of hard physical work in conflict with natural forces. It is a book which could hardly have been written by anyone who did not admire *Huckleberry Finn*; it is a book whose claim to survival rests mainly on detail, and it is all American detail.

Kipling always acknowledged that *Captains Courageous* owed much to Dr Conland, who had brought his elder daughter into the world. Conland had served in the fishing fleet of which the centre was Gloucester, Massachusetts, which lies, as the gull might fly, some thirty miles north-east of Boston. The fishing vessels were schooners, powered only by sail, going on voyages of some four to five months in the summer to the Grand Banks of Newfoundland, a thousand miles to the East. There they fished for cod, not by net but by line. A schooner would anchor on the Bank and send out a little fleet of seven or eight dinghies, each with one man, who might on a good day catch as many as two hundred big cod with hand lines and then row back to the schooner; sometimes they would 'trawl', which did not mean, as it would now, letting down a net, but paying out three hundred fathoms of line with a baited hook every few feet. In either case, the day's catch had to be cleaned and salted and packed in the hold that evening. It was hard work and of course there was danger; sometimes a schooner was lost, sometimes one of the dinghies, called dories; sometimes a man was washed overboard. In October of every year there was a memorial service at Gloucester when the names of the drowned were read out. There were few families who had not at some time lost one man at least.

Kipling questioned Dr Conland, with him explored the back ways and quays and wharves of Gloucester and Boston, talked to the fisher-folk, went out in their boats, watched cod cleaned and hooks baited, learnt how deep the banks lay on which the dories fished, how many fathoms of line went to a tub of trawl, what the men ate for breakfast. This was the admirable background to a story which is not quite convincing. Harvey Cheyne is the spoilt fifteen-year-old son of a man who by hard work, imagination and luck has made many millions in the expanding America of the 'nineties. No one has ever said no to young Harvey; he is 'pasty-faced', unhealthy, conceited, and a nuisance to his elders. In bravado, he tries a particularly villainous cigar—given him in malice by a man he has met in the smoking-room of a liner and whom he has irritated by his conceit—is violently sick and as he leans over the side is washed off the fore-deck by a big wave. He is picked up by a dinghy from the *We're Here*, a schooner from

Gloucester. No one on the *We're Here* believes him when he says that his father could buy the whole schooner and never miss the money and they laugh at his demand to be put ashore at once. He must stay till the hold is full. They are short of a hand who has been washed overboard, and the skipper offers him a place at ten-and-a-half dollars a month. His pocket-money had been two hundred. His conversion is instantaneous; one hard punch on the nose is enough, and from a horrid, whining, self-centred brat he becomes eager to learn and ready to admit when he is wrong. He serves his three months as extra ship's boy and learns a little of many seaman's skills but, more importantly, the virtues of hard work and of jumping to obey. A rope's end comes into some of the teaching, but less than might have been expected; that instantaneous conversion had been complete. When the *We're Here* — naturally the first of all the fleet to fill her hold — makes Gloucester and Harvey cables his parents, the story is really over, though there is thrown in a detailed account of just how Harvey Cheyne the elder broke all records for a run across America from California to Boston in his private car — which meant a private coach on the railway. This is the kind of thing over which Kipling liked to take trouble; he found a railway millionaire to show him just how it might be done and he was pleased when another railway millionaire set out to beat the fictitious record. But it is not essential to the story, and to me is frankly boring. It need hardly be said that from now on and for ever Harvey is a virtuous hardworking son, who as soon as he is out of college takes over a shipping line his father has recently acquired, while his companion as boy on the *We're Here* — who had been Huck to his Tom — becomes an officer in the line.

There is, in short, little merit in the story, but the atmosphere, the creation of the self-contained world of life on the *We're Here*, is altogether successful. It is to be read for the seascapes, the changes of light, and for one unforgettable scene in fog, when a great steamship with sirens shrieking is tearing through the muffled whiteness among the little schooners, with folk sleeping in the cabins who will never know they have sent men to the bottom before breakfast.

When he wrote this book, Kipling was still the journalist, collecting material with enormous devotion, using it brilliantly to build up a world quite different from anything he had known before, but a workaday world in which the men (each labelled:

New England skipper, old man-o'-war's man, Galway fisher) do their duty and play their parts. Each speaks in character, but they are flat characters and their different personalities do not affect the story, nor does the story—except for the moment in the fog—hold the reader in suspense. Neither as a boy nor today can I feel it is the equal—as a boy's adventure story—of, say, *Treasure Island*. There is a hard, frightening glitter to the whole of *Treasure Island* which holds the reader enslaved, and there are a dozen scenes in which we can hardly bear to wait for the end. And the squire, the captain, the doctor and Long John are ready to walk off the page, as bright and fresh as paint. Nor does *Captains Courageous* stand comparison with that other masterpiece of boy's adventure, *Huckleberry Finn*. Both are in a sense tracts; there is a moral to both. But *Huckleberry* is spontaneous; the story, preposterous though it often is, flows on like the river, one incident growing from the next, and held together by the life of the rivers, the glimpses of the shore, the smoke of distant fires, the sound of men talking across water at night, stars and lights on the water, eddies and snags and sandbanks, all blending together into a background like one of those stews in which, as Huck says, everything seemed to swop around. It is never *contrived*.

Kipling had enjoyed collecting the material for *Captains Courageous* and had enjoyed writing it. But if this book is compared with *The Light that Failed* or *Kim*, the other two full-length novels, it must be judged escapist; it was written from the top layer of the consciousness, it involved neither struggle nor growth. 'I revelled,' he said himself, 'in profligate abundance of detail.' And the moral of the tract—belief in work and discipline and hardship—is open to C. S. Lewis's criticism; it is perhaps an ingredient in the successful practice of any creed, but as a creed for its own sake it is barren and negative. This Kipling was just beginning to perceive; trying to explain why he had decided to leave Brattleboro, he said of his neighbours in Vermont that 'behind their desperate activities lay always, it seemed to me, immense and unacknowledged boredom—the deadweight of material things passionately worked up into Gods ... ' That surely was a reflection of something he had not yet fully perceived in himself.

How long the Kiplings would have hesitated about leaving Vermont if it had not been for the crisis which now developed, it is impossible to say. But there can be no doubt that it toppled them into the decision to leave the country, even though there was at first a reluctance to admit that the flight was permanent.

3. IGNOMINIOUS FLIGHT

Carrie had another brother, Beatty Balestier, well known as a character in Brattleboro and around. He drank too much, he cursed and swore, he was unreliable, generous, profligate, violent —but people forgave him. Not, however, his elder sister; she found it much more difficult than anyone else to condone his obstinate refusal to behave like a New Englander. She and he were temperamentally incompatible and there was continual trouble. It must have been she who eventually suggested a bargain; the Kiplings would support his wife and child if he would go away for a year, get a job—purge and leave sack, and live cleanly. It was not a suggestion that any man could accept and yet keep his self-respect; and he angrily refused it. Then there was a quarrel about a piece of land near their house which Beatty had sold his brother-in-law for a dollar to prevent anyone else building on it, on the understanding—so Beatty said—that he should keep the right to mow it. But Carrie decided to bring it into use; she had it terraced and planted with trees and virtually made part of the garden. Beatty thought this was a breach of the agreement. So relations were bad. The two households hardly spoke for a year. Then Beatty filed a petition in bankruptcy and there was a feeling abroad that the Kiplings should not have let it come to this. Kipling made a slighting remark to a neighbour about having carried Beatty by the seat of his pants for the last year. It was repeated to Beatty, who one day sighted Kipling out for a bicycle ride, galloped furiously up to him, abused him and threatened him with violence, indeed, so Kipling said, with murder.

If it had not been for the wives, perhaps no more would have been heard of this affair. That was the impression Charles Carrington formed after talking to those in the neighbourhood who remembered. But—whatever discussion may have taken place in the home— what Kipling did was as un-Stalkylike as could be. Think how carefully Stalky would have prepared a pit for his enemy to walk into! But Kipling walked himself with open eyes into just such a pit and put himself hopelessly in the wrong. He laid an information against his brother-in-law for threatening to murder

him; he had him arrested. It was an error in the fourth dimension.
By this act he sold himself into the enemy's hands; he, who hated
publicity, was the sole witness and now had to appear in court and
answer questions for a whole day—and they were shrewd, damag-
ing questions. Beatty was cast in the part which everyone likes—
open-handed, impulsive, an honest-to-God American farmer.
Rudyard was the cold, calculating stand-offish Englishman who
would trick his wife's brother out of land and let his family starve,
and who went to law at a hint of violence instead of fighting it out
like a man. Many newspapers welcomed the opportunity to hit at
the man who had criticized America and had refused to meet
reporters. Beatty was bound over to keep the peace but, in every
field except the legal, he had won. Kipling had been exposed to
laughter as woundingly as one of the local magnates of his own
tales. If, as seems likely, he had walked into the trap at Carrie's
bidding and against his better judgment, but loyally determined
that he would never say so, that would not reduce the sting. Did
he perhaps remember this affair, years later, when he wrote in
'Beauty Spots' of 'the first dry sob' of Major Kniveat, who had
hoped to attain some leadership in the village but for whom 'all
hope of office, influence and authority was stripped for ever—
drowned in the laughter in the lane'? It hurt him deeply. This was
in May and he left America for Britain in August 1896, only a few
weeks after the case was finished. He had been happy there and
leaving was a defeat; he felt sore and bruised; it was some time
before he could make up his mind that he had really abandoned
the house he had built in Vermont. 'I don't quite think of quitting
the land permanently', he wrote to a friend in June. 'It is hard to
go from where one has raised one's kids and builded a wall and
digged a well and planted a tree.'

During the next three years, the Kiplings moved from Torquay
to Rottingdean, where the Burne-Jones family and other relations
had houses for the holidays, and spent some desultory endeavour
in looking for a permanent home. They also began the custom—
which lasted till 1908—of going to South Africa for the worst of
the English weather. But in 1898 they decided at short notice to go
instead to America, to see Carrie's mother, deal with some business about copyrights, and finally dispose of the house. On arrival
in New York, in early February 1899, first the children, then
Carrie and finally Rudyard fell ill with pneumonia, while the news
arrived that Beatty was suing them for malicious prosecution.

Carrie threw off her illness quickly and with indomitable fortitude struggled to save her family. Rudyard's life hung long in the balance but he came through in the end. His elder daughter Josephine died. 'Months passed', wrote Carrington, 'before he recovered from his illness; from the shock of his daughter's death he never recovered … ' He never visited America again.

6

A Check to Growth

1. COMPLETE SURRENDER

In 1902 the Kiplings settled at Bateman's, near Burwash in Sussex. 'A grey stone lichened house – A.D. 1634 over the door – beamed, panelled, with old oak staircase, and all untouched and unfaked ... a good and peaceable place standing in terraced lawns ... a walled garden of old red brick ... two fat-headed oast-houses ... ' he wrote to C. E. Norton in America, and in the same letter: ' ... we discovered England which we had never done before ... It is the most marvellous of all foreign countries that I have ever been in. It is made up of trees and green fields and mud and the gentry, and at last I'm one of the gentry ... '

At last I'm one of the gentry; at last I've found a home. But in 'a foreign country' in which he had still to feel his way and find his feet, in which for a long time he was to make delighted discoveries, in which he had to keep reassuring himself that he *belonged*. Here he endured the First World War and the loss of his only son in 1915.

Those are the important facts, the outward events that influenced the development of Kipling's art. Of course there is a great deal more; the South African War and his popularity with the services, his world reputation, his enormous and growing sales overseas, his diminishing prestige with the literary world. In public affairs, there was the Liberal settlement in South Africa, which he took as a defeat, and the crisis in Ulster. But for the purpose of this book, Bateman's and the loss of his son are the essentials. These set the frame for the middle period.

I have differed already from Edmund Wilson, and I shall differ still more. None the less, he was right in connecting Kipling's life with his work and in seeing three broad periods in both. What he did not sufficiently recognize was that in all three periods there were different levels of Kipling's personality at work, that characteristics marked in the early stage persisted till the end, that compassion and irony were present in embryo· in the earlier stages long before they came to full fruition in the last phase, when, in my view, the whole stature of the writer was enhanced. You will see, throughout his life, samples of work side by side which represent quite different veins. There is some development in each vein; in some there are changes as marked as a change from male to female – but, as in male and female, vestigial organs in one represent what is fully developed in the other.

There was growth throughout Kipling's career. Even the best of the early period will not stand comparison with the best of the late. But there was a check in growth between the early and the middle periods. The luxuriant fertility of *Life's Handicap* and *Many Inventions* does not spread out into the richer and deeper fruition that might have been expected. At the end of Chapter IV I suggested that Kipling's marriage posed certain questions. Would he go on finding the kind of material that suited him best? Would marriage help him towards some fusion of the superficial and the deeper levels from which he worked? The middle period persuades me that the answer to both was no. Marriage, I believe, was the turning-point; marriage made him happier but it also shut him in and confined him. Then came the flight from Vermont and the realization that his first attempt at making a home and growing roots had proved abortive. The death of his daughter was the third event that turned him inwards. All his training had taught him that grief must be hidden. He had learnt, in the House of Desolation, at Westward Ho! and in the Punjab Club, lessons of caution and reserve that were quite foreign to his instincts as an artist. But the successes of the marvellous year 1890 had encouraged him to poke his head cautiously out from the horny carapace that had resulted. Now once again he withdrew.

The surrender in marriage had been complete and was a more enduring influence than the flight from Vermont. Here is the evidence of a friend, Viscount Castlerosse, who often stayed at Bateman's, quoted by Edmund Wilson. The Kiplings, he says:

> were among the few happy pairs I have ever met; but as far as Kipling was concerned, his married life was one of complete surrender. To him Carrie ... was more than a wife. She was a mistress, in the literal sense, a governess and a matron. In a lesser woman, I should have used the term 'nurse'. Kipling handed himself over bodily, financially and spiritually to his spouse. He had no banking account. All the money which he earned was handed over to her, and she, in turn, would dole him out so much pocket-money. He could not call his time, or even his stomach, his own ...
>
> Sometimes in the evening, enlivened by wine and company, he would take a glass more than he was accustomed to and then those great big eyes of his would shine brightly behind his strong spectacles, and Rud would take to talking

faster and his views would become even more emphatic. If Mrs. Kipling was with him, she would quickly note the change and, sure enough, in a decisive voice she would issue the word of command: 'Rud, it is time you went to bed,' and Rud always discovered that it was about time he went to bed.

I myself during the long years never once saw any signs of murmuring or even of incipient mutiny.

Carrington's account of the marriage was based on minute knowledge of the correspondence and on long talks with Rudyard's daughter and also his secretary. Though more tactfully expressed, it gives much the same impression as Lord Castlerosse's; Rudyard had found a mother, a dominant mother, who ruled his life and would not desert him at a House of Desolation, but who had very little contact with the deeper aspects of his art and personality. He was turned inwards. Then came the successive blows of defeat in America and the death of his daughter. He was like a plant whose early growth has been touched by frost; he had had a check—in fact, three checks in succession, but the roots were strong and threw up new shoots.

Kipling was a compulsive writer; he had to express himself in words. In the middle period, he drew on memory and looked back to boyhood at school and to India. Memory was one of three main shoots and was strong at first. But India remained a memory only. That brief visit in 1891 had lasted barely three weeks, and he never went back. Whether this was because of the association of that short visit with Wolcott's death, I cannot be sure. But it seems likely that he was reluctant to go for another reason too; it would not have been easy—during the cold-weather visit of a celebrity—to see the side of India he had loved, Kim and the dust of the Grand Trunk Road and the smoke of cowdung fires in low lines above the village thatch in the evening. Did he perceive that he would have been led instead into talking to Governors about duties on cotton and native education? At any rate he did not go, and drew on memory. There are four Indian stories in *The Day's Work*, and none of them is trivial; indeed, all are first-class entertainment, and one at least has attracted much attention from critics. Then there was *Stalky*, a return to boyhood, and then *Kim*, and in three of the later collections one Indian story each. Memory is not a well on which a writer can draw indefinitely.

In quantity, the most prolific shoot in this middle period was one which did not show great development in quality. More and more stories drew on technicalities—on details of seamanship and ships' engines; on the Navy and the contrast between discipline and the need for originality and initiative; on parts of engines and ships; on bridges and trains; Kipling even invents a whole new technical world of the future. These technicalities he wove into stories that are often entertaining and sometimes exciting; they are always concerned—I can think of no exception —with the relation of the part to the whole, the individual to the team; but they are not as a rule much concerned with man's relation to the infinite, nor do they display any growth of a deeper understanding of mankind.

No one can live all his life at full stretch. This is a point Kipling made, half-facetiously, in a very early story, 'The Conversion of Aurelian McGoggin'; it is the heart of Browning's long poem about Bishop Blougram, which occurs in the volume Crofts had thrown long ago at Kipling's head. It is natural to escape from the sublime or painful—but always laborious—confrontation of the soul with eternity into gardening or stamp-collecting, music or chess. Theologians in Victoria's reign used to memorize the timing of trains on obscure rural branch-lines, and philologists delighted in remembering the scores in first-class cricket matches. All these are what Aldous Huxley has called lateral escapes from the self. And from pain, too, there may be escape in hard work or in numbing, soul-cleansing routine. But it is at his peril that an artist introduces this kind of material into his work except as background. With Kipling what had begun as an escape came in this middle period near to idolatry, something worshipped for its own sake.

There was a third strong shoot from this vigorous stock. Now more than ever before Kipling allowed his imaginative free play in fable, in animal stories, in historical reconstruction, meant ostensibly for children but worked, as he said, at different levels for different kinds of reader. Both Henry James and Edmund Wilson criticized the Kipling of this period for writing for children, in terms which suggest that they regard work for such an audience as beneath serious consideration. But the best children's stories are always written on two levels, and it is surely far more worthwhile to write *Alice in Wonderland* or *Huckleberry Finn* than an indifferent novel for grown-ups. It is to the class of

Alice and Huck that the Mowgli tales belong; indeed, they are not only good in themselves and have held countless children enthralled; they released Kipling from the consciousness of an audience to whom he had to show off, and let him follow his fancy, free as air—and in following his fancy he often made his points on political organization in a more agreeable and convincing way than when he put them directly and explicitly. And of the Puck stories, it is not enough to say that they are good stories in themselves and fables of human life, as the Mowgli stories are, nor that they make history come alive; all that is true, but they also form the bridge to the best of the late Kipling. They introduce a new, warm, positive element, his love of the continuity of English country life and of its unspoken ethics. *Kim* too falls into this category of the untrammelled imagination; there is no intrusive 'I', no motor-car; no one in *Kim* is trying to get into a club to which he does not belong. It was these stories of fancy—'engendered in the eyes, With gazing fed ... ' that made possible the best stories of the last period, when personal loss and physical pain really had drained away both hate and self-consciousness.

2. ENGINES AND SCREWS

After the flight from Vermont, and before they bought Bateman's, there was an interval when the Kiplings lived at Rottingdean, surrounded by cousins, Poynters, Burne-Jones and Baldwins. They did not think this would be a permanent home; it brought little of that contact with tenant-farmers, with builders, with the odd-job man and the gardener, that was to come when they reached the true home. And Rottingdean was too close to Brighton; people came to stare at the colony of celebrities. Yet the Kiplings were increasingly clear that it was in Sussex that the permanent home must be found. The verses 'Sussex' were written in South Africa before they bought Bateman's.

It was while they were at Rottingdean that *Stalky* appeared, a deep draught from memory which I have discussed earlier because of its biographical importance. But it was also while they were at Rottingdean that *The Day's Work* was published. Much of this collection had been written earlier, before the flight from Vermont—which emphasizes my point that marriage was really the turning-point—but its appearance now, and perhaps even more its title, helped to foster one aspect of the legend about Kipling. It was put in words by G. K. Chesterton, who, after applauding Kipling as a man who had celebrated the poetry and romance of common things, went on: 'He has often written bad poetry, like Wordsworth. He has often said silly things, like Plato. He has often given way to mere political hysteria, like Gladstone. But no one can reasonably doubt that he means steadily and sincerely to say something ... ' and he goes on to conclude that *discipline* is Kipling's primary theme. C. S. Lewis, you will remember, said it was *work*. Of the two, discipline is a shade nearer the mark, and in the middle period it is certainly near enough the truth to impress the casual reader, particularly when driven home by Chesterton's technique of hammering on a single point with a succession of verbal ingenuities. Chesterton's essay impressed me deeply when I read it at the age of fifteen. But it is not quite true that discipline was the main theme; what divided Kipling all his life was the relationship between the individual and the team; he was on both sides. Though he was unusual, among writers and artists, in seeing the need for discipline and approving painful sacrifice by the individual for the good of the whole, the heroes to whom he comes back are always rebels against some aspect of the system. Stalky approves of the Headmaster but is always up against the housemaster; Mulvaney is all for the Army and for the old religion—but cannot stick to the discipline of either. Strickland and Pyecroft operate within a frame of discipline but both are rebels within it. And when Kipling turns to fancy, he chooses as his heroes Puck—that shrewd and knavish sprite, who was pleased when things befell preposterously—and Kim, a mischievous street-urchin, lords of misrule both. But of all the collections of stories, *The Day's Work* perhaps comes nearest to justifying Chesterton's point.

There is a story—it is called simply '.007'— about a new railway engine, which was treated like a new boy at school until it learnt to fit into the system of the American railroads; there is another, 'The Ship that Found Herself', about a ship that sails on her maiden voyage as a collection of girders, plates, rivets, engines and tubes, each speaking with its own voice. But by the time she had crossed the Atlantic, the ship spoke with one voice and the parts had learned that—with a little give and take—they must subordinate themselves to the whole. These exemplify two themes—what Henry James called 'engines-and-screws' and 'part-and-whole'—and their emphasis within the part-and-whole theme is on discipline. They have little interest beyond that; even as a boy, I did not find them much to my taste. There are two others—'The Devil and the Deep Sea' and 'Bread upon the Waters'—which combine the 'technicalities' theme with 'revenge'. They are about ships and ships' engines and the mysteries of insurance, and the Scots engineer who is a recurring figure in Kipling. There is 'An Error in the Fourth Dimension', already described, which is not concerned with technicalities; 'A Walking Delegate', which is a conversation between horses, a political fable I shall deal with elsewhere, to some extent technical; 'My Sunday at Home', a farce; four Indian stories and 'The Brushwood Boy'. The last is a dream story, important in any consideration of Kipling's work, and it is discussed later in this book. Only 'The Brushwood Boy', 'My Sunday at Home', and 'An Error in the Fourth Dimension' are *not* concerned in any way with work and discipline.

Of the Indian tales, 'The Maltese Cat' is first-class entertainment. It is the story of a polo match, the final of a tournament, in which the favourites, a rich regiment who have six ponies apiece, are beaten by a poor regiment, who have only three ponies each, so that each pony has to come out twice and in the second half are playing against fresh ponies. Most of it is told in the form of conversation between the ponies of the eventual winners, dominated by the Maltese Cat, who scores the winning goal practically by himself and teaches the other ponies to play up in the best public-school spirit. It is all rather absurd—but I loved it as a boy and when I came to read it to my children twenty-five years later found that we were all—reader and audience—almost in tears by the final goal. It is no use telling oneself that it is only a game, that it never really happened, that it was eighty years ago anyhow, that polo ponies don't think for themselves, still less talk, that the rules have all been changed since then. It is still as exciting as if one were there in the crowd, or even one of the players. It is one of the best examples I know of Kipling's ability to whip up emotion—in this case an emotion that reason will later altogether reject—by sheer virtuosity in the telling. Its only rival is 'Red Dog' in *The Second Jungle Book*. But it is no use pretending that it is original as a fable of human life; what the Maltese Cat teaches the other ponies is that they must play for the side and use their heads when they get a chance.

'The Tomb of His Ancestors' is another boyhood favourite to which I come back with pleasure, though again I rate it as excellent entertainment, and poetic rather than exact history, but am doubtful whether it is of great symbolic or psychological importance. It is about the tradition of serving in India, which in a few English families, lasted for the best part of two hundred years, and about the curious relationship which sometimes grew up between British officers and aboriginal tribes in India— primitive peoples despised by those of Aryan speech and Hindu religion. There are many patches of hilly or remote country dotted about India where such peoples survived for centuries. The hero of the story, John Chinn, came of such an English family and his grandfather, also John Chinn, had managed to win the confidence of just such a people, the Bhils, and had been buried among them. He had died young, but the government of the day had been impressed by his success in bringing the Bhils into reasonably peaceful relations with their neighbours, and had built a tomb over his body. It was treated as a shrine by the Bhils and the first John Chinn had become a local godling; the Bhils believed that he rode out at night, wearing his top-hat, on a clouded tiger—clouded not striped—when any fearful event was threatened. The second John Chinn was physically very like his grandfather and came to be regarded as his re-incarnation. He did not at first understand this but, when he did, he made use of the semi-divine honour in which the Bhils held him to save them from terrible trouble. They fell into a panic when a vaccinator came with his knives to protect them against smallpox. It was the kind of panic that might lead to raids on other villages, the theft of cattle and all kinds of madness, which in turn might have led to a punitive expedition. They might easily have killed the vaccinator. But it was all settled peacefully owing to John Chinn's divine status, his confident commonsense and his prowess with a rifle. He shot the clouded tiger, which was real, and laid the ghost of his grandfather.

This story may serve as one example of how Kipling played the sedulous jackdaw. There is a passage in Bishop Heber's account of his journeys in India in which he describes the achievement of a young man, Augustus Clevland (so Heber spells it), who had learned the language of the Sonthals, a primitive hill people in Bihar, persuaded them to sell 'wax and honey' to the people of the plains, to accept his authority, and submit to his judgment instead

of fighting—just like John Chinn the Elder. The Sonthals live
several hundred miles to the East of the Bhils and Augustus
Clevland in real life died sixty years before John Chinn in the
story—but the government of the day really did put up a monument to Clevland's memory, and he was remembered as something very like a deity a hundred and fifty years later. The younger
John Chinn found on his grandfather's tomb—hung about with
packets of wax and honey—a half-obliterated inscription, of
which the words come from Clevland's tomb; all Kipling has
done is to alter the name and date and a word or two and then
rub out some of the letters. On the other side, were 'ancient verses,
also very worn'. As much as Chinn could decipher said:

> ... the savage band
> Forsook their haunts and b ... at his Command
> ... mended ... rals check a ... st for spoil
> And .s.ing Hamlets prove his gene ... toil
> Humanit ... survey ... ights restore ...
> A nation ... ield ... subdued without a Sword.

This does not come from Clevland's monument, but from some
verses written about Clevland by Sir John Shore, who was
Governor-General of India after Lord Cornwallis. He was
Clevland's cousin and had been very fond of him. Shore wrote:

> ... the savage band
> Forsook their haunts and bowed to his Command
> And where the warrior's arm in vain assail'd
> His gentler skill o'er brutal force prevail'd ...
> Now mended morals check the lust for spoil
> And rising Hamlets prove his generous toil ...

But Clevland died when he was twenty-nine and unmarried. The
Chinns were a dynasty who all came to India; they were all first-
class shots and could sit up in the jungle all night without getting
fever. In all these respects (as Charles Carrington has recorded)
they reproduced the traditions of the Outram family. Kipling
took the facts about Clevland from Bishop Heber and the two
inscriptions from Clevland's tomb and Shore's funeral ode. To
them he added the tradition of the Outram family, shifting
Clevland's story sixty years later to suit his purpose. That is four
sources. I do not know where he found the clouded tiger, but

perhaps he had seen, as I have, on the walls of a village temple, the crudely drawn figure of an Englishman in a top-hat, strangely sedate by the side of Krishna and the milkmaids and Hanuman the monkey-god.

These were the ingredients—the bare list at the head of the recipe. But the skill to blend and cook them is a more mysterious process. To discover these ingredients—nuggets of fact, phrases heard in conversation, fragments from books—is an engrossing hobby for many devoted members of the Kipling Society, and the results of their toil are recorded in the Kipling Journal. This book is not written for these enthusiasts, and I do not intend to enter as a rule into such detail, but offer one example to illustrate Kipling's methods of work. He used such pebbles—but he changed them to suit his purpose. In this case, he achieved a story which seems to me of the highest quality as entertainment, and historically an admirable picture of the relationship with primitive peoples as the British in India liked to see it—and as it very often was. Exactly how the Bhils saw it at the time, no one will ever know, but it would be unhistorical to attribute to either party the idea—taken as dogma by so many people today—that the relationship was in any way degrading. As in 'The Man Who Would be King', there is here an imaginative, and in that sense poetic, perception of the essence of nineteenth-century imperialism, the bluff by which English officials with a minimum of physical force again and again established and maintained a supremacy over people from whose magic they were immune, and to whom their self-confidence therefore seemed supernatural.

'William the Conqueror'—a longer story, divided into two parts, each of almost the standard length—is the last, and the most completely successful, attempt to portray the discomfort, the dangers, the devotion, of the everyday life of British officers in India. It is in a sense a tract; Kipling believed that 'the English of the island' still pictured their servants in India as perhaps no longer the Nabobs of the eighteenth century, but as Jos Sedleys, dull, self-indulgent and second-rate. His tale begins with the now familiar picture of the discomforts of the hot weather in Lahore, but shifts to South India, where there is famine and Punjab officials are drafted in the hope of saving life. The three with whom he is concerned spent six terrible days in a train on the journey; when they got there, they worked very hard and everyone had fever and everything had to be improvised; they got back

5*

to Lahore in time for the Christmas week. Running through this perfectly ordinary account of sadly ordinary events is a perfectly ordinary love story. That, at least, is how it seems on cold analysis; in fact, I have always found the story unaccountably moving. It is not that William, the heroine, is very remarkable; Kipling was very pleased with her and she was supposed to be a new kind of woman, but surely it was only in fiction that she was new. She was not at all like Little Dorrit or Diana of the Crossways or Lady Glencora Palliser, but biographies and memoirs abound in women who stayed with their men and found their interest in their men's work; compared with Honoria Lawrence or Florentia Sale, William was 'new' only in having short hair and a man's name. She is said, incidentally, to have been written with Mrs Ted Hill in mind. Nor can I see that Scott, to whom she becomes engaged, is in any way different from a dozen other 'working sahibs'. The nostalgia which the English characters — exiles in Madras — feel for the North is admirably done, and this better than any other story brings out the homeless, uncomfortable life 'on the end of a telegraph wire', with everything ready to be packed at a moment's notice, the horrible sights, the constant danger of deadly disease; William, though she was only twenty-three, had been through an epidemic of cholera as well as a famine. But — though I still find it ultimately unaccountable — I believe that what is moving is the concern that William and Scott show for each other before either has acknowledged that they are in love.

'William the Conqueror' is in a sense the centre and heart of *The Day's Work*, the final statement of what Kipling wanted to say about the life of the working sahibs. But the whole collection — perhaps as a counter-balance to its title — is framed between two dream stories, 'The Bridge-Builders' and 'The Brushwood Boy', which is discussed later. Each of these stories in a different way provides a corrective to the main theme of work and discipline, but 'The Bridge-Builders' is the more direct and important commentary. Findlayson is a working sahib, quite indistinguishable from many others. He has been four years building his great bridge across the Ganges — apparently near Benares, since it is called the Kashi Bridge and Kashi is the Hindi name of Benares. There is much technical language about the bridge — the trusses, the revetments, the stone caps to the piers, the foundations of the piers eighty feet below the bed of the river. It is the crown of

Findlayson's career; he has endured many privations for its sake and he dreams of it night and day; it will last long after he is forgotten. It is his masterpiece; it will make him if it stands — and it *will* stand, for there is very little left to do now. But the river rises in spate 'two full months before her time'* and from a tiny trickle becomes a raging mile-wide flood. Findlayson cannot eat; he can only watch his bridge and go over the calculations. Almost unconsciously he accepts the opium pills offered him by Peroo the head lascar, who uses them as meat and drink in time of stress; the effect — on a fasting man unused to opium — is much more startling than Peroo had expected, and in a kind of trance he gets into a boat and with Peroo is swept downstream, landing by a kind of miracle on an island where he finds himself the spectator of a committee of the Hindu gods.

If the minutes of their discussion had been recorded, tersely, as good minutes should be, by a heavenly scribe, they would have shown four stages. First, Mother Ganges complains that she has been insulted by blasphemous intruders who have confined her within bounds and put a railway bridge over her waters. She demands redress; they must be slain. She has the support of Kali, goddess of death and destruction. But — and this is the second stage — several gods point out that the railways bring more pilgrims to their shrines and festivals; in any case, it is only dirt playing with dirt; in two thousand years, the intruders — who believe that their god is toil — will be forgotten; the new gods of these newcomers will be changed quickly into a familiar shape; already in the south their woman-goddess Mary is carved with twelve arms; what does it matter what names the gods are given? Then comes Krishna, the beloved, who lives among mortals and who knows what they think. He introduces the third stage of the discussion; he warns the august assemblage that though for the moment their pilgrims may increase, there are beginning to be murmurs of doubt, not about the virtues of this god or that, but about whether there is any need for gods at all. Here, the meeting appeals to Indra, the father of the gods. He replies that when Brahm ceases to dream, the Heavens and Hells and Earth will

* It is a minor point, but typical of Kipling's carelessness about time, that this 'two months before her time' cannot be reconciled with the opening of the story. Findlayson expects the Viceroy to open his bridge in less than three months' time. But viceroys do not open bridges before October, so we are late in June — as everything else in the story suggests. But that is just when the Ganges *does* rise, and Findlayson ought to have expected it.

disappear; Brahm still dreams and till He wakes the Gods die not. And on that oracular note they disperse.

Thus we have a fable within a story of the more familiar kind about a working sahib and his bridge. The fable is well knit into the outer story, not only by the bridge, which is the occasion of the gathering of the gods, but by Peroo's theological difficulties; he is a practical man of great ability and invaluable in the building of the bridge, and he has been in peril of his life in a typhoon at sea; he has looked down into the depths. He is sceptical about what his priest tells him but—with a pantheism that is characteristically Hindu—he had prayed in London to the dome of St Paul's and when at sea to the low-pressure cylinder in the engine-room. ('Not half a bad thing to pray to, either,' is Findlayson's flippant comment.) But he is uneasy, before the spate comes, at walling Mother Ganges up between man-made banks; after hearing the colloquy of the gods, he believes he knows a good deal more about divine purpose than his priest, whom he proposes to beat for talking riddles.

As to its meaning, the fable has several dimensions. On one level, it should be seen against the historical background of the British in India and the outbreak of reforming zeal that assailed some of them twenty years before Kipling was born. They had been then sharply divided; the Reformers, or Levellers as their opponents called them, were followers of Bentham and Mill and believed that enormous improvements could be made in human happiness simply by sweeping away any institution they regarded as anomalous—and India was full of what to an English rationalist seemed anomalies. Their opponents believed there was far more virtue in many Indian institutions than an Englishman might think, and that in any case change should be slow; they were less earnest, kindlier, more humorous, more human. John Lawrence was a Leveller, his brother Henry belonged to the other school. By Kipling's time, the division was nothing like so acute as it had been before the Mutiny, but it persisted; indeed, not only then but until the partition of India, it was possible to divide men into these two camps. The fable in 'The Bridge-Builders' is first of all a commentary on this division of opinion; Kipling belonged wholeheartedly to the school which believed that the ways of India would not be quickly changed.

But really the fable is more religious than political or social. Kipling had always been eclectic in religion, or perhaps more exactly had always believed that man makes God in his own image and therefore that, by whatever names they are called, all gods are only man's ideas of something that is One. This accords better with Hinduism than with Islam, with which he says elsewhere that he usually felt more at home. But in the mood in which this story was written he goes further; all is illusion, the dream of Brahm. In the extremity of stress, when the bridge which was his life might be destroyed and his honour washed down with it to the sea, Findlayson had perceived that in the eyes even of the man-made gods its life was nothing; the sea had once rolled where Ganges ran. And then, even beyond that, for a moment eternity had seemed real and all these things of no account. But with the morning, when he is rescued by the Rao Sahib's steam launch and the bright light that comes after rain is shining on its garish modern fittings, he is back again in the world of men and it is again very important that his bridge should stand. Presumably (as Miss Tompkins says) he was rewarded by the C.I.E. he had hoped for.

The bridge is the symbol of modern progress, science and technology; it has been built up at the cost of many lives, much toil and agony of spirit. But all that effort is only dirt digging in the dirt. None the less, the bridge is still standing, when we come back to the workaday world, and it joins the present to the past. There is a good deal in this story to which Kipling returns in *Kim*, notably the moment when Findlayson, lifted high on a cloud of opium, sees his body struggling in the water, as Kim's Lama was to see his. But while Kipling was always on the edge of an aware-ness of the infinite, there was never any true conflict in his mind about this; he was a son of Martha and like Findlayson con-cerned with stone and concrete, and the strength of good work-manlike building.

He put this story at the beginning of *The Day's Work*. It is about work and disciplined endeavour, like three-quarters of the book. But whereas '.007' and 'The Ship that Found Herself' suggest that work is good in itself and that man should work for work's sake, and 'William the Conqueror' goes a little further, saying that un-selfish work may lead to unselfish love, 'The Bridge-Builders' puts a question-mark against the whole idea of human effort, dis-playing its tininess and futility. Men scurrying about like ants busy themselves on things of desperate importance; but they are nothing in the face of eternity. Yet — the message goes — morning

will come and the bright sun and we must again be scurrying
about our important business.

3. THE SOUTH AFRICAN WAR

In the middle period, as I have said, the two decisive events are
the purchase of Bateman's and the death of Kipling's son. But
there are other influences, and the most important of these are his
immense popularity and the accompanying decline in his reputation among writers, the effect of both being heightened by the
South African War. It is easy to forget Kipling's fame and
popularity, which no writer could equal today unless he was also a
television star. As he came out of church after his almost furtive
wedding, he saw posters announcing the event; when he was ill
in New York in 1899, the newspapers made headlines of every
fluctuation in his illness. 'There were always fifteen or twenty
reporters in the hotel lobbies clamouring for news', writes
Carrington. 'Hushed crowds gathered outside the hotel ... prayers
were offered in the New York churches ... ' Throughout the
world, the press gave his illness the kind of attention given in
those days to the life and death of kings.

But though the public read him eagerly — and followed him
gaping to his great annoyance — even his friends in the literary
world, who in 1890 had hailed him as a Balzac or Dickens, began
to turn aside and express doubts. Henry James, in a light-hearted,
perhaps flippant, letter to a friend, which has been much quoted,
wrote: 'His talent I think still quite diabolically great; and this in
spite of the misguided, the unfortunate Stalky ... ' But, James
went on, in prose there was little of life Kipling could make use
of: 'Almost nothing civilized save steam and patriotism ... ' and
'almost nothing of the complicated soul or the female form or of
any question of *shades* ... ' He has 'come down steadily from the
simple in subject to the more simple — from the Anglo-Indians to
the natives, from the natives to the Tommies, from the Tommies
to the quadrupeds, from the quadrupeds to the fish and from the
fish to the engines and screws.' This was in 1897, and James was
still a personal friend writing most affectionate letters after
Rudyard's illness in 1899 and after the death of Josephine. But he
was disappointed. No doubt he would have expressed his dis-
appointment very differently if it had been meant for publication.
This was not a considered piece of criticism. Kipling's 'natives'

are not 'simpler' than his 'Anglo-Indians' nor his 'Tommies' than the 'natives'; indeed, the direct opposite is true. His 'working sahibs' are all of a piece; his Indians show far more life than they, and his soldiers, with their terrible moods of remorse and nostalgia, are, if you can bear the dialect, the most human of the three. The animals occur in fables — and Aesop and La Fontaine are names not to be despised; fables are essentially ironic, to be read by two audiences. As to the engines and screws, they too are always part of a fable; they are also to some extent, as I have said, an escape from pain.

But although James's letter was half-joking conversation, it none the less expressed something that he and many others felt — an irritated incomprehension that was fed by several springs. It was, they felt — the littérateurs at the Savile Club who had welcomed this clever young man, the Boston Brahmans who had followed the lead of Henry James and C. E. Norton — tiresome of a fledgling whom they had fed with such succulent morsels to develop into a great vulgar cuckoo, instead of the expected meadow pipit or dunnock. Why could he not write about 'the female form' — the raw material of all art — instead of such eccentric subjects as steam engines? And they would have been more than human if they had not felt that a writer who commanded such sales must appeal to an audience less discerning than their own. But it would be unfair to suggest that personal considerations were more than a small part of the reason for the loss of literary acclaim. There had been a genuine check in Kipling's growth, and the new development which now began did not grow out of the old. It would have taken a very sharp eye indeed to perceive at the time exactly what was happening. It was not only that there was this ultimately sterile line of stories about engines and ships but that the best of the old lines seemed to be petering out.

If you compared 'The Man who Would be King', first published in 1888, with 'The Tomb of His Ancestors', published in 1897, it would be difficult to say there was any advance. They are in the same line; both are concerned with the hold over unsophisticated peoples which Europeans did often establish in the nineteenth century; 'The Tomb' is perhaps a better story as immediate entertainment — I certainly preferred it as a boy — but it is less pregnant of character and ultimately less poetic. It takes for granted what for the two ruffians in Kafiristan was a thing of wonder, sustained by a brittle magic which broke under stress.

Dravot and Carnehan are adventurers, John Chinn a subaltern from Sandhurst doing his duty. The snowpeaks, red gold, raw turquoise, and flaming red beard which spring to mind from one story really overpower even a clouded tiger ridden by a man in a top-hat in the other. And this was the kind of subject with which Kipling's name had been associated. Henry James cannot be blamed for not foreseeing, when he wrote that letter, that new lines of development were in preparation—but throughout the middle period critics altogether missed the significance of what was happening. Today, the point can be seen more clearly.

Put 'A Wayside Comedy' (1888) beside 'Mrs Bathurst' (1904) and you have two stories about the destructive force of a woman's attraction, in both cases exercised by a woman who was essentially kind and who had done nothing to bring about disaster. The earlier story is beautifully built and finished, perfect of its kind, fitting neatly into a short period of time and into one obscure little corner of India. But it is a trifle cold and unreal. You might easily think at first reading that 'Mrs Bathurst' compared poorly, that it was a rambling, inconsequent affair, sprawling over three continents and several years, which left the reader in the end very much in the dark as to what had happened. But 'Mrs Bathurst' is the first of a new kind of story; it is highly experimental, deliber-ately told, not merely within a frame, with a narrator in the first person, like 'Love-o'-Women', but with three narrators for the main story, each of whom has something to add. Once you realize how carefully art has been concealed and how packed with meaning every sentence is, the effect is one of great richness. It has been argued that too much has been cut and that the reader has been tried too hard; and it is a fact that various people who have written about 'Mrs Bathurst' have come to different con-clusions about what really did happen. Personally, I think that the uncertainty was intended, and that it adds to the sense of wonder at the incomprehensibility and uniqueness of man. What we are shown is an interrupted series of fragmentary pictures, the kind of tantalizing glimpses that in real life we do suddenly get of other people's lives, and the effect of the fragmentation is cumulative and very powerful.

It was not surprising that the critics did not at the time under-stand the experiments that Kipling was making. He concealed this new art very carefully and they had been misled by the screws and engines, also by a great deal of the verse he poured out at this time and by his public attitudes. There is such a volume of work and it is so varied that it is easy to seize on one element and associate it with the name of Kipling, even though it may be almost exactly contradicted by something else. And since he wrote on such different levels, it was almost inevitable that verse on the smoking-room level should attract more attention than the rarer but often obscure verses that are better worth preserving. Beresford notes that, in his school-days, Kipling composed in verse more fluently and readily than in prose. Verse fitted his intuitive habit of mind. The method of the ballad — which suggests a whole story by a phrase or a line — was something that exactly suited him because he too saw things and felt them rather than reasoned about them. It was his method to start fitting words to a tune and to hum them to himself for a little until suddenly they began to flow. He threw away a great deal of verse but still published a great deal, and much of it was not set aside to drain, and revised and cut, with the ruthlessness he applied to his later prose.

In his last phase, he turned his visual images into meticulously hammered prose, and in that medium used the method of the ballad to suggest rather than tell a story. This was his best work. But in the middle period he published verse that was too fluently and easily written; words came to his mind that fitted the tune, and down they went. And if you set *The Five Nations*, the collection of verse published in 1903, beside *The Seven Seas*, published in 1896, there can be little doubt that the later volume has in it more verses that deal with public issues, more that is on the side of authority. There are verses about the inauguration of the Commonwealth of Australia, verses about Canada's celebration of her coming of age by the imposition of a tariff; mocking verses about military inefficiency; half-facetious verses about the virtues of the English, scolding verses about their complacency. In both collections, there was a good deal that contradicted the main note, but there can really be no doubt that in the second there was more of the kind of thing Edmund Wilson deplored.

All this was in part a result of South Africa and the South African War. The Kiplings, as you remember, had begun the habit of going to Cape Town for the worst of the English winter, and this had been interrupted by the visit to New York of 1899, by Rudyard's illness and Josephine's death. In Cape Town, Kipling had met Cecil Rhodes and had fallen under his spell. He was always ready to take his colour from men he liked and admired—and Rhodes was ready-made for his admiration. The self-made man, the millionaire who had opened the way to new territories, who had gathered thousands of men to build railways and bridges, who had led them to build cities in the wilderness— all this was to Kipling high romance and excitement. He was thrilled by the opening up of the West in the United States and Canada, by the spread of white occupation in Australia; the laying of deep-sea cables seemed to him a miracle of man's ingenuity and of his will to endure and achieve.

> I sent a message to my dear—
> A thousand leagues and more to Her—
> The dumb sea-levels thrilled to hear,
> And Lost Atlantis bore to Her.

That verse comes from a poem called *The Miracles*—cables, steamships, trains. There is a great deal of admiration for the kind of man who made such things possible in Kipling's early work. Daniel Dravot is a kind of Rhodes, long before Kipling had any thought of meeting him; his enthusiasm for the dreamer whose dreams come true is written into *The Naulahka* and *Captains Courageous*, 'The Mary Gloster', and a dozen sets of verses. Rhodes was the man who embodied all this. His dreams were not much different from the fantasies of scores of young men—but he had the steady persistence towards his end, the snake-like flexibility of method, above all the luck, to make them come true. He was inarticulate; he had the greatest difficulty in putting his meanings into words and Kipling often found words for him—and then accepted almost without question the thought or feeling he had helped to frame.

Rhodes often expressed a contempt for anyone who did not *do* things; writing for a living, he once said, was 'mere loafing'. At least since Westward Ho! Kipling had always nourished an uneasy agreement with this attitude. Rhodes thought in continents. As Chesterton pointed out, it is just as easy to think in continents as to think in cobblestones—but it is much more misleading; it means forgetting what the continents are like and what kind of people live in them. Kipling too at this time was inclined to think in continents. From the time he left India till the day when he bought Bateman's, he was basically rootless, inclined to spin the globe and wonder where he would go next, his mind flashing round the world even more eagerly than his body. Rhodes brushed aside objections to his plans, believing he could always do a deal; he must have encouraged in Kipling his tendency in the middle period to put labels on certain kinds of people and shut against them his mind and heart.

Kipling took his South Africa from Rhodes. He believed passionately that South Africa would have a great future as one of the five linked nations—four sisters beside a mother, in the recurring metaphor of the time. South Africa, like Canada, Australia, and New Zealand, would be independent:

> Daughter am I in my Mother's House
> But mistress in my own,

he had written. But this could only be if it was British; the Afrikaners of the Transvaal and the Orange Free State, the two Afrikaans- or Dutch-speaking republics, were obscurantist, enemies of progress. Some of their virtues he admired—independence, a fearless and uncompromising certainty as to what was right. But they obstinately stood in the way of the commercial and material development that to Rhodes was so important, keeping all power in the hands of those born in the republic—though the English-speakers paid three-quarters of the taxes. Kipling saw this as tyranny, and in some remarkable verses foretold the setting up of a police state in South Africa. It will be best to discuss this together with his 'imperialism', a little later; for the purpose of the present argument, it is enough to say that Kipling, who seldom sat down and thought out anything except his craftsmanship, did not sit down and think out his attitude to the South African War; he was, from the moment war was declared, passionately on the side of his country. But it is important to remember that he saw it not—as many Americans did—simply in terms of a powerful country against two very small ones, but as a war for progress and liberty, which could only be achieved by the mastery of South Africa. He wrote from South Africa to Dr Conland in Vermont:

> They make no secret of their intentions. They want to sweep the English into the sea, to lick their own nigger and to govern South Africa with a gun instead of a ballot-box. It is only the Little Englanders in London who say that the Transvaal is merely fighting for its independence; but out here both sides realise it is a question of which race is to run the country.

'Race' at that time, and indeed for another thirty years in South Africa, meant Afrikaans-speakers or English; what would now be called the question of race was then the question of colour, if it was a question at all. No one then supposed that Africans could have any real share in power, though the British in the Cape Province made no legal distinction between black and white and had fixed the qualification for the franchise at a level that gave a few Africans the vote. But the war was a white man's war; both sides were largely oblivious of the African people. Indeed, the country was organized on the broad assumption that Africans were not there. It was utterly different from India, where everything was done through or by Indians, and no one could forget that they were there. And in this too Kipling took his tone from Rhodes.

Charles Carrington has drawn a parallel between American attitudes to the Cuban war and British to the South African. In both countries, there were liberals and intellectuals opposed to their country's war; in both, there were leaders who saw it on the contrary as a war against obscurantism, corruption and tyranny, a war for progress and ultimately liberty. Probably a majority in both countries were influenced mainly by a determination that their side should win. In Britain, there were undoubtedly many whose minds were made up by the initial disasters; reverses like that, they felt, simply had to be wiped out. To that feeling, the disapproval expressed by foreigners added an edge. But in both countries there was a minority, not large in numbers, but intellectually important, who were disturbed by the war and could not feel convinced of its justice. This included a good many writers and critics who disliked Kipling's full-blooded support for it. And if the war as a cause made them turn against him, their attitude intensified his dislike of 'intellectuals', while the fact of war, the necessity of winning, intensified his tendency to see things in black-and-white, that rejection of all interest in 'shades' which Henry James had deplored. Rhodes made it worse; South Africa made it worse. It is in every sense a country of black and white.

Popularity made it worse too. The army and the navy had found their own special bard, their spokesman and their poet. He was 'carried at a canter round the quarter-deck', shoulder-high, in the Channel Squadron in 1898; he was rapturously received by soldiers wherever he went in South Africa. It would have taken a very strong head indeed to resist so whole-hearted a hero-worship. To an intuitive, who had always craved for affection, it was an encouragement to exaggerate just the qualities which endeared him to the soldiers and alienated the intellectuals. He did not outgrow the effect until after the loss of his son.

War was declared in October 1899, the year of disaster for the Kiplings. It had been in March that the world had learnt that he would live; soon afterwards he had learnt of his daughter's death. He threw himself into activity connected with the war with an energy which must surely have owed something to his desire to drown the pain. He wrote a song, 'The Absent-Minded Beggar' set by Sir Arthur Sullivan to a tune that 'would pull teeth from a barrel-organ', which was meant to raise money for comforts for the troops and their dependants. It did raise a quarter of a million pounds, and he worked at its administration and the distribution of blankets, pyjamas, newspapers, tobacco. He was rapturously welcomed in South Africa as the soldier's poet and the soldier's friend. Lord Roberts asked him to run a newspaper for the troops and he threw himself into this too, though not for long. By the end of April he was back in England, organizing rifle clubs, working for the Navy League, publishing in *The Times* odes in which his extraordinary facility with rhyme and rhythm, for long swinging jingling Swinburnian lines, is used to preach—in the spirit of his two Methodist grandfathers and with the intention of Isaiah or Jeremiah—a gospel of training for defence.

The swing and stamp of the verses are aggressive. But the aggression was directed at his own people. What he was saying at this period, again and again in these public poems, was that the peace and comfort and liberty of Edwardian England had been built by hard work and courage in the past and must not be taken for granted. They could only be preserved if Englishmen were ready to defend them. And defence could not be improvised at the last minute.

'These are the dykes our fathers made; we have never known a breach.' But no one will repair the dykes and the day will come when the sea will make a breach and those who did not mend them will have to say: 'Now, it may fall, we have slain our sons, as our fathers we have betrayed.' It was cricket and football that the English took seriously; the squires put preserving pheasants before anything else. The South African War had shown how ill-prepared they were; a great many young men had died who

might have lived if the English had taken defence seriously. They
had been shamed:

> At the hands of a little people, few but apt in the field ...

And this was because:

> Ye pushed them raw to the battle as ye picked them raw
> from the street ...

The note of denunciation rises. If 'the Lordliest life on earth' is to
be preserved, there must be one year's military training for every
able-bodied male: ' ... each man born in the island broke to the
matter of war ... ' but already they have turned back to 'the
flannelled fools at the wicket or the muddied oafs at the goal ... '
Still more fiercely the rulers of the land are questioned:

> Will the rabbit war with your foemen — the red deer horn
> them for hire?
> Your kept cock-pheasant keep you — he is master of many a
> shire —

It was this kind of note he was sounding in his public poems, and
much of it was included in *The Five Nations*, the collection of 1903.
It was not deep or original thinking; every colonel said the same,
but not with such verve or to such an audience. Kipling happened to have the knack of putting into eloquent and infectious
verse the kind of thing that hundreds of men wanted to put in
letters to *The Times*. It came from the superficial outer courts of
his spirit. But it would be wrong to speak of utterances of this
kind as proceeding altogether from hate — as Edmund Wilson
suggests. For the Boer fighting in the field, Kipling repeatedly
expresses admiration; he can shoot and fight, he can ride and
think; his courage is to be admired. Hate is reserved not for him
but for those who profess to be neutral or non-combatant but
secretly help the enemy, or for the Afrikaners of the Cape
Province, British subjects who profess loyalty but act on the other
side, or for politicians who want to throw away what young men
have died for.

So a picture was built up of a busy talkative man, rushing
vigorously about, organizing rifle clubs, preaching war, glori-
fying soldiers, wanting to paint the map red. And up to a point it
was true. But running through all this is another note, of pity for:

... the poor dead who look so old
And were so young an hour ago ...*

while beneath it was another man altogether, trying to escape from memories of his daughter, yet turning back to children's stories in which father and daughter are together; following his fancy into strange and magical worlds; secretly preparing an entirely new kind of story and new lines of interest.

4. GROWTH AND EXPERIMENT

It was in 1902 that the Kiplings settled at Bateman's, which they were never to leave. But though the period of rootlessness was over, Kipling was at first far from having settled. 'At last I'm one of the gentry', he had written, but the tales suggest an uneasiness as to whether he *was* accepted, either by the gentry or by the indigenous cottagers. It would have been strange if he had been confident, after his Vermont adventure; it would have been even stranger if Sussex folk had been ready to take for granted a new arrival, who was a celebrity, receiving fifty to a hundred letters every day, whose privacy was jealously preserved, whose wife was American, whose money was earned by writing. But gradually, as he went about the place, discussing the brook and its inroads, questions of hedging and ditching and draining, he listened and learned and acquired in the end a new kind of understanding, deeper, more real, less synthetic than what he had learnt from Scots engineers about steam, something that carried with it a balm to the soul and a knowledge of people that no one can learn from crank-throws, feed-pumps and main eccentrics. He put a good deal of this into Hobden of the Puck stories, but it went on developing, and in 'An Habitation Enforced', 'My Son's Wife', 'Friendly Brook' and 'The Wish House' there is an understanding of English country ways and of the meaning of things left unsaid which is of quite a different order from that manipulation of an acquired technical jargon which he displayed so often and with such brilliance. The first two of these stories, incidentally, are about learning to live in the country and learning to be accepted and, in both, the newcomers, though quite alien in habits of thought, have the advantage of hereditary connexions, which of course the Kiplings at Burwash had not.

* Again, I have de-cockneyfied.

Privacy was of increasing importance. There was that great pile of letters every day, some from lunatics, some from ambitious young writers; they came 'from every corner of the world' and 'dealt with every subject', as his surviving daughter later wrote. When those had been dealt with, the desire to be left alone must have been strong. With privacy went independence; years later, when he was installed Rector of St Andrews University, he told the students to cultivate 'a savage and thorny independence'. He assumed that most of his hearers were sons of the manse or, more generally, of professional parents with little cash to spare, and that they followed the ancient Scottish tradition of the sack of oatmeal behind the door. He advised them, by economy and hard work before breakfast, to build up their independence till they could decide what was worth doing. 'If a man has not his rations in advance, he has to stay with his tribe ... ' This creed had been formulated early in married life when his bank suspended payment. Even before that he had for a time lived it out on the Embankment, when tuppence would buy enough sausage and mash for a meal.

It was this creed that made Kipling refuse all honours from the Government, even a direct approach from the King. He could do his work better without such recognition, he said. There was also something deeper at the back of his mind. He had written in 'The Children of the Zodiac' of 'the indignity of horrible praise' that people gave Leo and the girl when they sang and of 'the silly wagging peacock feathers that they stuck in his cap, and the buttons and pieces of cloth they sewed on his coat.' He had a real distaste for such things. Perhaps he was also uneasily aware that his fellow-writers already regarded him as too heavily committed to the side of authority, and remembered what they had said of Wordsworth when he accepted the office of Poet Laureate. But there is no sign of uneasiness in 'The Last Rhyme of True Thomas', published in *The Seven Seas* in 1896, a rhyme in the manner of the Border Ballads, in which True Thomas scornfully rejects the King's offer.

> The King has called for priest and cup
> The King has taken spur and blade
> To dub True Thomas a belted knight
> And all for the sake o' the songs he made.

But he will have none of it:

And what should I make wi' blazon and belt
Wi' keep and tail and seizin and fee
And what should I do wi' page and squire
That am a King in my own countrie?

He harps to the King to show him his power over men and what
he means by his 'own countrie'. He ends:

I ha' harpit ye up to the throne of God,
I ha' harpit your midmost soul in three;
I ha' harpit ye down to the Hinges o' Hell,
And—ye—would—make—a Knight o' me!

What rings in that is not so much 'thorny independence' as fierce
arrogance. But in whatever proportion the motives were mixed,
of the facts there can be no doubt. He was discreetly sounded but
refused to be Poet Laureate in 1896; he made it clear that he would
not accept a knighthood in 1899 and again in 1917, and he refused
the Order of Merit in 1921. But honorary degrees were another
matter; these did not interfere with his independence. And—this
is pure surmise—no one could charge him with currying favour
with academics and intellectuals; tribute from a foe is less com-
promising than reward from a patron.

He was certainly independent. In the last months of 1913, the
Liberal Government was trying to push through a Home Rule
Bill for Ireland; the Protestants of the North regarded this as
betrayal and were ready to fight. Both Northern Protestants and
Southern Catholics were arming themselves and getting ready for
civil war. In March 1914, there was something very like mutiny
among officers of the British army at the Curragh; throughout
Britain, Conservatives collected signatures for the Ulster Coven-
ant, which pledged its signatories to resist any attempt to coerce
the Protestants into accepting a Home Rule that would put them
at the mercy of the Catholic majority. Kipling was active in the
cause of Ulster; he wrote for the journal of the Ulster party the
verses 'Ulster', later included in *The Years Between*. They are
intemperate in the extreme, and calculated to inflame feeling on
both sides:

The dark eleventh hour
Draws on and sees us sold
To every evil power
We fought against of old.

Rebellion, rapine, hate,
Oppression, wrong and greed
Are loosed to rule our fate
By England's act and deed.

There are six verses, all in that vein. Nor did he confine himself to
verse; he made a public speech, in May 1914, in which he attacked
the Liberal leaders in terms (says Charles Carrington) that were
'virulent even by the standard of those ill-tempered days'. He said,
among other things, that the Liberal leaders were reduced to the
necessity of handing over Ulster to a gang of criminals 'for no
other reason than that they might continue in enjoyment of their
salaries'. His speech was an embarrassment (Carrington continues) to his own party and 'a self-inflicted wound to his own
reputation', which never fell so low. It is perhaps not surprising
that three months later German leaders believed that an England
so bitterly divided would not dare to go to war.

Ireland presented a complex problem which has so far proved
insoluble. Kipling's feelings about the Southern Irish were, as
usual, mixed and inconsistent. But something forced the part of
him that showed above the water to take violent part in the con-
troversy, simplifying and overstating. Meanwhile, below the
surface, he was experimenting and moving towards new growths.
The vein which I have labelled 'fancy' I am putting into a separate
chapter. But there remain in the middle period two collections of
tales, *Traffics and Discoveries*, published in 1904, and *Actions and
Reactions*, published in 1909. The first of these has three stories
(out of eleven) about the South African War, and one, longer than
usual and in two parts, which is less a story than a tract in the form
of fiction, about the organization the British Army ought to adopt
if it was to be prepared for war. Four introduce Pyecroft, the
naval successor to Mulvaney. Three of these are farces, one –
'Steam Tactics' – I think, a rather ill-natured farce; one, however,
is 'Mrs Bathurst'. This, with 'Wireless', and 'They', are stories
of quite a different kind; they are the beginning of the late
manner.

In *Actions and Reactions* (which has only eight stories, two of
double length), the only story I would class as unquestionably in
the late manner is 'The House Surgeon', but there is also 'An
Habitation Enforced', a double-length story, one of the fuller
exercises on the theme of 'Hobdenism' and the ways of English

country folk. There are two stories about the colonial service in
Africa, which certainly show no advance on the Indian stories and
are without those brilliant evocations of the Indian scene which
redeem even the more trivial of these. There is a return to *Soldiers
Three* in a story about Ortheris and a dog; another farce, and a
fable about work and devotion to duty among bees who give
their lives to the hive. There is a long story about air transport in
the future, of which perhaps the most remarkable part is the
creation by means of answers to correspondents and advertise-
ments of a whole world of technicalities. A critic of 1909 would
have been justified in thinking that there had been little advance
since *Traffics and Discoveries*; a good deal of this collection must be
classed as 'lateral escape from the self'.

But — going back to *Traffics and Discoveries* — something must be
said of 'Wireless' and something more of 'Mrs Bathurst'. 'They'
is dealt with elsewhere. 'Wireless' is a tale that I read as a boy
without much interest; the surface of the story carried me along
sufficiently to finish it, but I did not pause to think about it or
perceive the complexity of its double set of parallels. The narrator
has made friends with the owner of a chemist's shop in a seaside
town; this man's nephew, Mr Cashell, is an enthusiast for the new
discovery, 'wireless', which is only just beginning. One evening,
he is going to try to get into contact with a fellow-enthusiast in
Poole. He explains that a wire at Poole charged with electricity
can give out waves that may be picked up by another wire parallel
to it and some distance away. This is an 'induced current'. The
power of those waves is tiny, but just enough to make possible a
connexion, which the receiving battery, if it is powerful enough,
can use to turn each pulse from space into a dot or dash recorded
on a heavy Morse instrument. It is on this point that Mr Cashell
insists; the waves from space are useless without a much stronger
power in the receiving battery; it is like a child's hand on the valve
that lets the steam into the engines of some great ship. He speaks
of 'Powers — whatever the Powers may be — at work — through
space — a long distance away.' It has to be remembered that the
whole idea of wireless was in its very earliest infancy.

This sounds like another of those technical discursions, but this
time it is quite different. Mr Cashell's explanation comes piece by
piece, interwoven, it seems casually, with the main part of the
story. This concerns Mr Shaynor, the chemist's assistant, who is
keeping the shop open late, this being Saturday night. He is what

was then called consumptive and coughs blood on to his handker-
chief; he is infatuated with a girl who has 'a singularly rich and
promising voice that well matched her outline'; her name is
Fanny Brand, and perhaps at this point it may occur to the reader
that Keats was a consumptive chemist who was infatuated with a
girl called Fanny Brawne. Once that has occurred to him, he will
be aware of a dozen carefully built-up details that recall the
imagery of *The Eve of St. Agnes*; there was, for instance, a hare
hanging up outside the poulterer's next door, and in the bitter
east wind its fur was 'blown apart in ridges and streaks as the wind
caught it, showing bluish skin underneath', and he will remember
that 'the hare limp'd trembling through the frozen grass.' Mr
Shaynor lights a pastille to relieve his cough; it smells like
incense—'pious incense from a censer old' and as the reader
visualizes the wavering blue lines of its fumes he may recall the
candle whose 'little smoke in pallid moonlight died'. As they wait
for the wireless message to come through, the atmosphere in the
chemist's front shop, with its great coloured jars and twinkling
bottles, builds up slowly into something that recalls Keats's poem,
with the moonlight shining through stained glass, much as a
crude advertisement might recall a Rubens or a Tintoretto. Mr
Shaynor sinks into a doze, and then in a coma begins to talk aloud
and to write down lines from Keats. They come slowly and painfully; sometimes they are wrong—he makes it, for instance 'The
little smoke that dies in moonlight cold'—but once he gets six
lines right as they stand in Keats's works. When he comes back
to his waking self, he says he had never read Keats, nor, it
appears, even heard of him. Mr Cashell, the wireless man, now
calls them to hear messages from two warships, who are both
transmitting messages—but in both cases the receiver is out of
order so that neither can get more than fragments of what the
other is trying to say.

It would be a mistake to try to draw from this story a conclusion
that can be expressed in precise logical terms. The parallel wires,
one in Poole and one in—is it Brighton? It is within sound of
the sea—can transfer something to each other, but a stronger
force is needed to make what is transferred significant, and both
transmitter and receiver must be in order. The other pair of
parallels, between Keats and Mr Shaynor, is even more mysterious, and the analogy cannot be pressed too far. At one stage, the
narrator keeps repeating to himself that of course 'like causes

must beget like effects'. But he does not really believe this explanation of what is happening. Nor does Kipling; if he did, he would be saying that the combination of consumptive chemist's assistant, ripe demanding young woman, a cold night, and certain visual images, would produce Keats's poem just as mixing two chemicals will produce a certain gas. Such crude determinism would be quite foreign to what Kipling felt at any level of his diverse personality. Indeed, he makes fun of an improved form of this theory, putting it into 'lofty words', which suggest that the circumstances 'in conjunction with the mainstream of unconscious thought common to all mankind had thrown up temporarily an induced Keats.'

But while I am confident that Kipling did not really suppose that it is enough to say 'like causes must beget like effects', it is more difficult to say what he did mean. It would surely be absurd to suppose that, on the exact analogy of Poole and Brighton, the soul of Keats was trying to get through to Mr Shaynor and rewrite the poem he had written much better once before. The reference to 'the main-stream of unconscious thought' is interesting, particularly when one remembers that this story was written in 1902 and that Jung's formulation of the collective unconscious was not published until some years later. But as Mr Shaynor struggles with Keats's lines, there is a strong sense of a power trying to get through to an imperfect human receiver, and this accords well with the view Kipling often expressed – and which indeed many poets have shared – that his best work was not his but came *through* him. But what is that power? The collective unconscious of mankind? Or some superhuman spiritual force? In either case, why dictate Keats to a man who never read poetry? And in either case, the analogy with the Poole-Brighton transmitters breaks down, since in their case purely human conscious agencies were concerned with talking to each other.

What emerges from this attempt at analysis then, is no exact correspondence between the two pairs of parallels, nor any clear idea of what was happening to Mr. Shaynor, but a broad suggestion of an analogy between the transfer of electric influence over distance and the transfer of thought through time; a still stronger impression – though very indeterminate – that artistic achievement is unaccountable and comes *through* the conscious personality, the part above the surface. This Kipling felt, but as usual he did not think it out in intellectual terms. What he did think about with great care was the construction of the tale and its surface detail. There is no longer an outer story as frame to the inner main story (as in 'Love-o'-Women' or 'On Greenhow Hill') but the slighter story is parallel to the main story and woven into and through it. And the visual images, scents and sounds that suggest 'The Eve of St Agnes' are built into an apparently casual account of rather pointless conversation with such skill that I could as a boy read it simply because it flowed, while now the richly lacquered effect—as of some delicate piece of chinoiserie—seems to me a masterpiece of craftsmanship. There is nothing else quite like it till 'The Eye of Allah', which has the same richness of varied, but congruent, detail, but is artistically far superior because it is set against a background of pain and loss as well as the travail of the artist, and because the central point carries conviction.

'Wireless' must be classed as a brilliant experiment in form, but not ultimately either moving or intellectually convincing; there can be no doubt about the importance of the central theme of 'Mrs Bathurst'. As I have said, it is a novel condensed into a series of single scenes with most of the intervening parts left out. There are widely differing interpretations of it, and some critics have assumed without question a conclusion which seems to me demonstrably wrong. And, critics apart, you will find intelligent Kipling devotees who have quite a variety of ideas about what happened. So it must be discussed. But to condense it any further is impossible, while it is equally impossible to discuss it without reminding the reader of the points which are in dispute. He must read the story again and form his own judgment—but that he should make such a personal rediscovery is one of the objects of this book.

As I have said already, the inner story is told to the narrator by three men, each of whom holds certain pieces of evidence. Most of the running is made by Pyecroft, but his companion, Pritchard, a sergeant of Marines, also remembers Mrs Bathurst well. She was a young widow who had kept a pub in Auckland, New Zealand, for warrant officers and sergeants. No one could forget her; she had *It*, a phrase then used for the first time; she was kindness itself and immensely attractive but basically good; Pritchard, indeed, who in a gigantic calf-like way is still half in love with her, keeps insisting that whatever happened could not have been her fault. The key phrase about her—which Kipling had heard ten years before in New Zealand — was that she 'never scrupled to feed a lame duck or set her foot on a scorpion ... ' Both Pyecroft and Pritchard also know Vickery, a warrant officer with only eighteen months to go before his honourable discharge with pension. He had four false teeth on the port side, his own having been carried away by an ammunition hoist; they clicked when he was excited and this gave him the name of 'Click' Vickery. Both also knew that Vickery recently went from Cape Town up the country to take delivery of some naval stores left there after the South African War. This he had done and seen them into trucks for return to the navy. Then he had disappeared.

So much was common knowledge. But Pyecroft, who had been serving in the same ship, could throw more light on his disappearance. Their ship was in Cape Town and they had leave to go ashore. Vickery had asked him to come, at his expense, to the most costly seat in a circus where there was an exciting novelty — something hardly any sailor had seen before — a cinematograph. It showed a train coming in to Paddington, and there, quite plain, was Mrs Bathurst, walking towards you. It was only for forty-five seconds but it was all that Vickery wanted. He led Pyecroft out of the circus at once and for the rest of the evening insisted that he should come with him, walking very fast, all round Cape Town, turning into every bar he saw for a drink, downing it without pause for conversation and then tearing on to the next. Next night and the next night for five nights running, Pyecroft went through the same demanding ritual. For most of the time, Vickery would not permit conversation, but once he did answer a question; yes, he knew what Mrs Bathurst was looking for; she was looking for him. But any further questions might lead to murder — and if that led to his own death he would not mind.

When Vickery got leave to go up country, he told Pyecroft that the cinematograph show would be at Worcester, which is about fifty miles from Cape Town up the line, 'so I shall see her yet once again'. He added that he was *not* a murderer because his wife had died in childbed six weeks after he left England. 'That much at least I am clear of.' He went clicking into the station with the words: 'The rest is silence.' It is now that the third man present, a railway engineer called Hooper, comes in with his contributory evidence. He had been in Rhodesia and had heard of two tramps on the railway line (near Wankie's on the way to

Victoria Falls); his informant had given them food and quinine.
('I don't envy that other man if—' said Pyecroft, but no one
finished his sentence.) Hooper had found the two tramps, both
near the line, struck by lightning and black as charcoal. What he
had just heard enabled him to identify one of the two, the one
who was standing up, by the four false teeth on the port side.
Those teeth Hooper had had in his pocket from the beginning of
the story, though he never showed them. The last words of the
story are spoken by Pyecroft: ' ... 'aving seen 'is face for five
consecutive nights on end, I'm inclined to finish what's left of the
beer and thank Gawd he's dead!' And since Pyecroft had said
that on those walks Vickery's face had reminded him of things
preserved in spirits in a bottle — 'White and crumply things —
previous to birth ... ' — we may be inclined to agree with
him.

Many readers have assumed without question that the second
tramp was Mrs Bathurst. But this is quite untenable. Vickery says
he is going to see her 'yet once again' in the cinema show at
Worcester. The two tramps were clearly men; there were a lot of
deserters wandering about after the war, and Hooper's informant
would have spoken of them quite differently if he had been talking
of a man and a woman — something very unusual. Pyecroft's
reference to 'that other man' goes unchecked. Hooper three times
distinguishes between the two tramps by phrases he would not
have used if one had been a man and one a woman. 'The man who
was standing up had the false teeth ... his mate who was squatting
down ... The false-toother was tattooed ... ' And if Vickery had
made an assignment to meet Mrs Bathurst in Rhodesia — he being
now a free man — his whole behaviour becomes incomprehensible.
He could have married her and taken his pension. The story
depends inescapably on the fact that he has lost her irrevocably
through some grievous fault of his own. That I take to be the
hinge to any understanding.

What that fault was we cannot say with certainty, but perhaps
he had persuaded her to sell up in New Zealand and come to
England without revealing that he was married. The cinema
camera had caught her by chance as her train steamed in to
Paddington and she got out, looking for Vickery. My own guess
is that he had contemplated murdering his wife and perhaps even
taken some steps towards carrying out the murder. Perhaps Mrs
Bathurst discovered, in one blow, the fact that he was married

and the plan for the murder. Perhaps he found he could not carry it through and confessed to her. They must have quarrelled and he must have believed it was for ever. There was the hard side to her nature; perhaps she had set her foot on him as a scorpion and he, when he understood the wrong he had done her and how he had misjudged her, dared not face her again. But most of that is guesswork.

Next comes the question of what Vickery had said to the captain of his ship. All we are told is that he asked for an interview and that the captain came out having shipped his court-martial face, went ashore and came back looking normal, after which Vickery was sent on his mission. Here again, one can only guess, but my suggestion is that Vickery had convinced the captain that he was going mad and likely to commit suicide or even to murder a comrade, and had asked for a way out that would not bring scandal on the navy and his ship—or on anyone else. When he went ashore, the captain was able to find a plausible reason for sending him away from his ship and giving him the opportunity to desert. He carried out the duty assigned him and then disappeared, meaning to find an unobtrusive way of ending his life. The other man he picked up by chance; we know that he still had a craving for company. It has been suggested (by Elliott Gilbert, who is right in thinking the second tramp was not a woman) that Vickery stood up in the midst of an intense electrical storm to attract the lightning, and that the second tramp, who was crouching, is there to emphasize that Vickery's death was voluntary. It may be, though again this is surmise, that the second tramp was not so much *put* in as *left* in. We know that one source of the tale was the phrase about Mrs Bathurst overheard in New Zealand years earlier; from what else we know of Kipling's methods of work, it seems likely that he had another pebble to add to that, and it *may* have been that someone had told him of two tramps killed by lightning and found by the side of the railway-track. It is just the kind of picture that Kipling had always looked for and used as a centre-piece (like the Other Man dead in the rickshaw) and just the kind of thing he might have heard over a drink in Cape Town. That is a guess; what I am sure of is that Vickery was seeking death.

There is one saying of Pritchard's which at first sight suggests that *he* thought the other tramp was Mrs Bathurst. When Vickery has been identified by the teeth, Pritchard 'covered his face with

6

his hands for a moment, like a child shutting out an ugliness. "And to think of her at Hauraki!" he murmured— ... ' remembering her as she had been in her bar in New Zealand. But it is not conclusive. He knew that—though *she* was not to blame—she had in some way been involved with Vickery, who had been destroyed by the involvement—burnt indeed to charcoal that fell to pieces when the corpse was moved. That surely was ugliness enough. It is brought out by contrast with a picnic party on the beach, who start for home as this tale of mental agony and physical disintegration comes to an end. They are 'sunburned, wet and sandy' after a day of happy idleness and they sing a popular song of the day, 'The Honeysuckle and the Bee', a song of sentimental prettiness, that goes with the thought of Mrs Bathurst, innocently flirtatious in her bar at Hauraki.

Many will say that this is not the way to tell a story, and that it is a blemish that learned critics have pronounced it unintelligible. But there has been a good deal of disagreement about *Hamlet*, and it is part of the attraction of the play. As Bridges says in his 'loose alexandrines':

> Hamlet himself would never have been aught to us, or we
>   to Hamlet, wer't not for the artful balance whereby
> Shakespeare so gingerly put his sanity in doubt
>   without the while confounding his Reason.

To me, on return to the story late in life, the interest has been enormously enhanced by the uncertainty as to what happened between the still shots we are shown. It may be that the part played by the cinematograph is no accident, and that someone had been explaining to Kipling how the illusion of motion was conveyed by a succession of single pictures.

But there is an older model in the Scottish ballads and in particular that powerful anonymous poem: *Edward, Edward*. I hope the reader will read it through and consider how it resembles a Kipling story. It opens, like 'Love-o'-Women', with a murder just committed.

> Why does your brand sae drop wi' blude,
>   Edward, Edward?
> Why does your brand sae drop wi' blude
>   And why sae sad gang ye, O?

O I hae killed my hawk sae gude,
Mither, mither;
O I hae killed my hawk sae gude,
And I had nae mair but he, O.

But his mother will not be put off, and presses him closer and closer with menacing questions, till at last he blurts out:

O I hae killed my father dear
Mither, mither;

She does not ask why or how nor utter any word of sorrow, surprise or reproach. She goes on questioning, coming a little closer at every question. What is he going to do now — about himself, his life being forfeit? What will he do, a banished man, about his towers and hall, his wife and children? And finally, what will he do about herself:

And what will ye leave to your ain mither dear,
Edward, Edward?
And what will ye leave to your ain mither dear,
My dear son, now tell me, O?
The curse of hell frae me sall ye bear,
Mither, mither;
The curse of hell frae me sall ye bear:
Sic counsels ye gave to me, O!

In that last half-stanza we suddenly understand the part this terrible old woman has played, driving him on to the murder, as much because she hates her husband as for the sake of the lands and castle she will get when her son is banished — for there can be no doubt she will make short work of the wife. But none of this is said. There are only seven stanzas — and apart from the refrain, each stanza has only two lines, each repeated. Fourteen effective lines — but each hammered home and the reader (or rather hearer) made to picture for himself the motives of a woman who combines in herself Clytemnestra, Lady Macbeth and Hedda Gabler!

Perhaps in 'Mrs Bathurst' Kipling carried this method too far. But that he meant to do what he did I have no doubt, nor have I any doubt that now — after reading it several times and thinking about it a good deal — I am left with an immensely strong impression of its three main themes: the devastating and destructive power which an extremely attractive woman may innocently exercise; the unaccountability of human affairs and the eccentricity of chance; and the difficulty of knowing anything of the lives of other people except what is revealed in a passing flash. It would be an interesting though laborious task to reconstruct 'Mrs Bathurst' as Henry James might have told it — surely at ten times the length — but for the moment let us turn to the other new line of development, free-flowering fancy.

PART TWO
The Search for a Home

7
Hallo My Fancy

'In conceit like Phaeton
I'll mount Phoebus' chair ...
... Fain would I hear his fiery horses neighing
And see how they on foamy bits are playing,
All the stars and planets I will be surveying! —
Hallo my fancy, whither wilt thou go?'
                WILLIAM CLELAND, 1661–1689

I. MOWGLI

In his biography of Kipling, Charles Carrington recounts the
experience of a young girl whose family had stayed with the
Kiplings in South Africa. She had then been at the age when the
nursery is a pleasant memory and the lunch table something from
which it is important not to be excluded, though it is regarded
with apprehension. On the first morning of her stay, this young
lady went to the beach with the younger children and it happened
that there came by a short dark man who stopped to play with
them and tell them stories. She was fascinated; this, she thought,
was the most enchanting person she had ever met. Kipling was
already her favourite author, and, now she had met him, life
would never be quite the same again. He was even more exciting
in the flesh than in his books. They went back to the house and
she made herself tidy for lunch; there at the head of the table was a
short dark man who looked just like the man on the beach. But
this man she did not much like; he disappointed her. He seemed to
be acting a part and would only talk about the technical details of
some cooking-stove.

Many others have spoken of the relaxation and happiness that
Kipling felt with children. And in some of his published stories
which were originally told to children, an older reader can feel
this release. But that he felt a release when writing for children
does not make these books unimportant. On the contrary, the
relaxation allowed him to free himself from the need to strike an
attitude, and to express himself more fully than ever before. The
children's stories provided a bed in which seeds could germinate
and young plants could grow without being clogged or distorted
by the rank top-growth of political opinions. They permitted the
appearance of a sanity and sweetness which in the last period was
again transmuted by pain into compassion. But the value of these
stories is not only that they prepared the way for the last period.

They were told to children in the first place, and meant to be read to children when they had been written, but they were all meant to be read by grown-ups too. They are all 'worked' on at least two levels, and because they come straight from the subconscious, they have an immediate and direct appeal to people of all ages.

This is particularly so of the Mowgli tales in the Jungle Books —apart from 'In the Rukh', which although it shows Mowgli as a grown man, was written before the others and had nothing to do with children. I shall assume that anyone who reads this book has at some time of his life made the voyage to the Seeonee Hills and remembers that warm evening when Father Wolf woke from his day's rest and a little brown baby, just able to walk, came out of the bushes, pushed his way in among the cubs and began to take Mother Wolf's milk. I need not summarize the tale; all we need do is to consider the strange world in which we find ourselves.

Mowgli's own parents do not look for him and are forgotten. But he finds new and loving foster-parents who stand by him and are ready to die for him. When Mowgli is taken to the Council Rock, on the fatal night when it is to be decided whether the pack will keep him or give him to the tiger, Mother Wolf 'got ready for what she knew would be her last fight' if the pack rejected him. When he is going back to men and she says good-bye, she tells him she has loved him more than ever she loved her cubs. But except for Mother Wolf and Messua—another foster-mother who loves him dearly while he is with the man-pack—there are no female figures in the Jungle. There are the Free People, the wolves in the pack, who are ruled—under the Law—by Akela, the wise old wolf who is leader. But he is far indeed from a tyrant; at the scene when Mowgli is accepted, Akela behaves like the Chairman of a Board, giving everyone a chance to speak and reminding them of the Law. The Free People form a rather austere republic, always subject to the Law, whose authority they invoke in any dispute. But without leadership and respect for the Law, they quickly become decadent and fawn on the wicked Shere Khan the tiger. The Bandar-log, the monkey people, are wholly outside the Law and even worse than a decadent republic; they are without honour or shame. Chaos is never far distant from Kipling's political imagination, and can only be kept at bay by discipline and leadership under the Law.

The Pack and the Council Rock constitute a male world, the world of the Club and the House of Commons; family life is apart from the Pack. And also outside the Pack—but under the Law—are Baloo the teacher of the Law and Bagheera the Black Panther, who was 'as cunning as Tabaqui, as bold as the wild buffalo, and as reckless as the wounded elephant. But he had a voice as soft as wild honey dripping from a tree, and a skin softer than down'. He is D'Artagnan, he is Alan Breck, the bonny fighter of every romantic story; he is the Master of Ballantrae and Rupert of Hentzau, and no tale of adventure is complete without him, while Baloo, the fubsy old pedagogue, is another kind of father with a touch of Lockwood Kipling, a touch of Uncle Crom, and more than a touch of Dr Johnson. And Akela too, who 'slew the slayer And will himself be slain', is an archetypal figure. Even stranger, more ancient, more magic, is the gigantic python Kaa.

In spite of five splendid foster-fathers, Mowgli cannot belong to the jungle. He wants to be a wolf—but the wolves keep reminding him that he is a man. They cannot look him in the eyes; they know he is a being of a higher order, and all but his inner circle of faithful friends and servants hate him just because he has pulled thorns from their feet. He is odd man out whichever way he turns, alone on his island, like Crusoe and Prospero, like the heroic white man alone among a thousand natives, who recognize his hateful superiority because he is immune from their magic. When Kaa by his dancing weaves a spell over the Bandar-log, so that they can do nothing except by his will, even Baloo and Bagheera are bewitched as well. They sway one step nearer with the lines of monkeys, till Mowgli lays a hand on their necks and they are released. But Mowgli's magic is too strong for any of them; they are all afraid of his eyes and of the Red Flower, the fire which only he can feed and control.

The Law under which the people of the Jungle live became one of Kipling's basic ideas. It was Natural Law, something that had grown very slowly—'it is by far the oldest law in the world'—and it had to exist if wolves were to live together in a pack and bring up their families, and if the different kinds of animal were also to live together within a framework that everyone understood. It kept chaos at bay. It had not been thought out by logical processes; it had evolved. And Kipling, who felt things but hardly ever thought them out, does not explain how the Law was applied or interpreted, though Hathi the elephant is sometimes a kind of judge and his sons are sometimes policemen. But, in the fragments he lets fall, it is possible to detect two main principles in the

Law. One is protection for family life, for property in hunting-grounds and kills, for cubs that are too weak to protect themselves; the other is for the restitution of a balance after it has been upset.

After Mowgli's rescue from the monkeys, he must be punished, not because he has knowingly done wrong but because by playing with the monkeys he has brought on Baloo and Bagheera pain, humiliation, and loss of hunting-time. It was not his fault, but he must be punished to put things right. And it is by this principle that Mowgli is brought into the Pack. To bring him in is to break the established order of things and makes a chink through which chaos may creep; a sacrifice is needed to restore the balance. He must be bought, as Ameera's child was bought by the goat Holden beheaded. Bagheera's bull is a scapegoat for Mowgli, on to which is transferred the guilt of the breach, and all cattle become forbidden to Mowgli for the rest of his life. All this is familiar to anyone who knows even a little about primitive societies and how primitive people think. But the point is that Kipling is not writing into his story what he had learnt from an anthropologist; he simply felt that this was natural and right, and it recurs in his later work in different forms.

The Mowgli stories have enthralled many thousands of children. They were written with that purpose, and they succeed because they give shape and form to archetypal fantasies about the self. They are not quite free from that knowing nudge that lets the reader into a secret—Mowgli, repeating his lessons to Baloo, gives 'the words the Bear accent which all the hunting-people use'. But children enjoy secrets, and the older reader need not be irritated when he knows that the secret has only just been made up; this is not the same as being told secrets about matrimony or sneered at because one does not know who dances the Halli-Hukk.

There are some absurdities. Mowgli's friends at the beginning argue that if Shere Khan is allowed to kill the boy, men will come with guns and disturb the whole jungle; but they assume that no one will worry if he disappears into a wolf's cave. It is thrown as an insult at the wicked Shere Khan that he kills cattle, but the heroic Bagheera has killed a bull only half a mile from the Council Rock. When Won-Tolla, the outlier, the wolf who lives with his wife and family away from the pack, brings news that the Red Dogs from the Dekkan are coming and are five times as many as the Seeonee wolf pack, he says they are hot on his trail. One of his

6*

paws is mangled by the teeth of a Red Dog, yet he has not only broken away from these implacable killers and trackers, who never abandon a blood trail, but left them so far behind that they do not arrive for thirty-six hours.

It would be easy to add other points of the same kind, but they are trivialities; the verve of the narrative carries the reader past this kind of thing. Nor need we stress the point that in the animal world we are always on the side of the predators. No one—except one witty fawn during the Water Truce—suggests that the deer might have a point of view. Why worry, when there are such marvellous pictures as the journey through the tree-tops—when the monkeys would rush Mowgli up a tree till he felt 'the thinnest topmost branches crackle and bend under them, and then with a cough and a whoop would fling themselves into the air outward and downward, and bring up, hanging by their hands or their feet to the lower limbs of the next tree'—or the gathering in the drought when the Peace Rock 'lay across the shallows like a long snake and the little tired ripples hissed as they dried on its hot sides'? Or, again from 'Red Dog', Kaa's thinking back into the past before he hits on the stratagem by which the Red Dogs are defeated.

'Red Dog', indeed, is superb. It has everything—every situation that has stirred the blood of imaginative youth since tales were first told. There is the threat of invasion by barbarian hordes —far more numerous than the Free People, pitiless in courage and tenacity, but despised and hated because, among other things, they had hair between their toes. (This, incidentally, they themselves seem to have regarded as a mark of racial inferiority; Mowgli was able to 'wake them to stupid rage' by twiddling his toes above their heads from a tree-top; 'those who have hair between their toes do not care to be reminded of it'.) There is the mustering of a whole people to fight in defence of homes and children; there is the wise old counsellor thinking back into the past; the brilliant exploit of one hero who 'pulls the very whiskers of death' and leads the enemy into a trap; the defence of a narrow place—Thermopylae, Horatius and the bridge, Alan Breck in the round house; there is the vengeance of Won-Tolla whose family have been killed by the Red Dogs; there is the death of the glorious old leader and Mowgli the victor left mourning on the battlefield. This tale too I could never read aloud to my children without everyone weeping. Every situation is archetypal; we have been there before a hundred times, but it is so fresh and original a setting that it compels identification.

It is the essence of the Mowgli myth that here concerns us — a hero who has no parents of his own, but loving foster-parents instead, who grows up strong and beautiful, but a stranger among beings of a lower order who cast him out because he is different. His own natural kind too repel him with stones. He has revenged himself on Shere Khan and now he revenges himself on the villagers by destroying their fields and houses; he goes back to the Jungle and lives there again — but now he is the Master of the Jungle. 'He had the good conscience that comes from paying a just debt;' before he goes all debts are paid. He would have to go back to men in the end — as everyone told him — but for the moment, he can pause in this enchanted world. Mowgli, the odd man out among wolves and men alike, who triumphs over his enemies and accomplishes his revenge, sums up a formula which repeats itself with variations in 'Rikki-Tikki-Tavi' and 'The White Seal'. It is true that the White Seal did have parents, not foster-parents. But not only was he white, and they were not, which made him different from all other seals, but he asked questions, which no other seal did. He had a mission and could not marry till it was accomplished. He was the genius who is quite different from his parents; he is a more serious version of 'The Elephant's Child'. In the story of that name (in *The Just-So Stories*) much the same formula was to reappear later. A young person who is different from his family and relations because he is always asking questions — for which they always punish him — finds a foster-parent in another gigantic python and eventually revenges himself on everyone who had punished him.

Fantasy need not believe its own tales. Kipling did not think he was Mowgli. But who can doubt that he put into Mowgli much that he longed for, much that he felt deeply, much that he half suspected about himself?

2. FOLK IN HOUSEN

The Puck stories were written in Sussex when the cure was beginning to work. 'Take of English earth as much ... ' Kipling wrote in the verses called 'A Charm':

> 'Lay that earth upon thy heart
> And thy sickness shall depart.'

He did find healing in the English countryside and the ways of its people. Late in life, in *Something of Myself* he spoke of the pleasure of finding traces of Roman, Dane, Norman and Saxon on the acres which the law now said were his. But this he had told us long before in *Puck* and *Rewards and Fairies*. These stories, unlike the Mowgli tales, are set in his usual structural frame of a story in a setting, but the setting is always the same, a corner of England with a hill behind the meadows, woods with pheasants calling, a winding stream overgrown with hazel and alder, the mill sluice and the mill, the fields called Three Cows and Long Slip, the old forge and Little Lindens farm. Here the two children find Puck; who else could they expect when they act *A Midsummer Night's Dream* on Midsummer Night? And, as everybody knows, through Puck they met people from every age who had come to that valley —and hear of quite a few, like Maximus and Talleyrand and George Washington, who had not.

There is one odd feature of these stories. There were other stories of the period in which children went back in time or were transported to distant places or strange worlds, taking with them the knowledge of their own world. But the Kipling stories of these two collections are different; a Norman knight or a Roman centurion comes to the children and tells his story. These strange visitors know nothing of what has happened since their own time; they have been plucked straight from the past. Indeed, in 'Marklake Witches', the girl who tells the story was dying of 'consumption' — that is, tuberculosis — at the time when it happened, and it becomes apparent, as she tells her story, that everyone but herself knows it. Even now, as she talks to Una a hundred years later, she still doesn't know the nature of her sickness. It never struck me as a boy that this was odd. The irony was moving, and I didn't stop to consider. But the implication is that all time is co-existent, that Parnesius, Philadelphia, Queen Elizabeth and the rest have come — *during* their lives, before they knew the end — to talk to the children. But I don't think Kipling stopped to think about this any more than I did when I first read these stories.

I do not propose to discuss these stories in detail. That is not because I do not admire them, nor because I do not think them important in Kipling's development. On the contrary, I think that, like the Mowgli stories, they helped his development enormously. Like the Mowgli stories, they seem to me usually free from the self-consciousness that so often blemishes Kipling's

work; they blend the poetic and historic imagination successfully, and I am thankful that no magic of oak and ash and thorn
obliterates them from my memory. They are a stage in the beginning of a new Kipling. He had found a home and began—very
slowly—to feel at home in it. And in these stories, because they
were for children, he does not need to proclaim so noisily that he
is at home. They held me as a child and still do. But I believe they
are much better known than the later stories, and those who read
them as children will hardly need to be re-introduced to them.
When I thought I disliked Kipling, I would have made an exception of all the stories I have here grouped under 'Fancy'—those
about Kim, Mowgli and Puck—and no doubt others will feel the
same. This book is written in the hope that such readers will turn
back to the later Kipling. Except for one story, all I mean to do
here is to emphasize the recurring themes.

These are the steadfast and enduring marriage of land and
people and the importance in a man's life of what he has tried to
do. The first point has been noticed by everyone; the land absorbs
the people who come, whether they are neolithic workers of
flint, Romans, Saxons, Danes or Normans. The Norman knight
sings:

> I followed my Duke ere I was a lover
> To take from England fief and fee;
> But now this game is the other way over—
> But now England hath taken me!

And not only men, but gods and fairies too become English, with
perhaps an echo of 'The Bridge-Builders' and India's absorptive
powers. The other point is perhaps less obvious. These are
imaginative reconstructions of history in which the actors are
deeply *responsible*; Sir Richard, the Norman knight, falls in love
with a Saxon lady, but he has a duty to his feudal lord and the
people of the manor, and the two sides of his life always have to
be balanced, the personal against the public. It is the same right
through the sequence about Norman and Saxon, and right
through the sequence about Romans on the Great Wall. Sebastian
Cabot wants guns for his naval venture; even the widow Whitgift
in Dymchurch Flit—a tale of a rather different kind, almost pure
magic and fancy—lends her sons because she knows it will help
all the people of Romney Marsh to regain their health and 'come
out fresh and shining all over the Marsh like snails after wet'. And

it is the same in *Rewards and Fairies*, though with a certain difference.

The one story on which we must dwell is the first of *Rewards and Fairies*, which is called 'Cold Iron'. It was of this in particular that Kipling said, in *Something of Myself*, that 'I worked the material in three or four overlaid tints and textures, which might or might not reveal themselves according to the shifting light of sex, youth, and experience.' The reasons he gives for this are that the stories 'had to be read by children, before people realized that they were meant for grown-ups'; and they 'had to be a sort of balance to, as well as a seal upon, my "imperialistic" output in the past'. Certainly, the impression of different levels is strong in 'Cold Iron', and I am far from sure that I have reached them all. It is a fable, quite different from the others.

'Cold Iron' begins within the usual outer frame. Dan and Una creep out of the house to look for an otter early in the morning of Midsummer Day before five o'clock. They take off their boots so as not to wet them in the dew. They have forgotten all last year's adventures – magicked away by oak and ash and thorn – but something suddenly brings them to the threshold of remembering, and then Puck is with them again. They talk of how last year he had made them forget, and Una asks if he could turn her into an otter. Not with her boots tied round her neck – there is cold iron in them. She throws them away. Nor when she has trusted him. This magic is not like Kaa's – it is as homely and earthy and kind as Puck himself. They didn't wear boots last year; Cold Iron has begun to separate them from the innocence of childhood. They hate their boots, but would they go back? 'No-o. I suppose I shouldn't – not for always. I'm growing up, you know,' said Una. And we begin to get a hint at what Cold Iron stands for.

The inner story grows almost imperceptibly out of the frame of the outer as the conversation goes on. The People of the Hills – which is the proper name, of course, for those whom you and I call fairies – have always wanted to 'act and influence on folk in housen'. So one day Puck suggests to Sir Huon, who was lost long ago on the road to Babylon and who succeeded King Oberon, that he should 'take some human cradle-babe by fair dealing', bring him up 'on the far side of Cold Iron', and send him out into the world with a splendid fortune. And before long, Puck finds a baby, born on Terrible Down to a slave-girl who had died. He had been left at a church door, so that no one was wronged by his taking; he had never been into a house and so — as long as they could keep him away from Cold Iron — the People of the Hills could bring him up as their own. Sir Huon and his Lady — the Lady Esclairmonde — welcomed The Boy with as much wonder and excitement as a pair of human lovers with their first child. But, soon after The Boy came, Puck heard a hammering down at the Forge and saw a Smith forging something from Cold Iron. He saw him toss it from him 'a longish quoit-throw down the valley', and he knew that some day someone would find it because the Smith was Thor.

The Boy grew up and at first he was allowed to go on night-walkings with Puck among folk in housen. But, though Puck never let him touch Cold Iron, they got into one or two scrapes together and the Lady Esclairmonde scolded Puck till at last he said he would let them bring The Boy up their own way and he would leave him alone till he had found his fortune. So he kept out of the way — but he watched The Boy, very lonely, poring over the big black books of magic he was set to learn, and playing with boy's magic, filling the valley with hawks and hounds, knights and ladies and castles, hungering all the time, of course, for folk in housen, his own mortal kind, whom he was not allowed to see. 'They always intended a fine fortune for him — but they could never find it in their heart to let him begin.' But one hot night, when the valley was full of his hounds giving tongue and packed with his knights in armour, and The Boy was roving about, 'wrapped in his flaming discontents', he stumbles in the fern on that *something* which the Smith had cast a quoit-throw down the valley. Sir Huon and his Lady and Puck were close at hand but they could not save him; it was Cold Iron, and he had picked it up. Whatever it was, they knew it would be his fortune, so they called out to know. Was it a sword, a sceptre, a plough, a great book with iron clasps? It was none of those, but a slave-ring, such as his mother must have worn, and before they could stop him he had put it on his neck and snapped home the lock. What else could he have done? So he went to work among folk in housen — doing what he knew they needed — and he married and had bushels of children.

This is one of many fables which it would be a mistake to inter-pret on too intellectual a plane. Kipling *felt* what he wanted to say, he did not think it; having felt it, he used his intellect to shape his feeling in words, but it would not proceed like a theorem of

Euclid. Nothing is exactly equal to anything else. When I was twelve, I read it, just as I was meant to at that age. The early morning dew, the home-baked bread; the smoke from Little Lindens farm, Hobden's simple breakfast of cold roast pheasant, frame the story of Sir Huon and Thor and the fate of The Boy who could make shadow-knights and shadow-castles but had to give it all up and live with folk in housen. I always thought I knew what was meant by folk in housen — the respectable world of grown-ups. But Cold Iron? Something hard and inescapable, that was alien to magic and to the escape I found in these stories from the hard real World of Work, in which I had to grind at Latin and Greek and Mathematics. That was as far as I went at first. On the next level, it is clear enough that the first meaning of the fable is not too far from Wordsworth's in the Immortality Ode. Cold Iron is the prison-house, whose shades begin to close on every boy.

> Why with such earnest pains dost thou provoke
> The years to bring the inevitable yoke,
> Thus blindly with thy blessedness at strife?
> Full soon thy soul shall have her earthly freight,
> And custom lie upon thee with a weight,
> Heavy as frost and deep almost as life!

But is there not something else here, something a good deal more personal? Once again we have a Boy with foster parents, like Mowgli, torn between two worlds; he snaps home the ring on his own neck and leaves his magic so that he may work for folk in housen and have bushels of children. Did Kipling remember, as he rejoiced in the healing power of English earth, those intensely confident verses he had written a few years before in *The Last Rhyme of True Thomas*?

> My lance is tipped o' the hammered flame,
> My shield is beat o' the moonlight cold;
> And I won my spurs in the Middle World,
> A thousand fathoms beneath the mould.

When he wrote that he still had the confidence to make boy's magic, but now he has snapped the catch on himself and lives with folk in housen. Carrie was very much folk-in-housen. It made no difference now whether he travelled first class by the Union Castle Line or stayed at home as the squire of Bateman's.

> There walks no wind 'neath Heaven
>   Nor wave that shall restore
> The old careening riot
> And the clamorous crowded shore —
> The fountain in the desert,
>   The cistern in the waste,
> The bread we ate in secret,
>   The cup we spilled in haste!

Cold Iron had cut him off from the old feckless days as surely as the burdens of his office had closed upon Diego Valdez, High Admiral of Spain.

But there are more levels still. 'Cold Iron' is a more elastic symbol than the x or z of an equation in algebra, whose value is constant. The story is followed by verses also called 'Cold Iron'. Incidentally, T. S. Eliot admired this linking of verse with a story in prose, which he called a new art-form; Edmund Wilson castigated it as a tasteless device. But whether you like it or not — and I think Eliot was far more perceptive than Wilson on this point — it is manifestly no accident, and, in the verses, Cold Iron has another meaning, indeed two meanings. The verses, like 'True Thomas', are cast as a ballad, with the refrain, only slightly varied to each verse: 'But Iron — Cold Iron — is the master of men all.' In the first two stanzas the Baron makes rebellion against the King his lord because Iron — Cold Iron — is the master of men all: that is to say, because he thinks he has the military strength to win and because he believes that force is the last arbiter in human affairs. But he is taken prisoner and prepares for the death which by his own creed he has earned.

> Tears are for the craven, prayers are for the clown —
> Halters for the silly neck that cannot keep a crown.

But his King gives him Bread and Wine and shows him Hands pierced with nails. The iron of those nails is the master of men in quite another sense. And the Baron kneels in submission, ackowledging that 'Iron, out of Calvary, is master of man all!'

The end of this song comes as a shock to the reader, and I suspect that it came as a shock to Kipling himself. It is surmise to suggest that it welled up, unbidden, but in part suggested by the ballad form and the recurring rhythms of the nursery rhyme. But, wherever it came from, Kipling the craftsman — the Kipling who selected from what was presented to him—did not reject it. He was never an orthodox Christian and was constant in his tolerance of other faiths. But as he grew older, he moved more and more towards the belief that suffering on behalf of others has an ultimate value of its own. He was to come back to this in the best of his late tales. It was something with deep emotional roots which could be expressed in Christian terms even though he knew that its mythological roots were pre-Christian. Thus the verses are an imaginative recognition that suffering on behalf of others and forgiveness of injury may in the end exert a more powerful compulsion than brute force.

But if Cold Iron is to be the symbol for the power of redemptive suffering as well as for the power of the sword, how can it also be the Cold Iron of custom and drudgery—all that separates golden youth and the confident artist from folk in housen? Here are three kinds of power that may affect man's life. The link between these three odd bedfellows is the compulsion that is exercised on a man by his own sense of his own honesty and duty. What else could he have done? That is The Boy's question as he snaps home the catch. He accepts the burden. And in a closely linked story, 'The Knife and the Naked Chalk', a flintworker on the chalk gives his eye to get the secret of making knives from the workers in iron. He has to let a priestess put out his right eye with a red-hot knife, but that is not all; he must also become a god and lose his girl and the right to marry and have children. But what else could he have done? It was for the sheep, and the sheep are the people. What else could Gloriana do but send two gallant boys to the Gascons' Graveyard to save Virginia from Philip of Spain? And what could they do but go? St Wilfred, near death by cold and starvation on a ledge of rock, is compelled by his own honesty to say that even a pagan should not change his faith—even a faith he does not believe in—when he is in adversity. Simple Simon uses the same phrase when the Armada has come up the Channel to the narrow seas off Rye and he stands out in his own ship with all the naval stores he can scutchel up to bring comfort to Sir Francis Drake, who has been fighting the Spanish for days. Pharaoh Lee, who is a smuggler and a gypsy, refuses to tell Talleyrand what he had overheard Washington tell his cabinet, because the secret was not his; it belonged to the Seneca chief under whose guidance and protection he heard it. 'What else could I have done?' he too asks. It was Kipling himself who said that this phrase 'What else could

I have done' was the theme of *Rewards and Fairies*. It is compulsion, but a compulsion which applies only to those with nobility of purpose, those capable of sacrifice for the honour of their craft and of honest craftsmanship, or for the people and the sheep, or for England, or for a village sick of the plague. You take up the ring and snap home the lock and there you are, bound for life to do what you know people need. You cannot lay down the burden and you have to pay the cost. But, without the phrase, the people of *Puck of Pook's Hill* had been just as firmly bound by the compulsion of their own integrity. Here is something very near the centre of what Kipling thought was the right behaviour for man, and it is a good deal more than a gospel of work and discipline for their own sake.

3. KIM

Kim is not a creation of the untrammelled imagination in the same sense as the Mowgli stories. It is firmly set in a world of men, not of beasts or magic. And let us be clear that it was published in 1901, nine years before *Rewards and Fairies*, five years before *Puck of Pook's Hill*. Kipling had long cherished a hope that one day he would write a book about India that would eclipse all others; he refers to it in the last of *Plain Tales*, and indeed began to write it when still in India. That unfinished work—*Mother Maturin*—perished and *Kim*, when it emerged, was nothing like what that would have been. But though it is the result of long brooding it is, as Kipling said himself, imposed from without, almost wholly the product of what he called his Daemon. By this he meant whatever it was that put ideas into his head, passed judgment on his work, and sometimes took charge and wrote the story for him. It was not himself and yet it was within him. 'When your Daemon is in charge,' he wrote in *Something of Myself*, 'do not try to think consciously. Drift, wait and obey.' It is just because it was wholly inspired by his Daemon that *Kim* is included in this chapter. It is spontaneous; it is free from self-consciousness; it is written from deep in the personality and with love. It is almost Kipling's last look at India; it is his last—and only successful—full-length novel, and makes a fit culmination to a chapter beginning with Mowgli. Once again, I assume that most readers have some knowledge of this book.

In a sense, it is the same story as that of Mowgli and 'Cold

Iron'. Both Kim's parents are dead, but the Lama and Mahbub Ali love him and become foster-parents. He is the Little Friend of All the World and loved by all; it is a gentler and more loving story than Mowgli's, for there is no Shere Khan and neither wolf-pack nor man-pack cast him out. But he is none the less caught between two pairs of opposed worlds. On one level, the Indian world of the bazaar and the Grand Trunk Road is set against the Europeanized world of St Xavier's School, the mathematics and trigonometry and the technicalities of collecting intelligence and getting it to the right quarter. That is one pair of worlds. On another level, there is Mahbub Ali's life of action, intrigue and excitement, set against the Lama's search for freedom from desire and anger and the vanity of created matter. But in neither case is there any doubt which he prefers. The Indian world is enjoyment, the Europeanized is duty. (Mowgli, too, had been much happier among the wolves.) And though Kim loves the Lama with a depth he cannot give Mahbub, no one can suppose for a moment that the Way of Renunciation is for Kim. Thus there is a counter-point between his personal ties to people and the attraction of what they stand for. It is Mahbub's world that draws him; what the Lama stands for has very little meaning for Kim. But on the personal level, there is no doubt at all that the Lama comes first. And the bond between saintly old man and mischievous worldly imp is curiously moving.

Kim is not a fable. It can first be read for itself, as a series of clearly sketched figures moving against brilliant scenes from the India that Kipling remembered. It is, Kipling said, plotless; as to the form, he mentions Cervantes. And others have compared it to Tom Jones, to Pickwick, to Huckleberry Finn. All these comparisons are to some extent apt; it is a string of incidents rather loosely linked to the Lama's search for his River and to the bond of love between Kim and the Lama, though rather more firmly organized than those illustrious models. But as in Pickwick and Quixote, the combination of the innocent master and the shrewd disciple is essential. The Lama is not as mad as Don Quixote, nor is Kim gross or stupid like Sancho; like Sam Weller he protects his master from the consequences of his innocence, but the fact that he is only an imp of a boy adds a piquancy. Sam in the last resort squares up with his fists; Kim wins hearts with his tongue.

It is in his criticism of Kim that Edmund Wilson goes most seriously astray. It falls in what he regards as the 'bad' period, and he comes to it obsessed with his dislike of imperialism. True, he begins by calling it an 'enchanting, almost a first-rate book, the work in which more perhaps than in any other [Kipling] gave the sympathies of the imagination free rein to remember and to explore ... ' But Wilson has to see everything to do with Kipling at this period in terms of the strong and the weak, the bully and the oppressed. He sees India in these terms. He expects the book to develop into a conflict which was quite foreign to Kipling's mind and quite unhistorical. He thinks Kim will come to realize that by acting as an intelligence agent for the government he is 'delivering into bondage to the British invaders those whom he has always considered his own people'. Kipling, Wilson thinks, has refused to face this fundamental conflict and Kim has thereby 'betrayed the Lama'. But the expectation is absurd; it is unhistorical, for hardly any Indian thought in such terms at that period, and it completely misunderstands Kipling, to whom there was no conflict here at all. Kim was helping in the task of sustaining an ordered society. Like his creator, he takes it for granted that the government is on the whole benevolent, and it does not occur to him that there is any alternative. One might as well berate Dickens because Mr Pickwick made no pronouncement on the rights of women when he found himself in that awkward predicament in a girls' school.

Wilson continues in this same rather ill-tempered vein, suggesting that Kim refuses the advances of the Woman of Shamlegh because she is a 'native' and he is a Sahib. There is no justification for this in the text. She has more than one husband of her own already, she is years older than he is, he is exhausted, and he has to look after the Lama. Kim, who is barely seventeen, puts his master's service first. Must a boy be a racist because he does not yield to the blandishments of every woman who makes eyes at him?

Much more perceptive is Nirad C. Chaudhuri, who considers *Kim* 'not only the finest novel in English with an Indian theme but also one of the greatest of English novels in spite of the theme.' He adds that Kipling 'was an intuitionist and I do not think he ever felt the need for intellectualizing his artistic motivation.' Perhaps he did not quite know what he was doing, but 'through his sincere primitiveness' he hit upon the greatest themes in India —'the life of the people and religion in the twin setting of the mountains and the plain. These four are the main and real characters in *Kim*.' But, since he was 'not that tiresome creature, the note-book novelist of India', he was able within that framework to introduce Russian spies, plotting princes, a jeweller with hypnotic powers, what you like. These were not important, mere stage properties. And he 'saved the book from all suggestion of pedantry and humbug by putting it in the most English of all English forms of fiction, a serio-comic saga.'

That rather odd phrase about 'sincere primitiveness' is to be cherished; it goes with André Maurois's 'permanent natural contact with the oldest and deepest layers of human consciousness'. Chaudhuri has understood, as Wilson did not, the true conflict in *Kim*, and what the book is about. But *Kim*, though it is 'about India' in the broadest sense, is also about identity. 'Who is Kim?' he asks himself 'till his head swam' — and three times in the book he returns to that question. It is a question many children ask — but it is much less often that it worries folk in housen who live under Cold Iron. It had immediate impact for me as a boy; here was an experience I knew and recognized, something I asked myself. Later I found that various English poets had had the same kind of experience — Vaughan, Traherne, Wordsworth — but not in quite the same way. Kim's self-questioning is not set against lakes and mountains but against the crowded millions of India, and there is a piquancy in this one tiny scrap of life asking such questions amidst the pullulating myriads — and a scrap that enjoys the immediate impact of life with such vigour. And again, the Buddhist background adds something; the Lama looks for a means to rid himself of that very identity that Kim wants to find as an anchorage or dwelling-place. With Kipling, the mysterious nature of identity was to become more important as he grew older until, in his last years, the point at which the personality disintegrates under strain becomes his main preoccupation.

But, on the whole, coming back to *Kim* after many years, I am inclined to think that, at this stage and in relation to this book, it is easy to make too much of such questionings. They fly into the book, they stalk there happily, picking up crumbs, fluttering and chirping, but essentially as intruders, like the sparrows who nest in an Indian bedroom. It is essentially a happy book. It is quite free from hatred or revenge. There are not even any unpleasant characters; the evangelical Anglican chaplain with the regiment is narrow, insensitive and stupid, but he is not malicious, and in any case he is of little importance; the drummer-boys are coarse and dull but not cruel; the Russian spies do not emerge as people. There is tolerance for all and an enormous zest for the life of the road, for the life of this 'great and beautiful land'. Kim, waking at the first halt on the Grand Trunk Road, saw 'life as he would have it – bustling and shouting, the buckling of belts and beating of bullocks, and creaking of wheels, lighting of fires and cooking of food, and new sights at every turn of the approving eye.' It is a rich frieze of varied and happy life, moving continually, strong in scent and sound and colour. The whole spirit of the book is warm, positive, loving. It does not at all fit Wilson's picture of a man crushed by the American disasters.

Next to the Jungle Books it has been the most widely loved of Kipling's works. Chaudhuri, a Bengali, salutes it as a book about India, and it has been loved also by people who have never seen India at all. It combines the scents and sounds and smells that Kipling had known and loved before he was six with the glimpses he had seen again as a young man and put into 'Beyond the Pale' and 'In the House of Suddhoo'. But as a young man, he had shied away; he dared not be thought to have gone native. Now he could give rein to his fancy and draw the India he had loved; he could forget the squalor and depression, the intense heat, the continual sickness, all he had endured in that terrible hot weather when he felt he could bear the country no longer. Time had ironed out that unhappiness. This merciful oblivion was a common experience. Among those English who had spent most of their life in India, anyone who ever read a book at all would say: 'Of course, I love *Kim*.' And so they did; it pictured a happy India, as they liked to remember it, as they wished it to be. Yet it is romantic without being sentimental. There is trickery and bribery and sudden death.

As far back as Westward Ho!, Kipling had been interested in the parlour Buddhism he had picked up from his Pre-Raphaelite friends. He read *The Light of Asia* and talked about it to M'Turk. He had been in charge for six weeks of the Museum at Lahore and had admired the Buddhist carvings there. His father had told him a good deal about the early traditions of Buddha Gautama's sayings and travels in India. These were good reasons for linking Kim's wanderings to a Buddhist lama rather than to a Hindu ascetic. And, as Chaudhuri suggests, there is perhaps another reason; the Buddhist search for union with the Absolute is a shade more divorced from all that Kim stands for than the Hindu. And

this contrast between Kim's world and the Lama's, set against the
love each feels for the other, is the heart of the book. Kipling was
far indeed from being a Buddhist; he was one of the sons of
Martha. That he felt for the time an appreciation of what he
believed to be Buddhism can hardly be doubted. How convincing
a Buddhist would find the Lama's final sacrifice, I cannot say.
Having attained union with the Great Soul, the Lama's own soul
withdrew itself 'with strivings and yearnings and retchings and
agonies not to be told', so that Kim too might find the Way. I
suspect that this is more Christian than Buddhist. But that does
not matter. The Lama is a man whose holiness shines through
him, and such men may be of any faith. His creator was in touch
with something very far from hatred.

PART TWO
The Search for a Home

8
The Other Side

1. EXCOMMUNICATORY HATREDS

Yet the paradox remains. The man who drew the Lama was also the man with a pipe and a dog who wrote patriotic songs, thundered his disapproval on complex issues of which he did not always show full understanding, and seemed to think a political discussion was ended if his opponent could be knocked about or held to ridicule. 'A Walking Delegate' (1894) is Kipling near his worst. It is set in Vermont, in a rough pasture where a number of horses are grazing. The owner brings them salt on a Sunday morning and overhears their conversation. They are joined by an outsider, a horse from a livery stable who has been sent there for the summer; he preaches a subversive doctrine about the inalienable rights of Horse and the duty of all horses to rise against their oppressors. The others are honest working horses who have found out that it doesn't pay to rebel against man. Long ago when they were colts, they had tried rearing in harness; someone yanked them over backwards and it hurt. So now they unite to half kick the intruder to death. The story is said to show verbal virtuosity in contrasting dialects from various parts of the United States, but it must surely be judged as a political fable. And it is a bad political fable. The intruding yellow horse is ugly, idle, greedy and murderous – he wants to attack and kill the owner of the other horses – and his vague communism is of the silliest kind. He is pure stage villain. There is no suggestion that there might be real ills which communism sought to put right and which could be righted by some better means, and the only answer to the fatuous talk of the villain is the recognition of where force lies and an appeal to more force. This is not a persuasive way of defending the fabric of society.

Let us also recognize that there is often a spiteful rancorous note in Kipling's treatment of those who disagree with him. Liberal Members of Parliament are a class he detests; they are almost as bad as the yellow horse. They are always grossly fat and physically repulsive. Mr Lethabie Groombridge of 'Little Foxes', for instance, was 'loose-lipped', breathed in people's faces, 'sputtered visibly' and 'emitted spray from his mouth' in speaking. He is childishly credulous, and needless to say is eventually exposed to public ridicule. Again, when Kipling became 'a motorist', village policemen became almost as much a target for malice as politicians. Kipling had joined a rich but persecuted minority. There was a good deal of feeling against motor-cars; they were smelly, noisy and dangerous to horse-drawn traffic; they killed chickens and dogs and sometimes children; they must have been seen by many as a threat to the peace of the English countryside and all that Kipling admired in old Hobden. But he sees none of this. He had a toy which he enjoyed using, and anyone who questioned his right to enjoy it just as he pleased was anathema. The speed limit was absurdly low by modern standards; it was raised from 12 miles an hour to 20 in 1903. The police set traps to catch motorists who drove faster than the limit—and no doubt some magistrates were hostile. Kipling, however, of all men, should have recognized that obedience to the Law is a virtue and that the police were doing what they had been told to do. Far from it; the unfortunate policeman in 'Steam Tactics' is taken many miles from his home and left, a long way off the road and late at night, in the middle of a private park filled with zebras and kangaroos. Kipling is back in the world of Beetle, gleefully indulging in a fantasy about what he would like to do to policemen, who have become natural enemies, just like assistant masters.

Some time before this, he had written:

> Something I owe to the soil that grew —
> More to the life that fed —
> But most to Allah Who gave me two
> Separate sides to my head.

What did he mean by this? Certainly not that he could look on both sides of the case if he thought he was personally wronged, nor that there would be any hesitation about making up his mind where he stood on any public question. There are few hate poems more effective than 'Cleared' (1890) and 'Gehazi' (1913), in both of which he pronounced a venomous verdict of guilty on people who had been acquitted by processes of law. It would really be nearer the mark to say that he had two separate levels to his soul. The Kipling whom Charles Carrington's young lady met at the lunch-table, and did not like, was the conscious performer; he was much influenced by all that went on around him and he expressed the views of a comfortably-placed middle-aged conservative; he had at his command immense resources of vocabulary and powers of expression, but what he said — when the man at the lunch-table was in charge — was what was to be heard in every mess and smoking-room. What he added to it was often an extra

edge of rancour and vindictiveness. But somewhere deeper down
—on the far side of Cold Iron—was someone else, the man who
could play with children as a child and who was in mysterious
touch with the springs of human emotion. The smoking-room
Kipling could dismiss whole classes of people from existence. In
Something of Myself, written when he was nearly seventy, he writes
of a bulldog in South Africa who went for walks with the children.
'There was a legend that he had once taken hold of a native and,
when at last removed, came away with his mouth full of the
native.' Politicians who ask questions about the Empire, policemen who try to take motorists before magistrates, natives of
Africa—none of them are really people. These are what Wilson
called 'excommunicatory hatreds'.

Wilson wrote: 'The tales of hatred—hatred of Americans and
the Germans: "Sea Constables" and "Mary Postgate"—become
murderous at the time of the war ... ' The First World War was
of course a time when most Englishmen hated; Zeppelins were
bombing open towns and submarines sinking unarmed vessels—
and submarines could not pick up survivors. Kipling's reaction
was certainly one that does not suggest two sides to his head.
'Sea Constables' is the story of a yachtsman turned naval officer
who hunts a so-called neutral into a tiny Irish harbour. The
neutral was carrying oil which he meant for a German submarine,
which was practising unrestricted warfare. By the time he gives
in and sells his oil to the British, the captain of this ship is seriously
ill and knows he will die unless the narrator of the story will take
him to a place where there are doctors and a hospital. The
narrator refuses; he knows he is condemning him to almost
certain death, but that oil, if it had gone where it was intended,
would have condemned many men to death no less certain.

War is an ugly business, but there are conventions. The overt
and acknowledged reason for anger against the Germans was that
they had broken in war conventions to which they had agreed in
peace. The international law of sea warfare suited the British.
Their naval power commanded the sea's surface; they were
dependent on imports by sea. Indiscriminate sinking by submarines and mines killed women and children and civilians as well
as combatants, and that made them very angry. It also threatened
their existence, and that reinforced their anger with fear.

That the Germans should do such things was bad enough, but
it was even worse that a neutral should help them for his own

profit. This man had relied on his legal rights as a neutral so long as they operated to his advantage. When he surrendered, he expected to be treated with the chivalry traditionally extended to a beaten foe. Chivalry — foe — the words are archaic and his adversary, Maddingham, who tells most of the story, does not think it is any longer that kind of war. In any case, the neutral has put himself out of court; he has claimed rights as a neutral by the strict letter of the law and Maddingham will keep the strict letter. He is not now going to stretch a point for a man who has relied on his keeping exactly to the rules. He is in command of a warship and he has carried out his orders; he has no instructions to take neutrals to doctors. So he condemns him to death 'as surely as if he had hanged him'. It is a personal decision, and no doubt in war many men would have taken the same view. There is no question in my mind that his hearers in the story approved of the decision and — with rather less certainty — I think that Kipling too approved.

But can it be said that the story shows 'murderous hatred?' War is murderous, and when men are fighting for their lives and the existence of all they value, the niceties are apt to be blurred. If it is considered with more care than I think Edmund Wilson can have given it, the story concerns the criss-crossing of the legal conventions that are supposed to govern warfare with the unwritten standards of decent behaviour that before 1914 had been taken for granted, and with the passions that arise in a struggle for existence. An artist cannot honestly shrink from recording what is ugly, nor need he be exempt from the emotions of the time in which he lives. This story was conceived and first written in 1915, and it would be absurd to expect from Kipling — that far from balanced man — a balanced discussion of international law at sea as it affected England and Germany. He saw clearly enough the neutral's astonishment at his adversary's reaction; he understood and shared the anger felt by sailors, who risked their lives to save ships, against a man who for profit would help their enemies to sink ships and drown men — and not only men but women and children. He drew what he saw in 1915, when there was certainly hot anger against neutrals who made profit from the sinking of British ships. It is incidentally Edmund Wilson's own gloss that the 'neutral' was American; he is never so described, and the anger is directed not at Americans as such but at a particular kind of neutrality. But the story was not published in hot anger; it was held back until 1926. Most reminiscences of that war were by that time directed with anger at the horrors the system forced men on either side to perpetrate. In this tale, the anger is still that felt during the war, and the only indication that it is to be regarded as a historical piece is in the sub-title: 'A Tale of '15'. All the same, I am not quite sure that 'murderous hatred' is the right description.

'Mary Postgate', also written in 1915, but published much earlier than 'Sea Constables' in 1917 in *A Diversity of Creatures*, is a very different matter. Artistically it is one of the most successful stories Kipling ever wrote, while 'Sea Constables' is so compressed, and so soaked in technicalities and naval slang of the period that it is hard to follow and, even when one has mastered it, emotionally inconclusive. I have already referred to 'Mary Postgate' and I do not propose to describe it in detail. It is told directly, with no intervening narrators, and convinces the reader entirely. Mary Postgate is between forty and fifty, unmarried and quite without physical attraction. She has been all her life a 'companion' to elderly ladies. We recognize her unimaginative sense of duty, her utter devotion to Wynn, her employer's nephew, whom she has helped to bring up, the desolation which his death has brought her. She has loved him with a far more complete dedication than his aunt has given him, and yet of the two she is the stronger in the face of loss. It is she who collects all the remnants of his boyhood—his toys, cricket bats, books and clothes—goes to the village for paraffin and takes them out to the incinerator for destruction: 'The shrubbery was filling with twilight by the time she had completed her arrangements and sprinkled the sacrificial oil. As she lit the match that would burn her heart to ashes, she heard a groan or grunt behind the dense Portugal laurels.' This was a German airman who, like Wynn, had fallen from his aircraft and whose back or neck was broken. But before he came down he had unloaded a bomb which had killed a child in the village, and Mary had seen that child less than an hour ago. All her love for Wynn turned to hate for the man who had done that dreadful thing. *That* she has seen, *that* she understands and—unimaginative and indeed stupid as she is—she thinks that he too has seen what he has done. She explicitly thinks that Wynn would never have done *that*. She refuses to fetch the doctor or do anything to ease the last hours of the German airman. She has never been wife or mother, but to deny him that mercy is something which she, as a woman, can do and a man would be too soft to do. A man would have helped him—but she, no, she will not. No, she waits for his death, in the soaking rain, 'while an increasing rapture laid hold on her'. When she is quite sure he is dead, she 'drew her breath short between her teeth and shivered from head to foot'. Then she went back to the house and 'scandalized the whole routine by taking a luxurious hot bath before tea', and came down looking, as her employer said when she saw her 'lying all relaxed on the other sofa, "quite handsome!" '

'So close must any life-filling passion lie to its opposite.' That Kipling had written when he said he was drained for life of any capacity for real personal hate. And it is that point he rams home in this dreadful story; the starved loveless woman loves Wynn with single-hearted strength—all her own people are dead—and when he falls from four thousand feet to instant death the one emotional channel left to her is choked until it turns to hatred and finds a consummation she has never found with a man. It is one of the most powerful stories Kipling ever wrote. It has been called 'the wickedest story ever written', but I find that judgment hard to understand. It is certainly a story about hate—but does not hate exist? And is not this transformation of love into hate psychologically convincing? The emotional strength of the woman and her limited intelligence, her ungainly figure and clumsy movements, are brought out by tiny touches; she had waited in agony for other deaths, but as she waited for this death, she wielded the poker on those sacrificial ashes with fierce lunges, 'her underlip caught up by one faded canine' ... One faded canine! Every detail is visualized and recorded.

It is certainly murderous hate, and of an intensity hard to parallel. It has been said that Kipling, who despised women, put his own hate into a woman's breast and could then stand back and feel superior; only a woman could be capable of *that*. But he did not despise women so much as fear and wonder at them. Certainly he thought women were, by the evolutionary process, far more directly aimed at one purpose than men. He had put the point, half facetiously, in the long set of verses called 'The Female of the Species'. It begins, almost entirely in mockery:

When the Himalayan peasant meets the he-bear in his pride,
He shouts to scare the monster who will often turn aside.
But the she-bear thus accosted rends the peasant tooth and nail.
For the female of the species is more deadly than the male.

And after more in that vein, he approaches closer to seriousness, pointing out that 'Man propounds negotiations, Man accepts the compromise ...'

> Fear, or foolishness, impels him, ere he lay the wicked low
> To concede some form of trial, even to his dearest foe ...
> But the Woman that God gave him, every fibre of her frame
> Proves her launched for one sole issue, armed and engined for
>   the same ...
> She who faces Death by torture for each life beneath her breast
> May not deal in doubt or pity—must not swerve for fact or
>   jest ...

Those verses were written in 1911 and had particular reference to the movement for women's votes; they must be ranked with the semi-public verses of the middle period, which can seldom be held to have much poetic merit; they are highly quotable newspaper articles tossed off with that fatal facility in verse which damaged his reputation. Like most of the 'public' poems, they were written from near the surface of his consciousness; they were an elaboration of the kind of thing most comfortably placed conservative males would say. But in this case the verses did also say a good deal that came from much deeper in his personality. He *did* at all levels believe that women were more formidable than men because more concentrated. The point constantly recurs: it is to be found, for instance, in the opening pages of 'Mowgli's Brothers': 'Shere Khan might have faced Father Wolf but he could not stand up against Mother Wolf ... ' And it seems unlikely that his experience in marriage had done anything to modify his views. Carrie *was* concentrated; she *was* formidable. To say that Kipling despised women is thus a misrepresentation even in the middle period, and in the late period, on the contrary, it is often on a woman that he focuses most closely and in regard to a woman that he produces his subtlest and most understanding work. Nor does it seem justifiable to suggest that he felt any need to shift to anyone else the blame for the hatred which he portrayed in 'Mary Postgate'.

One question the story raises in my mind after several readings is whether Kipling meant us to perceive that the dying German had not in fact *seen* the little girl his bomb had killed, that he had got rid of the bomb simply to help his own chance of survival when he crashed, and that Wynn would in fact have done just the same thing; in short, that what seems bestial cruelty may be mere lack of imagination. Mary, of course, sees none of this; 'I have seen the dead child,' she says in atrocious German, taking it for granted that he too has seen the child and knows what he has done. Taking the story by itself, I incline more and more to regard it not as an exhibition of Kipling's murderous hate for Germans, but as a psychological study of the relation of love to hate in a repressed middle-aged woman, who is far from clever but capable of powerful emotion. The note of sexual satisfaction resulting from gratified hate—with its echo of *Stalky**—is remarkable at a time when Freud had not become part of everyone's intellectual currency. I have to admit, however, that this perhaps cold and clinical view does not accord with the set of verses that follows the story; they are called 'The Beginnings', the refrain being: 'When the English began to hate.' This set of verses seems to me Kipling near his worst; he has taken a stale cliché—that the English are slow to anger but terrible when roused—and turned it into verse, this time in deadly seriousness. It had been half-facetious in an earlier piece ('Et Dona Ferentes') with the conclusion:

'Cock the gun that is not loaded, cook the frozen dynamite —
But oh, beware my country, when my country grows polite!

But the link between a story and the accompanying verses, sometimes very close, is also sometimes very loose, and in the case of 'Mary Postgate' and 'The Beginnings', though both story and verses deal with hate, the verses seem to be superficial and of quite a different order from the tale, which comes from the depths and is most carefully considered and worked on.

But it is impossible to discuss Kipling and hatred fully without looking at the later period and linking it with revenge and the restitution of balance, which we shall do in the third Part.

2. THE IMPERIALIST

There was a change during the middle period in Kipling's imperialism. When he was in India, he had taken it for granted that British rule was for the good of Indians—which at that time was the view of practically every Englishman and of a good many Indians. He looked on it much as he looked later on Roman rule

* Already mentioned on p. 41.

7

in Britain; it maintained order, it advanced civilization. Occasionally, the smoking-room Kipling allowed something from the smoking-room to take charge and become a story. There is, for instance, 'The Head of the District',* in which a liberal Viceroy appoints a Bengali to the charge of a district on the frontier; there is an immediate rising, the Bengali runs away, and the tribesmen try to take off his head but by mistake take his brother's head. They roll it on the table before the self-effacing hard-working Englishman, who ought to have had charge of the district and has by now quelled the rising and knows he will get the blame for everything that has happened. It is a story in which all the ideas are clichés from the smoking-room, redeemed only by brilliantly observed detail. But in India for a good deal of the time, the other Kipling, who had loved his *ayah*, is in charge and his imperialism is Roman; he sees British rule as an administrative framework, free from racial extremism, superimposed on the existing life of India.

In Africa, however, as the friend of Cecil Rhodes, he fell under the sway of something quite different; white imperialism. It was an essential part of Rhodes's dream that enormous stretches of Africa should be actually *owned* by white men; they were to be farmers, miners, artisans, who would take over the country as white men had taken the United States and Canada from the red men. The native races would cease to exist as distinct free peoples; they would become labourers and servants or be banished to reserves, away from the line of rail. The only ladder of advance for individual Africans would be by adopting every feature of the white man's culture. Nothing could be more different from India, where nearly all land was in Indian hands and there were very few English except the tiny band of administrators.† This new kind of imperialism was embodied in Rhodes himself, a man of great force of character who, like Kipling, shut parts of his mind as close as a camel shuts its nostrils against a sandstorm. And Kipling was very susceptible to influence; he was surely thinking of himself when he wrote of the Apostle Paul that he 'had the woman's trick of taking the tone and colour of whoever he talked to'. He took tone and colour from Rhodes, and his imperialism grew brassier.

* Already mentioned on p. 105.

† There were a few small areas, in Assam, in Bihar, and in the Nilgiris where there were British 'planters' for special crops such as tea and indigo. They were exceptions to the general pattern. Fortunately, they were never in political control as white settlers came to be in Africa.

None the less, there is often an unexpected turn to the prophetic pronouncements of his imperialist period, a turn which does not fit at all well with the picture of him generally held. 'Recessional,' as everyone knows, is a warning against just the kind of imperialism that Kipling was generally thought guilty of. 'For frantic boast and foolish word—Thy Mercy on Thy People, Lord!' On the other hand, as Elliott Gilbert has perceptively pointed out, it *sounds* as though it meant the opposite of what it actually says, because it rehearses, in glorious rounded cadences, all those material splendours about which we are adjured not to boast. It does also conceive of the Empire as a trust, bestowed by God upon a chosen People—note the capital—on whom there is a consequent obligation to administer it with justice and humility. At the time when it was written, just after the Diamond Jubilee, it was the humility of 'Recessional' that was found startling, and people who normally disapproved of Kipling's politics wrote to thank him for it. But it will not strike many readers today as humble. 'The Old Issue', on the other hand, is still surprising. It was inspired by the outbreak of the South African War and its theme is that throughout their history the English have sought to replace tyranny by rule of Law. That is the message which the trumpets sing:

Trumpets round the scaffold at the dawning by Whitehall!

And Kruger in the Transvaal is just as much a tyrant as Charles I had been. It is the old issue, and what will grow up in South Africa, if we let it, will be the Police State:

He shall peep and mutter; and the night shall bring
Watchers 'neath our window, lest we mock the King—

Hate and all division; hosts of hurrying spies;
Money poured in secret, carrion breeding flies ...

Cruel in the shadow, crafty in the sun,
Far beyond his borders shall his teachers run.

What Kipling foresaw was a tyranny of Afrikaners over Englishmen; what has come to pass is a tyranny of white over black. But he was nearly right; it is a police state with the whole apparatus of hurrying spies. Black Africans did not come on to his radar-screen at all, but his view of what that war was about turned out to be surprisingly true, and should be set beside the widespread

American and Continental picture of the big bully attacking the plucky little Afrikaner republics.

There is no reason why a writer should not hold strong views on politics, nor indeed why he should not give support to a party which he thinks can put his views into effect. No one holds it against Milton or Marvell that they took part in a political movement. Swift and Johnson had strong views, which they expressed with vigour. Kipling was no more intemperate than they, and it cannot be said that he changed his politics from self-interest; his politics were always in keeping with his subconscious philosophy of tidying things up and keeping chaos at bay. But his politics had a great deal to do with the low esteem in which so many critics held him for so long. His was a losing cause, unfashionable among intellectuals, but that in itself would not have been enough to account for the bitterness with which politics affected literary judgment.

The critics, one must admit, could hardly have been expected to love him. 'But I consort with long-haired things' was not the only proof of his hostility to them and their kind; there had been plenty of indications that he thought 'intellectuals' little better than politicians, and 'My Son's Wife', written as late as 1913, begins with a long sneering attack on a group of middle-class urban intellectuals whom he calls the Immoderate Left. It was not only that he had hardly a point of agreement — on marriage, on work, on politics and society — with Shaw or Wells or the Bloomsbury Group. More infuriatingly, he was committing a crime against all the values for which he ought to have stood as a writer. It was a crime which he had himself described in one of his early stories, 'A Conference of the Powers', published in 1893. In this, an eminent novelist, Eustace Cleever, is introduced by the narrator to a group of subalterns just back from the war in Burma. He was a great man, a success, but he had only *written*; he had never *done* anything. And these boys had *done* things. He was so impressed by what they told him that he summed up his feelings in a quotation to the effect that 'few lips would be moved to song if they could find a sufficiency of kissing'. 'Whereby I understood that Eustace Cleever, decorator and colourman in words, was blaspheming his own Art ... ' That surely was what added venom to the dislike intellectuals felt for Kipling. He would insist on belittling writers and artists and thinkers and expressing his preference for soldiers and engineers and 'people who do things'.

Doing things was better than writing about them. It was contempt for intellectuals as much as imperialism that made him obnoxious. 'You'll be a man, my son ... ' was the ideal he set before youth—and it was clear to most writers and intellectuals that they would not be included in the category.

Imperialism, however, was the charge most often preferred against him and the one that is remembered. What did it mean? Today it is often a Marxist term of abuse—paradoxically directed most often at the United States, whose citizens at least up till 1917 regarded themselves as essentially the enemies of imperialism. But it is really an anachronism to regard Kipling as an imperialist in the Marxist sense, because the term implies an economic theory of which he never showed the least consciousness. Again, the word is often used in a more general sense, without any very clear definition in mind, but with the general implication of something big and bad opposed to something small and good. As a child I was encouraged to admire Robert Bruce and William Tell and the Spartans who died at Thermopylae, all heroes of a dawning nationalism. And as long as it is someone else who is the big attacking bully, that feeling is very widespread; 'Plucky little Belgium!' and 'Gallant little Serbia!' we cried in 1914. But the tables have a way of being turned; Serbs have been looked on as imperialists by Croats and Slovenes; the gallant little Afrikaner republics have become tyrannies to black Africans. In the cold light of reason, an imperialist is a person who believes in uniting a number of political systems under one central authority; this is a respectable political faith. Indeed, the course of human history suggests that it is only under a strong and wide-reaching empire that people have enjoyed peace for any period of time, or that minorities have been able to live in some security. This is what I have called Roman imperialism, which Kipling accepted without question in his Indian days.

But an empire, or a monarchy, or a republic, or a democracy may degenerate into a tyranny. What Kipling never perceived was that after the Age of Reason and the French Revolution, no empire that was not based on willing participation could be more than a temporary phase. In the sense that he could put himself into the position of Queen Elizabeth or a Roman centurion, he was a magnificent historian, but he was no historian at all in the sense of perceiving the currents of thought in history. He did not see the vulgarity and greed of the kind of imperialism that came in with

Cecil Rhodes. How different from the pattern set in India by such
men as Elphinstone and Metcalfe, and followed—with the same
devotion if not the same vision—by the working sahibs of his
own tales! He did not really understand that people on the whole
do like to feel they have some hand in their own government.

In his two tales of politico-science fiction, he pictures a future in
which the mass of people have surrendered all political rights in
return for benevolent government by an international board of
technocrats. The population of the world has been immensely
reduced and the most serious of all crimes is 'invasion of privacy'.
This, we are told by Carrington, was not his vision of what he
wanted to happen, but it looks very like it. He hated the thought
of a hysterical mob, and in 'As Easy as ABC', the more important
of these prophetic visions, the symbol for the bad old days of
democracy is a sculpture of a lynching, called 'The Nigger in
Flames'. There had been a song which men had sung when they
brought the bad old days to an end:

> Holy State or Holy King
>   Or Holy People's Will—
> Have no truck with the senseless thing.
>   Order the guns and kill!

To sing that song is forbidden at the time of the story, a hundred
years from now, and the narrator says that 'every silly word of it'
is 'loaded to sparking-point with the Planet's inherited memories
of horror, panic, fear and cruelty.' But the whole story is loaded
with fear and dislike for crowds and the mob. Things had reached
such a pitch that the Planet had decided it would have no more
committees, no more parliaments, no more voting. The passion
for privacy has become so extreme that men hate the thought of
being touched in a crowd.

I have not seen it suggested that Kipling himself hated to be
touched in a crowd. But in this story, the desire for privacy—
raised to a pitch most people would regard as neurotic—has
become the one political fact; everyone is rich, everyone is tall;
they all live to be a hundred. But all they want is to be left alone.
Hatred of democracy has gone beyond all reason. And the four
lines just quoted from the song underline neatly the point which is
really the centre of politics—where does authority rest? You
reject Holy State and Holy King, you reject the Holy People's
Will—but who orders the guns? If you hate mob violence, there

must be some form of police—and all that has happened in Kipling's story is that you have put a Holy Board of Control in the place of the Holy People. Yet surely the element in him that admired Puck and Hobden, Kim and Stalky, would have been the first to hate the soulless tyranny of a board of technocrats. It is an incidental point in this story, not pertinent to the main theme, that Illinois is a backward agricultural area and Chicago a place so unimportant that no one can remember where it is. London, A.D. 2065, is the cultural capital of the world. This can only be another spurt of hostility directed at the country he could not forgive for that error in the fourth dimension he had made about his brother-in-law in 1896.

It would be absurd to regard Kipling as a political philosopher. His mind was essentially concrete, and he was at his best when writing about individuals and their deepest feelings. If 'politics' is understood in the widest sense, his almost subconscious instinct in regard to politics was that the essential task for man was to keep order; he believed that happiness and freedom were only to be found in disciplined personal submission to the Law. Thus he admired what I have called Roman imperialism, which he had encountered in India. But because he never worked things out intellectually and was easily influenced by those among whom he spent his time, he drifted in the middle period into imperialism of the Rhodesian brand, coupled with a neurotic hatred of crowds and a passion for privacy. His explicit politics in this period come from the surface of his mind, and to me are distasteful. But it is a mistake to allow this to influence one's judgment of his best work, which comes from quite a different level.

3. THE FARCES

There are stories from the beginning to the end of Kipling's work which can only be called farces. There are several in *Plain Tales*, and then they continue with 'Brugglesmith' (1893) and 'My Sunday at Home' (1898) to 'Aunt Ellen' and—perhaps—'The Miracle of St Jubanus' in the last collection of all, in 1932. It was Kipling's belief that laughter is a healing process—and few would quarrel with this if the laughter is good-humoured. There are stories in Kipling where this is hardly so, where the laughter comes because revenge has been carried out successfully. It is not at all good-humoured, for instance, when the carrier's stones fly through King's window and Beetle pours gum all over the Persian carpet and scars the backs of his leather-bound volumes. On the whole, I class 'The Village that Voted the Earth was Flat' and 'Beauty Spots' as stories of revenge rather than farces, but they can be regarded as either. In the pure farces, the laughter is not usually malicious. None the less, coming back to Kipling after long absence, I have found them disappointing. In the best stories, there is more than I remembered; they are much better than I had thought. But in the farces, it is still the schoolboy we meet, writing better as he gets older, becoming a little more restrained, but still a schoolboy.

It is not so much that the misfortunes into which the victims are plunged are purely physical. Nothing could be more physical than the fate of the successful lover in *The Miller's Tale*, who sticks his bottom out of the window in his rival's face and gets it branded with a hot iron. There follows a tumultuous scene with everyone at cross purposes—just what Kipling would have enjoyed—but Chaucer takes one line to say that the townspeople in the story laughed, and one line in the next story to say that the pilgrims laughed at the story. Nobody stamped and shouted and rolled on the ground with laughter. Contrast this with 'My Sunday at Home'. In the course of a leisurely train journey through the English midsummer country-side on a Sunday, an American doctor hears that someone has taken a bottle of poison. What is meant is that he has taken it by mistake from the train, leaving a bottle of medicine instead, but the American thinks it has been taken internally. He springs out of the train and administers a powerful emetic to a gigantic navvy who is sitting on the platform rather drunk and ready to drink anything he is offered. The navvy is violently sick—and there is a purple passage about the blowing-up of Hell Gate and the geysers in the Yellowstone Park. The doctor has some difficulty in escaping from the navvy's resentment, and later the navvy tries to revenge himself on someone he thinks is the doctor but who is not. The narrator of the story—who for reasons I have given must be identified with Kipling—walked two miles from the station to the village—'and I waked the holy calm of the evening every step of that way with shouts and yells, casting myself down in the flank of the good green hedge when I was too weak to stand.' Even when he reaches the village and orders supper at the inn, he has to have a room to himself so that he can go on laughing between mouthfuls.

Nearly forty years later, 'Aunt Ellen' appeared. It is about a rolled-up eiderdown quilt which falls off the back of a car and is run over by two undergraduates in a second car driving from Cambridge to a dance in London. Everyone has been dining but the driver of the second car has been dining more lavishly than the other three, who persuade him that he has run over an old lady; the final hilarity is that the down comes out of the quilt and covers a policeman with fine white fluff. All good clean fun compared with Chaucer, and Kipling is now a little more restrained in his appreciation. 'I do not laugh when I drive, which is why I was as nearly as possible dead ... ' when at last the party reached London. 'St Jubanus', also in the last collection, is about a French curé's umbrella, of which the whalebone spokes had been repaired by a travelling pedlar in such a way that they were liable to entangle themselves in anything they touched. And on the saint's-day of St Jubanus, they become enmeshed with the lace collars of two acolytes and the beard of the village atheist, and the three go up the aisle in a frenzied *pas de trois*, each imploring the others to be still. The laughter brings about the cure of a shell-shocked soldier, so perhaps it is not a farce after all. It is also a story of revenge not taken and thus of forgiveness. But to the farcical part I feel the same objection as to the others. It takes the curé a page of beautiful prose to explain how funny they all found it. I think it *is* funny, but I should have enjoyed it more if I had not been told how they all ached and hiccoughed and how the curé 'beat his head against the back of a prie-Dieu'.

4.   FLAWED OPALS

There is some delicate work in the middle period which does not quite succeed, sometimes because of that fatal self-consciousness when the man at the lunch-table intrudes, or sometimes because the story at some point crosses the line, very hard to define, between deep human emotion and sentimental cliché. This was a transitional period, transitional in the first place in style and crafts-manship. In his early days he had used flat bright colours and often achieved the vigour of a primitive painting. He had done it by sheer exuberance. In the best work of his late period, he writes with extreme restraint, every word weighed; his story is pared down to a skeleton. While he was feeling his way towards the late style, he sometimes produced effects that seem artificial, like a

7*

shop window in which lay-figures are arranged in attitudes not
quite natural. But the period was also transitional for the writer's
personality. His outer self was reflecting the new surroundings of
Edwardian England, not with whole-hearted approval. Withinsides, there was painful growth and turmoil which only occasionally appears. It is not surprising that there were flaws and inconsistencies. Let us look briefly at two stories, of which 'The
Brushwood Boy' must be judged sentimental, while 'They',
which as a child I did not understand, now seems to me beautiful
and moving.

George Cottar, the hero of 'The Brushwood Boy', is Kipling's
perfect young man. His father is the squire of an estate with
several miles of trout-fishing, with stables and horses, gardens and
gardeners, velvet lawns, rose-beds, billiard-room, terraces and so
on. George is an only child and everyone adores him; he is a
success at his prep school and public school; he is Head of the
School and Captain of Games, and everyone swoons in admiration, from the humblest fags to visiting mothers on Speech Day.
At Sandhurst and in India with his regiment, it is the same story.
The men worship the ground he treads on — it is impossible not to
talk of him in clichés — and even the wives sink their grumbles and
jealousies to pay a tribute to George. He doesn't go to dances or
rot like that, preferring to study his profession and move lead
blocks about a four-inch map with the Major. He has never been
kissed. He gets a brevet and a D.S.O. and becomes the youngest
major in the army.

But he has strange dreams, which come in sequences and have
recurred since childhood. They always start in the same place and
they always lead to a country with a dreamlike geography of its
own; sea and downs and then, farther inland, dangerous territories where there are enemies, places where there are hard
unfeeling people sitting at tables, who don't understand; wide
seas where the islands slide about under one's feet, places where
absurd and funny things happen, places of pure horror, pursuits
and escapes. In these dreams everything links up and hangs together. He knows at once when it is going to be one of *those*
dreams. He has a companion in the dreams, a girl, whom he
always meets in the same place, by a pile of brushwood on the
downs at the beginning of a night's adventures. It is a world he
goes back to again and again and of which he can draw a map in
his head. This is his secret life. And then, when he goes home on

his first leave from India, he hears a girl sing, in his mother's drawing-room, a song about the dream country. And, of course, this was the girl who had been his companion in the dream adventures. He remembers every look and gesture of hers. She can remember all their adventures together and the absurd things people said.

In this story, it is the dreams that are real. They are probably based on actual dreams of Kipling's and they certainly convey that feeling of having been there before that is so common in dreams; they melt into each other in a way that is convincingly dream-like. It is the framework to the dreams which is unreal, the waking-life part of the story. Two fantasies have been combined, the perfect school-prefect and subaltern that Kipling would like to have been himself, and that not-impossible-she, the dream-girl who is recognized at first sight and who instantly responds with life-long and adoring love. Kipling thought this fantasy had come true when he met Flo Garrard, whose clear-cut ivory features and dark hair growing in a widow's peak reappear in the descriptions of Maisie in *The Light that Failed* and Miriam the Brushwood Girl. Both fantasies are really more appropriate at eighteen than at thirty-three, in a man five years married. They are both sentimental; they appeal to widely felt and facile emotions but do not correspond with reality. There was never anyone who fitted Kipling's stereotype of the perfect young man so completely as George Cottar. He is like an advertisement for the hire of men's evening wear. Nor is companionship in dream adventures a good recipe for lasting marriage; it is boy's magic—and Kipling, who had now lived among folk in housen and under Cold Iron for five years, ought to have known better.

The tale incidentally contains a sentence which has been described as the worst Kipling ever wrote. When George came home as the youngest major in the army—'who should come to tuck him up for the night but the mother? And she sat down on the bed, and they talked for a long hour, as mother and son should, if there is to be any future for our Empire.' If that does not make you squirm, nothing will. But what is it that is so awful? There is the coyness of 'who should come … ?'; there is '*the* mother', the same self-conscious depersonalization he had learnt at school; there is the absurdity of introducing 'our Empire'; there is the further point, revealed in the next paragraph, that George's mother was after something. She wanted to know if it was true that he had never been kissed. There is the strange idea—an assumption behind the whole story—that it is something much to be admired in a healthy man in his thirties that he should still be a child, adoring his mother, wanting to be tucked up, and sexually innocent. But absurd though it may seem a hundred years later, it is a historical fact that the Empire and the need for an imperial class of rulers—unencumbered by families, hardy of body and selfless in service—had produced this as an ideal picture of what was to be admired.

What is more, a great many young men identified themselves with the Brushwood Boy and tried to be as like him as they could. I have spoken to survivors from this period who have told me so. And perhaps this story illustrates the contradictions in Kipling better than most. His outer surface reflected the shiny public-school and army image of George Cottar but withinsides something obscurely moved; the dreams always have a hint of terror in the background, and sometimes they turn into terror. Did he simply add his own dreams to the idealized figure of George, or did he recognize that such glossy perfection could only be realized at the expense of hidden strain? Someone who had read Kipling eagerly in youth, and then neglected him, asked me if I had paid enough attention to George Cottar's nervous break-down. In fact, there is no nervous breakdown in the story—only one sleepless night. But she had felt that there *ought* to be a nervous breakdown and had built that in to her memory of the story. And perhaps the unconscious recognition of this strain and cost is what has made this story appeal so widely to that generation of whom many died in France.

'They' is more delicately conceived, and the contrast between the waking world and the imaginative creation is subtler, though it is here, to my mind, that the story runs into danger. That familiar figure of the middle period, the comfortably placed, middle-aged man in search of experience, driving alone in his motor-car—and to all appearances a bachelor—finds himself at the wrong end of the county, sixty miles from home. He is lost. The lane he is following through the woods brings him to a house which is to other houses as the Brushwood Boy is to other men. It is like Bateman's but with a little more of everything—mullioned windows, lichened stone and roofs of rose-red tile, with great still smooth lawns, and knights and peacocks of clipped yew. There are toys scattered here and there and he hears the noises children make as they play, scuffles and giggles and the sound of running feet. The narrator catches a glimpse of a child here and there, from the corner of an eye; a child at a window of the house waves a friendly hand but he never really sees them face to face.

A woman comes out, neither young nor old; she is blind and has always been blind, but she is beautiful. She talks about the children she has never seen; they are very shy and never come close but she is pleased—and also perhaps a little surprised—that he has heard them and a little envious that he has seen them. He comes again a month or so later and again hears the children and catches a glimpse here and there, but they won't come close. He talks to the blind woman again and a sense builds up of something he does not understand; she says things that are faintly puzzling, and so does the butler. There is a secret about the children that everyone shares but himself, and yet a feeling that in some way, though excluded from that knowledge, he is included in a fellowship which has to do with the children. It is as though in sleep he had been initiated into some secret society of which he does not know the password or the purpose. He has a right to come, they seem to say, even though he doesn't yet understand. It is only when he comes for the third time that he goes inside the house. There the children are more elusive than ever as he goes round the upper storeys; they are always in the next room or the corridor beyond. Then, in the dusk, he and the blind woman come down the staircase to the hall for tea and from above he sees them. They are in the hall, hiding behind a screen, away from the light of the fire. He pretends not to see them and sits near the screen. He taps it gently for a little to show he is not really deceived and then lets his hand hang ... 'I felt my relaxed hand taken and turned softly between the soft hands of a child ... '

'The little brushing kiss fell in the centre of my palm—as a gift on which the fingers were, once, expected to close: as the all-faithful half-reproachful signal of a waiting child not used to neglect even when grown-ups were busiest—a fragment of the mute code devised very long ago.'

Then he knew. Here my summary stops and comment follows. His own dead child had been at the window and had looked out when he first came. The butler's dead child was there too and some from the village; they came because the blind woman loved children so much and knew she would have none of her own; the butler and his wife saw them and, when the visitor in the car said he had seen them, they knew that he had lost a child too and that his child too would come to the blind woman who loved children so much. There are touches in the manner of the late stories, which only reveal their meaning on a careful re-reading, and then they add to the total effect. The welcoming hand from the child at the window is one; he saw this before he met the blind woman. And there is a remark, quite incomprehensible at the time, made by a woman he meets on the drive: 'You'll find yours indoors, I reckon.' There is no unpassable iron on the hearth of that house, and you have to punch the fire into life with a charred hedge-stake.

The story ends with his resolve that he must go and never come back, 'though that was like the very parting of spirit and flesh.' For him it would be wrong to come again — but what she had done was not wrong for her. I cannot be sure that I understand this, but I remember the Lama, who came back for Kim's sake, and I think that to live among loved children who were dead was right for the blind woman who could not have children of her own and had no other powers of creation to fall back on, but not for the narrator, who — though he appears as a quite solitary figure — must be identified with Kipling and taken to have both.

It was a time when there was much talk of mediums, but Kipling emphatically rejected conventional spiritualism in his verses 'En-Dor'. There is only one other reference in his writings to the daughter he had lost in New York. It is in 'Merrow Down', which is about Taffy, the little girl in one of *The Just-So Stories*, and her father Tegumai; two verses run:

> In moccasins and deer-skin cloak,
> 　　Unfearing, free and fair she flits,
> And lights her little damp-wood smoke
> 　　To show her Daddy where she flits.

> For far — oh, very far behind,
> 　　So far she cannot call to him
> Comes Tegumai alone to find
> 　　The daughter that was all to him.

'They', as I have said, I now find very moving. Although published in 1904, it has much in common with the late stories and is rewarding to read again; it is tender and there is compassion, for the blind woman, for the 'draggle-tailed wench' in the nearest

village who loses an illegitimate child, for all who have lost
children. Yet I have included it under the head 'flawed opals'. It is
not sentimental; the feeling behind it is deep and it cannot be
called conventional. It is the links with the everyday world that
create a feeling of slight unease. If this were a ghost story, meant
merely to entertain, then by all means it is right to add every
detail that will anchor the story to waking life and freeze the
blood. The aim in that case would be to create a suspension of disbelief — but a suspension only. It is not, in a ghost story, meant to
be permanent. But 'They' is not a ghost story. It is partly a fable;
it is partly an approach to that personal loss that had scarred him
so deeply. It is trying to say something that we shall go on believing — even if we don't altogether believe in the framework. I have
a feeling that one should go into that garden through a yew-hedge
rather as Alice went through the Looking-Glass, as Dan and Una
went into another world when they met Puck and came out of it
when they went back to folk in housen. That is a personal feeling.
That it should not be so was undoubtedly Kipling's conscious
decision; he wants the reader to believe in the house, which is on
the ordnance map, and to believe he saw the children.

Just before the child's kiss, which is the climax of the story,
there is the intrusion of a tenant-farmer, who is frightened of
coming at dusk. He has no children; he is not one of the fellowship. To him the atmosphere of the house, so friendly and welcoming to the narrator, is uncanny, terrifying. This incident does
not grate; something is needed at that moment to take the reader's
attention from the children, to push the narrator back out of the
firelight, to relax his expectations. This is perfectly achieved. But
there is a shade too long an interlude about the draggle-tailed
wench's child, a little too much emphasis on the bond of class
between the narrator and the blind woman, who really does
belong to the county gentry of Sussex. Perhaps the feeling would
not be there if it had not been for other stories about motor-cars in
which there is a recurring consciousness that the narrator has
friends who have chauffeurs and large gardens, that he has to
insist that he too has come to be landed gentry. And there are a
few, a very few, sentences which stick in the gullet. 'You're fond
of children?' the blind woman had asked him right at the
beginning.

'I gave her one or two reasons why I did not altogether hate
them.'

This kind of understatement is just the thing for an after-dinner speech. But it has a coy, facetious note quite out of place in a story of this delicacy. None the less, 'They' is a forerunner of the best of the late stories, and deserves to stand beside them.

PART THREE
Retribution and Compassion

9
Restoring
the Balance

I. THE LATE STORIES

Enough has been said already to show that the stories that are 'late' in style do not all fit into the late period. It is not to be supposed that one searing experience transformed all Kipling's work at a blow. But the First World War changed the lives of all who survived it, and Kipling's more than most. His only son was reported missing in 1915 and was at last presumed killed; his body was never found. It hit him very hard. As a kind of penance for his loss—perhaps from a feeling that death as much as birth demands a sacrifice—Kipling undertook the tasks of writing a War History of the Irish Guards (his son's regiment) and of serving on the War Graves Commission. Neither was the kind of work he had previously found congenial. The personal loss, the burden of those years when older men had to watch the young queuing up for death, the sense of a world in which all that was best was being destroyed—all these he endured and survived; he emerged, with his stature as man and writer enhanced, to add to his books the three last collections. The two last are *Debits and Credits*, published in 1926, and *Limits and Renewals*, in 1932. I am here excluding stories for scouts and some other writings and including *A Diversity of Creatures*, which was published in 1917 and contains some stories from before the war.

There are fourteen stories in each collection and, of these forty-two, eight seem to me in the top rank. Such judgments are a matter of personal taste, and some would include in their first team some I would put in the second. But this is my choice:

> 'Friendly Brook'
> 'Mary Postgate'
> 'The Wish House'
> 'The Bull that Thought'
> 'A Madonna of the Trenches'
> 'The Eye of Allah'
> 'The Gardener'
> 'Dayspring Mishandled'

This is the order in which they appear in the collection. My reserve team would also include eight: 'In the Same Boat', 'The Dog Hervey', 'The Janeites', 'On the Gate', 'The Church that was at Antioch', 'The Manner of Men', 'The Tender Achilles', 'Uncovenanted Mercies'. All these sixteen are stories about important things, and repay reading more than once; indeed, it would be a very acute reader who discovered the full flavour of any of them at first reading. There are several others in these forty-two which are of high quality as entertainment. 'The Village that Voted the Earth was Flat' is probably the best of the farces, if it is thought of as farce; I found it funny as a boy and do still find much of it funny. But there is something distasteful about so gigantic a revenge so laboriously plotted over so long a period and involving so many innocent people. It is all aimed at one magistrate who has had the audacity to fine motorists. It is true that he has gone further and has dared not only to fine them but to mock and deride them from the bench, but the punishment seems out of proportion. He and the whole village are held up to the mockery of the world; his career in Parliament is ruined. It would have been better to kill him quickly with a thunderbolt.

'Regulus' again is one of the best of the Stalky stories, and there are others which score high in their particular kind. The first point to be stressed is variety. Of these forty-two stories, five are farces — to which might be added 'Beauty Spots' and 'The Village', which are primarily stories of revenge; four are returns to the old Stalky theme, and two — 'The Tie' and 'A Naval Mutiny' — are quite trivial. The rest include two attempts at reconstructing the world in which the Apostle Paul lived; one is set in a medieval abbey; there are two fables about an after-life; three — all in my first team — concern the emotions of elderly women living alone; two are mainly (and several others in varying degrees) about doctors. In no less than eleven stories, war strain in various forms is important; in several, the stress of war has produced some degree of breakdown which can only be released by the patient's recognition of what is troubling him. In *A Diversity of Creatures*, no less than eight are about revenge, or, perhaps it would be fairer to say, restoring a balance by some kind of punishment. In *Debits and Credits*, there are two stories in which that theme is strong, and in these there is no relenting. But in *Limits and Renewals*, while there are three stories in which revenge is important, all three close on a note of pity. In 'Dayspring Mishandled', certainly one of Kipling's finest stories, revenge pursued over many years, with a tenacity of purpose almost unbelievable, turns full circle on itself. The motive had been principally to avenge the memory of a woman once selflessly

adored about whom the intended victim had uttered an un-
forgivable slander. But the avenger finds himself defending the
man he had meant to destroy against the enmity of his own wife,
which is wholly self-centred and malicious. This is the culmination of the stories about revenge and retribution.

Kipling's development is like a change of season in England,
which is never abrupt or exclusive. The earliest primrose comes
long before its proper time, the last lingers untimely on. One
cuckoo cries faintly in the distance and, a fortnight later, the
woods and fields ring with their shouts. The first frost kills some
tender shoots but warmth and sunshine return for many single
lovely days before winter sets in. Not all of these late stories are
wise or kind, but compassion and understanding grow more
frequent; personal revenge is slowly transmuted into impersonal
retribution. In style, however, the onset of maturity is far more
regular and gradual. 'I think this tale is like the woods, getting
darker and twistier every minute,' said Dan in the last story of
Rewards and Fairies. Certainly the later stories become more and
more elliptical, ironic and obscure, partly due to a policy of
repeated excision, partly I think to an increasing desire of the
craftsman to keep his most precious wares for a chosen audience
who will take the trouble to penetrate below the surface layer.
The reader must therefore always be on the look-out for clues,
unobtrusive sentences which may seem pointless but which may
later reveal an essential point in the story.

Kipling has said a good deal in *Something of Myself* about his
method of working, and his daughter has told us something too.
He kept a file of ideas or fragments that might some day be used
and drew on these for material. So, in a poem he called 'The
Craftsman', in a metre taken from Horace, he pictured Shakespeare assembling his materials and transmuting everyday incidents into high art. Talking to Jonson 'after long-drawn revel' at
the Mermaid, he recounts where he had first heard Cleopatra;
where he had 'listened to gipsy Juliet Rail at the dawning'; and

> How at Bankside, a boy drowning kittens
> Winced at the business; whereupon his sister
> (Lady Macbeth aged seven) thrust 'em under
> Sombrely scornful.

So Kipling too fettled together his pebbles and fragments till he
had his story written. Then he would take, not a pen, but a brush,

and go through it cutting everything that could be cut. Then the story would be set aside 'to drain' and after a time shortened again. 'I have had tales by me three or five years which have shortened themselves almost yearly.' 'A tale from which pieces have been raked out is', he wrote, 'like a fire that has been poked.'

This was craftsmanship, in which the conscious self was involved. But he was always conscious of something without which craftsmanship would be no use. He wrote in 'The Bull that Thought' of 'the detachment of the true artist who knows he is but the vessel of an emotion whence others, not he, must drink'. It was a point he often made. Once, in 1918, Rider Haggard, perhaps his most intimate friend, spoke to him of the loss of his son, and then of his fame; that perhaps was something left on which to dwell with pleasure. 'He thrust the idea away with a gesture of disgust. "What is it worth?—What is it all worth?" ' And he went on to 'show that anything any of us did well was no credit to us; that it came from somewhere else, that we were, in fact, only telephone wires ... ' This, says Miss Tompkins, is the most conclusive statement of something which is implicit in many stories and verses. It is never any use cross-questioning Kipling, because his ideas are never worked out in intellectual terms, but I think he believed that *all* creative work was inspired, or came *through* the writer, and that it was by a *further* grace that his personal Daemon was sometimes present and sometimes gave him instructions. 'My Daemon was with me in the Jungle Books, *Kim* and both Puck books,' he wrote. 'When your Daemon is in charge, do not try to think consciously. Drift, wait and obey.' But it seems that the Daemon could be sometimes more present or sometimes less:

> This is the doom of the Makers—their Daemon lives in their pen.
> If he be absent or sleeping, they are even as other men.
> But if he be utterly present, and they swerve not from his behest ...

The fourth line is an anti-climax and the verses remain a fragment, quoted in *Something of Myself*.

All through the late stories, then, we must picture the conscious craftsman trying to arrange his fragments of experience, but always as the instrument of some unknown force trying to express itself through him, always with an ear cocked for the advice or instruction of his personal Daemon. But let us turn to the idea of revenge or retribution and how it developed.

2. REVENGE AND RETRIBUTION

Revenge bulks large in Kipling's stories from the start. There are tales where it is disguised in a jocular or facetious form, as in 'Pig' (*Plain Tales*, 1888), a story of a young civilian in India who sold a horse for more than it was worth to a man who ought to have known better and then laughed about it; the man who had been stuck devised an elaborate official revenge which involved his adversary in interminable work and final humiliation. There is 'A Friend's Friend', again slight, about a man who got drunk at a dance; his drunkenness was insulting to the ladies to whom he had been introduced; he was punished by being tied up, after many indignities, in a roll of carpet, and sent away on a handcart. But other tales of revenge—in most of which the actors are Asian— are far more grim. 'Dray Wara Yow Dee' (*In Black and White*, 1888) is the tale of a Pathan whose wife has been unfaithful; her he has killed but the man he is still pursuing, until he can see his face in daylight and kill him with his bare hands. 'The Limitations of Pambé Serang' is a similar story of a Malay whose honour has been soiled by a drunken Zanzibari seaman, whom he follows round the world till at last, when he is sick and dying in a London lodging, he hears the voice of his enemy in the street, and begs that he shall be brought to his bedside; then with his last strength he drives home the knife he had kept under his pillow.

But it is really in the Jungle Books and particularly the Mowgli stories—in which fancy is given free rein—that the idea of the Law and the need to pay debts becomes clear. Not only must Mowgli be bought into the pack by a sacrifice—for which he owes a debt all his life—but his account with Shere Khan must be settled, and later his account with the villagers who had thrown stones at Messua, the woman who had loved him as a mother. He lets in the Jungle and utterly destroys their village; the rains fall and within a month it is 'only a dimpled mound, covered with soft, green young stuff'. It was after this that 'the pleasantest part of Mowgli's life began. He had the good conscience that comes from paying debts … ' And the same note is sounded in *Stalky*: 'Everybody paid in full—beautiful feelin',' said M'Turk absently.

An injury must be avenged—but there is more to it than that.

The balance must be restored and a remote all-seeing something —
The Law, perhaps — must be appeased. This is very marked in
Stalky. The regulation pattern for a Stalky story is that the Three
suffer some injustice or humiliation at the hands of Prout or King,
and skilfully avenge the injury without being detected or without
breaking the letter of the school code. But the all-knowing Head,
having indicated his basic sympathy and understanding, proceeds
none the less to lick them. It is flagrant injustice — or so he says.
But the boys recognize the true justice behind their punishment.
To lead their housemaster into an ambush was a proper revenge
for his behaviour, and they enjoyed their triumph, but they do
feel in an obscure way that it is an outrage against the law, or
more prosaically, the way a school ought to be run. In terms of a
wider justice, the balance has to be restored.

Until *Puck of Pook's Hill*, it is hard to think of a story in which a
person who has been injured holds his hand from taking revenge.
There is one complicated exception to this, in 'A Sahibs' War',
(1901, published in *Traffics and Discoveries*, 1904) when the apparition of a British officer just killed forbids two Indian soldiers
who have loved him from hanging his murderers, who are Boers.
There were orders that Indian troops should not take part in the
South African war, and the dead man, killed by treachery, had
again and again insisted on this; what they saw may have been
their vivid memory of his admonitions. And even this is not truly
an exception, because vengeance was taken, very completely, and
immediately afterwards, by Australians. But in the second story of
Puck, 'Young Men at the Manor', the Norman Sir Richard holds
his hand from vengeance on the Saxons who have held him roped
for hanging. It is the key point in the story. And Parnesius, the
Roman centurion, refuses to kill a soldier who has just been
insolent to him, because Maximus the Emperor has taken the
men out of his command. That marks the beginning of a change —
though an intermittent change — in attitude towards revenge.

Six years later, 'In the Presence', written in 1912, though
published in collected form in *A Diversity of Creatures* (1917),
marks another step. The story is told in a gathering of Sikh
soldiers of the Indian Army. One of them has been in England
and has to be told of what has happened in his absence; two
soldiers of the regiment, brothers, have taken leave and have
killed no less than seventeen of their mother's kin, who had for a
long time been endeavouring to force them to leave their land and

had refused all attempts at reconciliation. Then they went to the
flat roof of their house, sent reports of what they had done to the
police and in due course, after waiting for a proper time and after
performing the proper ceremonies, killed themselves. That is
the first part of the story; the two Sikh soldiers have upheld the
honour of the regiment and their own honour, and both the
regiment and the village approve of their conduct. Then the Sikh
who has been in England tells a story of the ordeal endured by the
four King's Indian Orderly Officers who were in England at the
time of the death of Edward VII and at the time of his lying-in-
state. There were only these four to provide a guard from the
Indian Army at the catafalque; the British army had of course
thousands of men on whom to draw. The British guards found the
strain intense and each man's watch was limited to thirty minutes.
But the four Indian Orderly Officers — actually two of them were
Gurkhas and two Garhwalis, but Kipling makes them all Gurkhas
for simplicity — usually stand a full hour each with three hours off.
They decide that they must take a wreath of flowers to Windsor
and it is not fitting that the wreath should be taken by only one
man. So the three senior go to Windsor, leaving the youngest on
guard four hours while the British guards are changed eight times.
The incident occurred in real life very much as described in the
tale, but a summary cannot do justice to the sense of strain which
the guards found so severe; it was the strain of standing motion-
less with the head bowed and watching the unending procession
of feet. The man who endured four hours came off with his eyes
working 'like weaver's shuttles ... So it was done — not in hot
blood, not for a little while, nor yet with the smell of slaughter
and the sound of shouting to sustain, but in silence, for a very
long time, rooted to one place before the Presence among the
most terrible feet of the multitude'.

The Sikhs who hear this story have only one regret, that it had
not been Sikhs to whom this honour had fallen. But it is surely
important that it is introduced by a tale of conventional revenge,
conceived as a means of preserving honour. The impact of the
whole is that patient endurance is as honourable as restoring the
balance by killing an enemy. 'Friendly Brook', written in 1914,
carries one stage further the concept of impersonal retribution
rather than personal revenge. It is a story set in the Sussex
countryside and entirely concerned with Sussex folk, daily
labourers, woodmen, smallholders, people like old Hobden whose

ancestors have lived in the neighbourhood for centuries. It keeps wholly to one key and to my mind is quite free from blemishes.

The opening is one of the best in Kipling. Two woodmen are sizing up a hedge they have to trim, and in a few sentences you get the impression of rain and fog — 'one could hardly see a cow's length across a field' — of the brook rising in the valley — 'every blade, twig, bracken frond and hoof print carried water' — of the highly skilled craftsmanship of the two men and of their professional respect for each other. One says that, if the brook rises only a little more, it will get Jim Wickenden's haystack at the bottom of the meadow. And it comes out in the conversation that each of them separately had warned Jim that he had put it too near the Brook. And what did he say in reply? A curious answer, which at first neither would repeat, which both had puzzled over, though the elder, who at one time had lodged with Jim Wickenden, clearly had a shrewd idea what it meant. But, at last, after cautious soundings, each tells the answer he had been given, and, as they both expected, each had had the same answer. Jim had said: 'The Brook's been good friends to me and if she be minded to take a snatch at my hay, I ain't settin' out to withstand her.' Then, over their midday packets of food, Jesse, the elder of the two woodmen, told what he knew.

Jim's wife had 'never made nor mended aught' till she died. When that happened, some years back, Jim asked his mother to keep house for him. She had been living with a daughter but now she came to live with Jim. He was one of those cottagers — once common throughout England and of whom even today a few still survive, to my personal knowledge in Western Hampshire and Dorset and no doubt elsewhere — with a field or two, some pigs and poultry, perhaps a cow, men of independence who eke out the proceeds of their holding by occasional daily labour as a woodman or the like. He had no child and his mother persuaded him to ask for a child from 'one o' those Lunnon societies', and Mary Wickenden had come to them in a candle-box. It seems he had not formally adopted her and the society too had perhaps been content to leave the matter vague. But Jim and his mother 'mothered up Mary no bounds, till it looked at last like they'd forgot she wasn't their own flesh and blood'. And many of the neighbours thought she was their own, as she did herself. Jesse, telling the story, thought her hard, cold and unloving; she seemed to have 'no rightful feelings' and had shown no kindness or concern even when Jim's mother was 'took dumb' and was reduced to writing on a slate. Mary was studying to be a school-teacher; she had set her heart on that and it seemed all she wanted. She was no beauty—but there was Jim's place that would come to her and four cottages an uncle had left him, so perhaps there would be men after her.

So there was the household, down by the brook and some distance from any neighbours—the old mother, masterful and very careful of the money and desperately frustrated at being forced to write all her thoughts on a slate, Jim, and Mary, their darling, but she set only on her studies, resenting any help she was asked to give 'in the kitchen or the hen-house.' Upon this strange trio, there burst one day a visitor, Mary's Lunnon father, whom they had forgotten all about. Her mother had died in her infancy, the father was a hopeless drunkard, and perhaps the society had supposed he would never reappear. He had the law on his side and in the end Jim bought him off. He had once done six months in Lewes gaol because he had thrown out a man who had fallen on his head. So violence was ruled out and what was left but bribery? Though Jesse added: 'I'd ha' packed her off with any man that would ha' took her—an' God's pity on him!'

But for Jim that too was ruled out. The girl was determined not to go and for Jim the idea of giving her up just did not occur. So he kept on paying, a little at a time, though it got a little more every time, and his mother scolded him on her slate for being so weak, and Mary scolded them both for not having told her, and scolded her father even more savagely for neglecting his duty all these years. Jim lay awake at night till he'd 'sweated his sheets into a sop' but he could think of no way out but hoping the man would drink himself to death. Then one November, in just such weather as the tale begins in—'rain atop o' rain after a wet October'—the brook began to rise and the stuff coming down in the flood jammed on top of a piece of the bank that had fallen in below Jim's place, and it looked as though a field of winter wheat would be drowned. The farmer came in haste to ask Jesse to clear that corner and let the water get away. So he began and, about noon, Jim came along with an axe over his shoulder and began to help him. Mary's Lunnon father had sent a postcard to say he was coming and he felt he just could not face the talking and the crying and his mother blaming him afterwards on the slate. So he had run and left his mother to tackle him herself.

By four o'clock they had made a channel for the brook to get round the corner, and they were getting ready to go when Jim saw in the half-light something that he thought was the white top of one of his straw bee-skeps, which he painted to keep them dry. But when he tried to 'pook' at it and bring it to shore, it was Mary's Lunnon father, whose bald head had caught the light. He had fallen off the plank bridge by the cottage after seeing Jim's mother; Jim looked in his waistcoat pocket and found that his mother, in spite of all she said, had given him more than he had ever done. They pushed him back into the stream and let him go on down. So Jim had good cause to be grateful to the Brook and would not grudge it a mouthful of hay. 'Hark!' says Jesse and the story ends:

'The Brook had changed her note again. It sounded as though she were mumbling something soft.'

'Friendly Brook' has not had the critical attention which I think it deserves. It is an artistic whole, all of a piece, with the Brook running through it all and the sense of saturated wet, and the soft blurred speech of the woodmen. This is very different from Mulvaney's stage Irish, which is really a literary convention of the period and does not at all convey the sound of an Irish voice; here the sound of a southern countryman's voice comes through by the use of words and phrases and with a minimum of mis-spelling.* The woodmen have the cautious good manners of people whose world lies within a radius of two or three miles — so that you have to be careful what you say, because who knows what damage may be done among people with whom you will live all the rest of your life. And consider that strange trio, Jim and his dumbstruck mother, the ugly duckling they thought a swan, and the determination of all three not to be separated! How easy it would have been, and how much the story would have lost, if Mary had shown some spark of affection! Jim's character comes out indirectly; both the two woodmen know him and it is by little touches that the picture emerges. Not a drinking man, careful of his money, though much less sharp after money than his mother, a friendly man ready to help a neighbour, patient, one feels, with his feckless wife, sharp mother and the shrewish Mary, a hater of scenes, he is none the less a man of strong passions. His hate for Mary's Lunnon father comes out only in his treatment of the body

* A Sussex friend tells me that the talk is authentic Sussex and identifiably East Sussex not West.

which — once he has recovered the money his mother had given
him — he pushes back into the water, saying: 'I've done with him.'

Jim's hate (says Miss Tompkins) is 'impotent and unprogressive
as nowhere else in Kipling.' But to my mind this negative judgment is not enough. Jim had progressed from the violence that
had ended him in Lewes gaol; Kipling had made progress too.
The story is written with a deep understanding, one of those
which most strikingly bears out André Maurois's saying about
Kipling's closeness to the depths of human emotion. Contrast
Jim's grounds for hate in this 'deep' story with those of the party
who take such cosmic vengeance on a rude and pompous magistrate in 'The Village that Voted the Earth was Flat'. That, though
much more ambitious, is a 'shallow' story. The two woodmen
understand Jim's feeling that the Brook deserves a sacrificial
victim; their primitive, and barely spoken, religion sceptically and
half humorously recognizes a personality in the Brook. The haystack, like the Bull that bought Mowgli, restores the balance, pays
the scheme of things for an unexpected favour. It is superficial to
dismiss their feeling as mere rural animism. They do not really
think the Brook is a water-spirit, but they do think that something
is due to something. It is just, it is retribution, and there is no
need for revenge.

3. DAYSPRING MISHANDLED

This story is of such importance that it deserves separate treatment. It is about revenge and brings to a climax the development
of revenge into retribution. No summary can be a substitute for
reading the story; it needs to be read carefully and more than
once, but it is no use discussing it without some sketch of its
outline.

It begins nostalgically 'in the days beyond compare and before
the Judgments.' We are back in 1890, or thereabouts, and a group
of young writers meet once a week for supper at Neminaka's
Café. They are ambitious but impoverished and are glad to write
under assumed names for a literary entrepreneur who suggests
subjects to them and places their work. Among these young
writers are the two principal people of the story, Manallace and
Castorley. Castorley is a 'mannered, bellied person' with a 'high
affected voice' and 'gifts of waking dislike'. Manallace is 'a darkish
slow northerner of the type that does not ignite but must be

detonated.' Slow-burning oak, one comes to think of as the metaphor for Manallace. Manallace is in love with a woman who is never named but always referred to as the mother of Vidal Benzuaquen; Vidal is the star that the music halls are crazy about in 'The Village that Voted the Earth was Flat'. Miss Tompkins must be right in thinking that Vidal's mother is never named because we are not meant to dwell on her personality, but only on what she meant to the two men. But I have an impression that she too was an actress and won many hearts.

At the supper which is the beginning of the story, Castorley announces that he has been left a legacy that makes him independent; he is going to leave 'hackwork' to follow 'Literature.' He leaves the supper early and unlamented, and that evening proposes to Vidal's mother and is refused. Manallace has produced nothing for the syndicate that week; he had been given a batch of prints to weave a story round—stereotyped medieval subjects, 'a knight, a castle, a young girl'—but they have 'turned into poetry in his hands'. None the less, he is elevated and excited; he drinks too much and tries to recite his verses but the others roll him under the sofa and go away. One man stays to see him home; this proves later to be the narrator, who in this story is most unobtrusive. Manallace, to this reduced audience, is allowed to recite the poetry to which the pictures had led him.

During the next few years, Manallace sticks to his production of pseudonymous romances; 'his line was the jocundly sentimental Wardour Street brand of adventure, told in a style that exactly met, but never exceeded, every expectation.' Vidal's mother is deserted by her husband and paralysed; Manallace takes all responsibility for her, looks after her and pays for her treatment. In the end, 'only her eyes could move, and those always looked for the husband who had left her. She died thus in Manallace's arms ... ' This was early in the War. Meanwhile, Castorley had used his independence to make himself an authority on Chaucer. His knowledge was genuine; he was no impostor. But he was blatant in seeking his own glorification. During the War, he and Manallace both worked as temporary civil servants, and in the same Ministry. Castorley 'cadged lumps of sugar for his tea from a typist, and when she took to giving them to a younger man, arranged that she should be reported for smoking.' One night the two men found themselves side by side waiting for an air raid and began to talk of the past as human beings. Then

Castorley said something about Vidal's mother, and 'from that hour—as was learned several years later—Manallace's real life-work and interests began.'

What Castorley said we are never told; perhaps, with embellishments, that she had set her cap at him but he had been too clever to fall into the trap. Be that as it may, after the war he methodically set about making himself the Supreme Pontiff on Chaucer, while Manallace seemed to have been left, by the death of Vidal's mother, with nothing but 'fleeting interests in trifles', 'experiments of uncertain outcome, which, he said, rested him after a day's gadzooking and vitalstapping'. The narrator finds him trying to make ink from bark and wine; grinding corn with a stone quern; experimenting with book-binding and the colouring of initial letters in late medieval manuscripts. He takes the narrator to hear Castorley lecture—impressive in his detailed knowledge of such things as the idiosyncrasies of spelling and penmanship in Chaucer's copyists, repellent in his self-advertisement. Then it bursts on the world that no less than 107 lines of a previously unknown Canterbury Tale have been discovered. The narrator calls on Castorley, whom he finds 'made young again by joy'. Yes, he had been in on it from the start, as soon as the spoiled page of manuscript had been discovered in New York; it had been used as stiffening for the side of an old Bible. And the marvellous thing is that every detail to do with this new manuscript supports some point Castorley had made in his lectures; analysis showed that the paste had been made from stone-ground wheat, the ink from a recipe with bark and wine which he had quoted, while oddities of spelling and penmanship at once identified a particular scribe on whom he had dwelt. And what, asked the narrator, were the verses about? Oh, it was unquestionably Chaucer; 'the freshness, the fun, the humanity, the fragrance of it all, cries—no, shouts—itself as Dan's work.' But, as Castorley gives the substance of the discovery, the narrator begins to remember Neminaka's and the verses Manallace had insisted on reciting when everyone had gone home.

So far the story is straightforward enough. This is the second crucial point, the first of course being when Castorley made that remark about Vidal's mother which turned Manallace's dislike to deep-smouldering hate. It is from now on that it grows darker and twistier. The narrator went to Manallace, who filled in the details of how he had worked and planted the forgery. What was he

going to do? Well, the first step was to get Castorley knighted and
then—he hesitated between revealing the whole thing secretly to
the press, which would bring Castorley's reputation about his ears
some breakfast-time, or telling him in a private conversation and
forcing him to back the forgery as long as he lived. To tell this
would kill him, says the narrator. 'I intend that,' Manallace
replies. He adds that he himself has been dead since—and he gives
the date when Vidal's mother died. *

Castorley becomes Sir Alured, and Lady Castorley calls on all
her friends with her new visiting-cards that very afternoon. But
Manallace does not pull the string. Castorley is ill and that seems a
reason for delay—as good perhaps as Hamlet discovered when he
came on Claudius at his prayers. And Lady Castorley begins to
utter strange hints; she says that Sir Alured owes more to Manallace than even *he* knows; she tells Manallace that she knows all
Sir Alured has told him about Chaucer. Manallace begins to
perceive that she knows his secret and is egging him on to pull the
string. He is more than ever inclined to delay and he agrees to
help Sir Alured assemble into a book a full account of his find.
It will help him in his revenge, he says, to have all the evidence
neatly laid out; his own task of exposing it can be the more
elegantly arranged. But as work on the book proceeds, and
Castorley's illnesses become more frequent, Manallace becomes
at last aware that Lady Castorley, too, has a secret; she and
Gleeag, Castorley's surgeon, are lovers. And a strange duel ensues,
she inciting Manallace to get the book finished, make his exposure
and kill her husband, he now trying to protect the man for whom
he has so long nourished so bitter and consuming a hate. 'I'm not
going to have him killed,' he says, having come to feel that this is
his prey. But she has access to him when Manallace has not, and
she is greedy; Gleeag, we are told, was content to wait. She begins
to hint directly to Castorley that the discovery is too perfect, has
come too pat. On his death-bed, he is distraught by anxiety on this
score and by suspicion of all those round him, and, becoming
oblivious of time, wants to go out and see Vidal's mother, in
order to put right some old wrong of which he felt guilty. For a
time, too, he appears to become detached from the body like

* At least, he means to. He says April Fourteen—but it had been April Fifteen a
few pages back. It is extraordinary that Kipling, with all the minute care he took over
detail—he actually forged a Chaucer manuscript, just as Manallace does—could
make this mistake and go over it a dozen times without noticing. But he had a blind
spot about times and dates.

Findlayson and the Lama. Manallace's attempt to save him fails.
Manallace says at the cremation: 'She is going to be known as his
widow—for a while at any rate ... ' With that, 'he took out his
black gloves.'

'As ... the coffin crawled sideways through the noiselessly
closing door-flaps, I saw Lady Castorley's eyes turn towards
Gleeag.'

The title of the story comes from 'Gertrude's Prayer', a song
put by Manallace in the mouth of his heroine in the forged page
of Chaucer. Gertrude's father is trying to make her marry a rich
old man; the refrain of her song—in a modernized form of
Manallace's Chaucer—is: 'Dayspring mishandled cometh not
againe.' All three stanzas make the point, the second applying
most directly to Manallace and his revenge.

If the 'slender sterting spray' from an oak is 'to-bruizèd', what
might have been a branch 'of girt and goodliness' will be turned
on itself:

> And knotted like some gall or veiney wen.
> Dayspring mishandled cometh not agen.

Manallace's deep and tender love is 'to-bruizèd' and turned in on
itself, twisted into a passion for revenge. 'So close must any life-
filling passion lie to its opposite'—a key sentence in *Something of
Myself* which applied to 'Mary Postgate'. But here it is carried a
good deal further. Love turns to hate which inspires revenge—
not 'to make honour clean' as in the Indian stories, but revenge
pure and simple, revenge meant to appease hatred. But the
revenge too is all turned on itself and wired and knotted, first by
Manallace's character; he has a quick mind to hatch a plot or
perceive a shade of meaning, but he shrinks from the decisive act
that will bring down the whole edifice. He is what Pope John XXII
called 'amletico' or Hamlet-like. But there is more in it than that.
An old Kipling theme reappears—the bond of shared work.
Obsessed though he is by self-glorification, Castorley is a genuine
scholar; his only likeable characteristic is his devotion to his
work. He is perhaps just saved by this, as a rather similar character, Wentworth, in Charles Williams's *Descent into Hell*, takes the
final and decisive downward step because he does not trouble to
point out a detail that is wrong in his own special subject. Shared
work, coupled with Lady Castorley's impatience for Castorley's
death, turns Manallace's destructive hatred to a possessive urge

to protect. But the desire to do justice is not extinguished, and Manallace means Lady Castorley to bear the burden of being his widow. He takes out his black gloves with the air of a judge putting on the Black Cap. But it seems unlikely that he will be any more successful in this attempt than in the former. She will escape him; he has no chance against her deadly concentration.

There is a moment in the story when it appears to be a gigantic ambush from the days of Stalky. Castorley has some of the less endearing characteristics of King, and there is something reminiscent about the manner in which he is led on, 'specifying in minutest detail every trap that was to be set for his own feet.' But even in the Stalky days, it was not enough that the trap should be sprung; the balance had to be restored by the divine Head. This device was not available to the Kipling of the late 'twenties, and the Head's part is played by far more subtle and impersonal forces.

The dayspring theme of joyous youth and opportunity recurs when Castorley's guilt about Vidal's mother is revealed on his death-bed. It is painful to remember that morning bliss at this time of physical torture, of suspicion and deception, but it is essential to the story as a whole that revenge should be seen to have grown from dayspring mishandled, and that the two themes should be threaded together right through to the end. The rather mysterious opening verse, as well as 'Gertrude's Prayer' at the end, stress the dayspring theme, not revenge:

> C'est moi, c'est moi, c'est moi!
> Je suis la Mandragore!
> La fille des beaux jours qui s'éveille à l'aurore
> Et qui chante pour toi!

Only the third line has any relevance unless one has read either the tale by C. Nodier in which this verse appears or Miss Tompkins's admirable exposition of it. Nodier's tale concerns a 'melancholic' who comes on a bed of mandrakes, of which many have been pulled up; he pulls up one more and a young man appears who asks him whether it sang. If so, its song would be this verse: 'C'est moi, c'est moi, c'est moi!' It had not; then it is not the right mandrake for him. The melancholic goes away dispirited and meets a doctor, who gives him a learned disquisition on the properties of the mandrake. It is anodyne and kills pain; it is narcotic and induces loss of consciousness; it is a purge and

8

emetic, but unless used with extreme care may cause death. In
Nodier's story, the mandrake is a symbol for poetic illusion, but
in Kipling's (says Miss Tompkins) it becomes a far more powerful symbol for revenge.

It is easy to follow Nodier's broad idea, that in the first flush of
enthusiastic youth, poetic illusion offers release from pain and
even from consciousness; but not everyone is a Keats, and for
many the mandrake will not sing and the drug will prove fatal.
I find it hard to believe that Kipling really meant the mandrake to
be the symbol of revenge throughout this tale. There is no mention of mandrakes in the story itself. To attach central symbolic
significance to something that does not even appear is surely to
extend the bounds of literary criticism beyond reason. What
vistas open! The immense importance of the soup-tureen in
Hamlet ... the poisoned daggers in *Alice in Wonderland* ... ! The
verses attached to Kipling's stories are sometimes very closely
linked to the story, but sometimes very loosely, and here I think
the association is simply that joyous dawn may lead to attempts to
kill pain and destroy consciousness—which will mostly prove
barren and indeed poisonous to whoever employs them. Nodier
implies that for one in very many the mandrake will sing; for
Keats it is right to use the mandrake. But Kipling did not mean to
suggest that there was one perfect form of revenge which might
be the salvation of someone other than Manallace. Further, what
most people know about mandrakes is that they were supposed to
shriek when torn from the ground; they 'were engendered under
the ground from the seed of some dead person put to death for
murder.'* Mandrakes were also an aphrodisiac, and produced
fertility in women. They were used in spells as a substitute for
man.

> Goe and catch a falling starre,
> Get with child a mandrake root ...

Mandrakes are far more rich in symbolism than Nodier's tale
suggests, and Kipling was far from ignorant of such matters.
Altogether, I do not think the analogy with Nodier should be
pursued far; it is a glancing reference, no more. If, indeed, Kipling
meant a full understanding of his story to depend on having read
someone else's, it was a blemish.

'Dayspring Mishandled' seems to me, as I have said, among

---

* Thomas Newton's Herball to the Bible. And see Genesis 30 vv. 14-16.

Kipling's very best stories. It is complex and highly finished, with many recurring details and interlocking minor themes. As one quite trivial example, Manallace says after the supper at Neminaka's that he might turn his Chaucerian verses into a comic opera—but it would be no use because Gilbert and Sullivan had command of the market. In his elation over the discovery, Castorley exclaims that the verses, though handled as only Chaucer could, are 'as modern as Gilbert and Sullivan'. The essence of the story, however, is simple; it is that individual efforts at putting right the offensiveness of such a man as Castorley turn back on the revenger. Personal revenge is self-defeating or abortive; retribution must be left to forces that appear impersonal. 'Vengeance is mine, I will repay, saith the Lord.'

It would be wrong to think that this was an intellectual conclusion that applied to all kinds of revenge. In 'A Friend of the Family' (1924) revenge is complete and successful, but it is taken on behalf of someone else and by a man who, as is continually insisted, is not quite like other people, having lived in the northern parts of Australia, among sheep and aborigines, and having never seen 'a table-cloth, a china plate, or a dozen white people together' till he was thirty. And 'Beauty Spots', later than 'Dayspring', takes us back to an earlier model; a tiresome and malicious man is destroyed, so far as all local influence is concerned, quite pitilessly, almost casually, not from hatred, not to make honour clean, but simply to get rid of a nuisance. But that story trembles on the edge of farce. The point that revenge may be more complete if not taken is also made in 'The Miracle of St Jubanus', which appears in the same collection as 'Dayspring'. But that is in comparison a slight story. In 'Dayspring', on the other hand, Kipling is writing at his best and deepest, and this must be thought of as his last word on revenge and retribution. But it could live in his mind alongside manifestations on quite another level.

4. LONELINESS AND PAIN

The outstanding fact in Kipling's life after his son's death was physical pain. Nothing of much biographical importance happened in the twenty years from 1915 on; he finished the sacrificial task of writing about the Irish Guards, he worked on the War Graves Commission; he continued to refuse honours from the

Government but was honoured by many universities; he travelled
in France and elsewhere and stayed on the Riviera, living the life
of a wealthy Englishman of his time. But there was an attack of
some gastric trouble in 1915; he was already ill when the news
came that his son was missing, and although he partly recovered,
he suffered from intermittent pain for the rest of his life. In 1922
there was a severe recurrence; he underwent an operation in
November and in February 1923 there was a serious relapse. His
daughter wrote:

> The strain of the war ... and my brother's death left both my
> parents in poor health in 1918 and my father subject to severe
> attacks of internal pain. Numbers of doctors tried to cure him
> but with little success ... The courage and patience with
> which he bore the recurring pain and the cures that were
> tried were truly heroic. His self-control was superb and the
> sweetness of his temper unfailing; he would only ask to be
> left alone until the pain was over. It was not till 1933 when he
> was terribly ill while in Paris that a French doctor found that
> for some fifteen years he had been suffering from duodenal
> ulcers. What endless pain and suffering he could have been
> saved had this conclusion been arrived at earlier; now he was
> too exhausted to undergo an operation.*

With this went pain of another kind and an increasing loneliness. Something of the strain and horror — not only at his personal
loss but at what was endured by all his generation — comes through
in the last verse of 'The Children' (1917):

> That flesh we had nursed from the first in all cleanness was
>   given
> To corruption unveiled and assailed by the malice of Heaven
> By the heart-shaking jests of Decay where it lolled on the
>   wires —
> To be blanched or gay-painted by fumes — to be cindered by
>   fires —
> To be senselessly tossed and re-tossed in stale mutilation
> From crater to crater. For this we shall take expiation.
>   *But who shall return us our children?*

This was shared with Carrie. But the impression is strong with me
that it was not fully shared. Mrs Bambridge wrote: 'The two

* Memoir by Mrs George Bambridge, quoted by Carrington as an Appendix.

great sorrows of their lives, my parents bore bravely and silently, perhaps too silently for their own good. My mother hardly ever spoke of her two lost children, but sometimes my father would talk of them to me.' And again she wrote:

> My mother introduced into everything she did, and even permeated the life of her family with, a sense of strain and worry amounting to hysteria. Her possessive and rather jealous nature, both with regard to my father and to us children, made our lives very difficult while her uncertain moods kept us apprehensively on the alert for possible storms. There is no doubt that her difficult temperament sometimes reacted adversely on my father and exhausted him, but his kindly nature, patience and utter loyalty to her prevented his ever questioning this bondage and they were seldom apart ... *

It would be easy to build up a superficial case refuting my judgment that loneliness was an important fact of Kipling's life in these years after the war. There was a stream of visitors to Bateman's — relations, celebrities of many kinds, children, young men in the Irish Guards. Carrington notes that the average number of visitors in the nineteen-twenties was a hundred and fifty a year, 'of whom many were invited to stay the night; and many more would have come if they had got past Carrie's scrutiny.' His clubs too provided him with company in London; he has written with pleasure of those he met at the Athenaeum, and he was later elected to the Beefsteak Club and to that group of distinguished persons meeting periodically to dine which was known, for more than a century-and-a-half, simply as 'The Club'. He loved talking and listening at such gatherings; long ago as a child, he had leaned over the balusters at the top of the stairs and listened to 'the loveliest sound in the world — deep-voiced men laughing together over dinner.'

There was no lack of vivacity at these gatherings. A French writer with whom he had corresponded, M. Joseph-Renaud, met him at the Author's Club, where, he said, 'this little dark man with the blinding gold spectacles and the enormous eyebrows, came up and shot a rapid fire of questions at me ... "Are the duels in Dumas correct in detail? Are there any such Bretons as those described by Pierre Loti? Is it true that Madame Bovary was a real

* Carrington's Appendix.

person? Tell me about this Colette whose animal stories are so
much better than mine!" And so on and so on ... When he had
drained me dry he turned abruptly away with a quick "good-
night". I had never met so tenacious an interviewer.' It sounds
very like the small boy in 'Baa Baa, Black Sheep', who demanded
of an astonished Aunty Rosa: 'What is a "falchion"? What is a
"e-wee lamb"? What is a "base ussurper"? What is a "verdant
mead"?' — and had been crossly told he was showing off.

But that is not really to answer the point. He was never a
solitary, he enjoyed company, but his nature was one of those
which call out for intimate affection. After the war, some of his
closest friends died, notably Colonel Feilden, a neighbour in
Sussex, and Rider Haggard. That is the common fate of the
elderly; he was sixty when Haggard died. Its special effect in
Kipling's case arose from the nature of his marriage. About this,
no one can reasonably be dogmatic. Both the partners were
stoics who disliked showing their feelings; no one knows what
they talked about when they were alone. It was in one sense a
thoroughly happy marriage; they did not quarrel, they were
'seldom apart'. But, reading between the lines, it does not sound
like a marriage of minds. No doubt they exchanged ideas fully
about how money should be invested and where they should go
on their winter expeditions in search of the sun. And no doubt
there are many couples generally thought to be happily married
who do not exchange thoughts on levels much deeper than this.
But there are not many couples of whom one partner is turning
over in his mind anything at all like 'Dayspring Mishandled'. I
find it hard to believe that Rudyard fully shared with Carrie the
gradual transformation of his feelings about revenge, his gropings
towards a conviction about an after-life, his growing belief that
suffering and love have some kind of redemptive value. But it
cannot be proved.

Pictures of the two together have much in common. I have
already quoted Lord Castlerosse on Rudyard's complete surrender (see p. 133). Miss Dorothy Ponton, who at one time lived
at Bateman's, teaching mathematics to John and Latin and
German to Elsie, draws a picture more discreet, but not in essence
very different, from that just quoted from Mrs Bambridge. Here
too the children's mother appears rather tense, possessive and
managing. Miss Ponton speaks of the two Kiplings going for
walks to inspect the farms on the estate, and Mrs Bambridge says:

' "Farm walks" were often taken and while C.K. discussed with the foreman ditches to be cleaned out, barns to be repaired or crops to be sown, he stood by listening and only sometimes making a suggestion.' He, who had so passionate an interest in technical detail, must stand by and listen! But he had picked up Cold Iron and snapped the ring home on his neck. 'My father's much exaggerated reputation as a recluse,' wrote his daughter elsewhere, 'sprang, to a certain extent, from her (my mother's) domination of his life and the way in which she tried to shelter him from the world.'

There is a glimpse of him seen by Hugh Walpole,* at a party at a great country house in Kent. 'Kipling ... ' he writes, 'is like a little gnome ... ' There were many celebrities present.

> Not that Kipling cares in the least about any of them. He is kindly, genial, ready apparently to be friends with anyone but keeping all the time his own guard ... Hates opening up reserves. All the same he'd had friends once and again he'd done more for than for any woman. Luckily Ma Kipling doesn't hear this ... She's a good strong-minded woman who has played watch-dog to him so long that she knows just how to save him any kind of disturbance, mental physical or spiritual. That's her job and she does it superbly ...
>
> He really, I think, has no vanity. He's a zealous propagandist who, having discovered that the things for which he must propagand are now all out of fashion, guards them jealously and lovingly in his heart, but won't any more trail them about in public. He walks about the garden, his eyebrows all that are really visible of him. His body is nothing, but his eyes terrific, lambent, kindly, gentle and exceedingly proud. Good to us all and we are all shadows to him.
>
> 'Carrie,' he says, turning to Mrs. K. and at once you see that she is the only real person here to him — so she takes him, wraps him up in her bosom and conveys him back to their uncomfortable hard-chaired home. He is quite content.

The only real person here to him — and they are seldom apart. But the impression persists that when he was at his desk they *were* apart. There he did escape. In the late stories, the narrator is always alone, a bachelor or widower — though often identified as a writer of some repute — while in three of *The Just-So Stories,* a

* *Hugh Walpole* by Rupert Hart-Davis (quoted by Carrington).

father and daughter have escaped from the control of wife and mother for joyous adventure on their own. There is also a poem, 'The Penalty' which appeared in *Limits and Renewals* (1932), as an epilogue to 'The Tender Achilles'. It is not easy to be sure what is meant by the Star of this poem. In relation to the story, it appears to stand for a man's particular bent, his own special art or skill or craft.

> Once in life I watched a Star;
> But I whistled, 'Let her go!'

But it sounds to me as though it should also be read with an application to Kipling himself. If so, it must stand for the vision of life which he renounced when he married and came to live with folk in housen on the hither side of Cold Iron. It ends grimly:

> I had loved myself, and I
> Have not lived and dare not die!

The anguish of wasted opportunity, of loss and remorse, was something of which he wrote often and felt deeply. 'Dayspring Mishandled' is one of the most persistent themes in his writings. It goes right back to Mulvaney and recurs again and again, particularly in relation to sexual love. This was what gnawed at Vickery's heart; he had lost Mrs Bathurst by folly and deception just as Love-o'-Women had lost Diamonds-and-Pearls. In a Kipling love story of any depth, either the pair are doomed, like Holden and Ameera, or the passion is one-sided, the partnership uneven, as in 'The Wish House'. That a writer should turn back, five years after marriage, to juvenile fantasy like 'The Brushwood Boy' — which is not a love story at all — makes the same point.

'In the days beyond compare and before the Judgments', he had written at the beginning of 'Dayspring Mishandled' — and who can doubt that he was thinking of the days before his marriage. Men of his class and generation liked to picture themselves as slaves to their women-folk. They would break away from a gathering of men in the club or the mess or the pub with some half-facetious remark about getting into trouble at home if they were late. It was an atonement for the woman's exclusion from the male world of real work and real companionship. If the woman was in bondage, then the man too, if he had any decent feeling, must accept some degree of bondage. Kipling often shows us men who talk in this kind of way—but in his own case, there was something not far from a reversal of the general rule. *They* pretended; he really *was* in bondage—as many women were—and, like many women, he revenged himself by excluding the tyrant from some areas of the imagination: in his case it was a very vivid and active imagination. It is in this sense that Kipling was lonely, and the loneliness echoes in the words he wrote to his surviving daughter when she had married and left Bateman's; the house, he said was 'resonant, silent and enormously empty'.

Even in his early days, he had been aware that physical pain might be welcome as a cure for mental pain, but it is nowhere stated so explicitly as in the 'Hymn to Physical Pain' (1932), the introduction to 'The Tender Achilles':

> Dread Mother of Forgetfulness
> Who, when Thy reign begins,
> Wipest away the Soul's distress,
> And memory of her sins ...

To pain, remorse and loneliness, must be added a lifelong dread of nightmare, for which the evidence is scattered throughout his writings. It lies at the very heart of 'At the End of the Passage' (1890), and 'In the Same Boat' (1911); it is strong in 'The Brushwood Boy' (1895), and dotted here and there in other stories. I do not see how anyone could doubt—simply on the evidence of what he wrote—that the kind of fear encountered in nightmare was terribly real to Kipling. So was the extreme depression he had once encountered in a house at Torquay and of which he wrote in 'The House Surgeon', a depression which he believed was due to the brooding of some human spirit on a wrong done in that house. No less real was that other depression, which was once called Accidie or Wanhope and, because it sprang from sloth or torpor, was counted by the church a sin. In the verses called 'Rahere' it is said to spring from a surfeit of 'Wealth or Wit or Power or Fame'. 'Hence the dulled eye's deep self-loathing—hence the loaded leaden brow;'—so to Rahere in these verses speaks Gilbert the Physician, 'who had seen him wince and whiten as he turned to walk alone'.

There is one other aspect of Kipling's personal life that must have influenced his concern with healing and mental health in his last years. His sister, named, like his mother, Alice, but known in the family as Trix, had been his companion at the House of

Desolation and again had been one corner of the Family Square
in Lahore. She was a girl of great promise; she married in India
and (says Carrington) was for many years 'at the hub of Simla
Society, as gracious as her mother and far more beautiful. A
person of extreme sensibility—imaginative and nervous—she was,
in the expression of those days, "psychic", so unworldly that she
seemed sometimes to live in a world of phantoms.' In December
1898, 'her mind gave way' and she had to be placed under her
mother's care at Tisbury. She recovered two years later and
rejoined her husband, but was 'hardly able to live a normal life'.
Her illness recurred early in the War and Rudyard made himself
responsible for her care. I know of no direct reference to her case
in his writings, but it can hardly be supposed that such an illness
in one so near to him did not occupy his thoughts.

5. HEALING

It is against this background of pain and loneliness that Kipling's
interest in healing must be seen. There are two healing stories in
Rewards and Fairies (1910), 'Marklake Witches' and 'A Doctor of
Medicine'. 'Marklake Witches' is told by a girl of the Napoleonic
period who during the events she recounts is dying of what was
then called consumption, something everyone in the story knows
except herself. The medical part is about the discovery of the
stethoscope and the angry opposition of the orthodox and the
superstitious; in some ways, it looks forward to 'The Eye of
Allah', which deals far more effectively with an invention produced before its time. 'A Doctor of Medicine' moves a step
closer to what were to be Kipling's later preoccupations with
healing, but it is a short step. A village in Sussex—it is Burwash—
is hit by the plague during the Civil War and Nicholas Culpeper,
herbalist and astrologer, joins the villagers in their isolation; he
fights the plague by reasoning based on observation of the stars,
reasoning that most modern readers would regard as absurd, but
which leads him to declare war on the rats, organize all the able-
bodied for rat-hunts, persuade them to clean up the village, stop
up the rat-holes, and take the sick into the open. The plague is
checked, and it is partly because the able-bodied are too busy to
think about getting ill themselves. Thus the story links the
health of the body with the health of the spirit, and is so far in the
line of Kipling's development. But the attitude to astrology is

superficial and conventional; it was a theme to which he returned with a more enquiring mind in 'Unprofessional' (1930).

Two other stories are about healing, though not about doctors of medicine: 'An Habitation Enforced' (1905) and 'My Son's Wife' (1917). Both centre on men who are sick at heart or in spirit. One is an American millionaire, struck down in the middle of a big deal by a complete mental and nervous collapse, something that doctors recognize. The other does not know he is ill, but he 'had suffered from the disease of the century since his early youth, and before he was thirty he was heavily marked with it'. The disease was a form of that same Accidie or Wanhope which had attacked Rahere, but in Frank Midmore it was a still more deadly sin because it involved association with the Immoderate Left. Both men are healed by becoming absorbed in the life of the English countryside, George Chapin and his wife by the shades of meaning and emphasis in English country behaviour, by the things said and more often left unsaid by an established way of society centuries old; their conversion sometimes hovers on the brink of the sentimental, but I find it more convincing than Frank Midmore's. His begins with the novels of Surtees, which he had never read before; he has inherited a house with a gunroom and a library and all the appurtenances thereof, and he finds himself gradually sucked into a world of fox-hunting solicitors and estate-agents, a shamelessly polygamous small farmer, floods and mud and rain, dark November evenings, poached eggs after hunting, the gravel churned up by horses' feet, illegitimate relationships unexpectedly revealed. All this makes rather a sharp change from making love 'to women whose hair smelt of cigarette smoke', which had been Frank's principal recreation before, and I find it hard to believe he would have taken to it so quickly. To my mind, this would have been a better, and a more convincing, story if Frank had been less committed to the Immoderate Left and if his Bloomsbury associations had been mildly indicated in the lightest colour-wash instead of being drawn in hard lines, limned in bright colours and then assailed with rancour. The country part is done in the late manner, with interconnected clues as to relationships which hardly appear till second reading. Both these stories are variations on the theme of 'A Charm': 'Take of English earth as much As either hand may rightly clutch ... Lay that earth upon thy heart And thy sickness shall depart,' but 'My Son's Wife' shows development only in style. In substance, it is saying that it is morally better to splash about in the mud hunting foxes than to sit on committees trying to improve the world; this is not new, while its attack on the intellectuals of Bloomsbury is shrill and uncomprehending.

It is with 'The House Surgeon' (1909) and 'In the Same Boat' (1911) that we come to the close link of mental health with physical and to the theme of release from disease by bringing to the surface the cause of a deep and secret wound. 'The House Surgeon' must have had its origin in that inexplicable depression that the Kiplings had felt in a house near Torquay which they had leased when they first came back from Vermont. In the story, the narrator meets in a steamship a man who has bought an expensive suburban house standing in its own grounds and has spent a good deal of money on improving and furnishing it. But it is haunted by a terrible feeling of depression, and of something trying to tell something. The narrator goes to stay in this house and as soon as he enters his bedroom is hit by a sensation of blackness and misery. Incidentally, he does not appear to have wife, family or home, has leisure to go to stay with anyone who asks him, and gives up a good deal of time to learning golf with an elderly solicitor from whom he wants information. He becomes friendly with this solicitor, who is the cousin as well as the legal adviser of the previous occupant, Miss Mary Moultrie. The narrator contrives to meet Miss Moultrie and discovers that she believes that her younger sister had committed suicide by throwing herself from the window of the very room where he had slept. Miss Moultrie is a hard, suspicious woman and a rigid evangelical; she believes that her sister has gone to everlasting damnation and broods constantly on the act of suicide and the house where she thought it had happened. By a singular coincidence, she is taken ill at night with an attack of asthma, and, desperate for breath, tries to open a sash window of which the sill is too low and almost falls out. Everyone thinks she was trying to kill herself and the narrator, whom she takes for a doctor, tries to make her see that this must be what had happened to her sister. He at last persuades her to visit the house and see the window in her sister's room. She does and is convinced; the curse is lifted. The title of the story is a rather feeble joke; the narrator has cured the house and has been thought to be a doctor.

Apart from the virtuosity of the telling—notably the gradual emergence of the character of Mr L. Maxwell M'Leod, a Jewish

dealer in furs, the owner of the house – the most striking part of
the story is the description of the oppression when the narrator
first goes into the bedroom. It needs to be read in full and I shall
quote only one or two scattered sentences to give the flavour of it:

> I was aware of a little grey shadow, as it might have been a
> snow-flake seen against the light, floating at an immense
> distance in the background of my brain ... my brain tele-
> graphed that it was the fore-runner of a swift-striding gloom
> ... I moved towards the bed, every nerve already aching with
> the foreknowledge of the pain that was to be dealt it, and sat
> down, while my amazed and angry soul dropped, gulf by
> gulf, into that horror of great darkness which is spoken of in
> the Bible ... Despair upon despair, misery upon misery, fear
> after fear, each causing their distinct and separate woe,
> packed in upon me ...

It came again on the M'Leods and their guest when they were at
dinner – but once Miss Mary Moultrie's suspicion is removed and
the spirit of her dead sister satisfied that all is understood, the
house becomes 'light, spacious, airy', 'full of the sense of well-
being and peace'. It is a complete cure.

'In the Same Boat' is also convincing about the Horror. There
are two people, a man and a woman, Conroy and Miss Henschil.
They had never met. Both have taken to drugs to keep it off. Both
at last go to nerve specialists. Conroy's is the more sympathetic
and imaginative; Miss Henschil's consultant thinks that all drug
addicts lie and invent the symptoms as an excuse for the habit.
Fortunately, the two consultants compare notes. Conroy's man
tells him that it may help to take a long journey by train on the
night when the Horror is due; vibration and the change of scene
may make a difference. Then, by an inspiration, he suggests that
Miss Henschil should go too and he puts her in Conroy's charge.
The responsibility for her will steady him.

The two start on their journey together and discover that they
have both been using a drug to make the Horror less. Step by
step, they tell each other the nature of their fear. For both, there
is what one calls sentence and the other notice. It is a long,
shuddering sigh. Once that had passed the lips, the thing was
inevitable; neither hard exercise nor drink nor anything else
could prevent it coming. Both knew how long it would be
between sentence and execution and in that interval walked in

torment — cut off from ordinary folk not under sentence —
counting the days, hours and minutes till it should have passed,
unable to count change nor to talk about dates and times without
turning the numbers into the hours and minutes that remained.
When the Horror came, it was nightmare, a sequence of sounds
and pictures — different for each of them — but culminating for each
in a moment of awful shock — 'as though your soul were being
stopped ... as though you were a violin-string — vibrating — and
someone put his finger on you.' 'As if a finger were put on the
naked soul!' Each had tried to make that shock less terrible by
drugs — each had found that drugs meant losing everything else
too. For him it is the sixty-seventh time, for her the thirty-ninth.
But *this* time it did not happen — icy cold, paralysis, darkness, fell
on them both but not the Horror. It was partly because they had
told it, as they had never been able to tell anyone before, partly
because they had faced it together. Six times they made this
journey together when sentence was given, and each time it was a
little less terrible. Then, when they are cured for the moment but
apprehensive that it may return, Miss Henschil's nurse reveals
something she has just discovered. Three months before she was
born, Miss Henschil's mother had an experience corresponding
almost exactly with her nightmare and culminating in panic and a
moment of shock, when someone touched her. Conroy at once
takes the first train to his mother's home, where he is able to
find that in her case too, before he was born, there had been a
series of terrifying events and the panic-stricken shock of being
touched.

Why their dates should coincide is never satisfactorily explained; it is no explanation to say, as the nurse tells them:
'Because a child is born somewhere every second of the clock'.
But was it chance? Or was it laid on them? 'Chance' implies that
there is no explanation, while if it was 'laid on them' some divine
or devilish person or purpose is implied. The uncertainty is never
resolved. It brought intense suffering and it was flagrantly unjust
— but, again by what appears to be chance, they broke out of it,
first by the shared experience and eventually by bringing the truth
to the surface. But they are not saved by love nor by laughter,
as an earlier Kipling might have suggested. The more cynical and
less imaginative of the two doctors thinks love between them is
inevitable and is concerned about his responsibility for the children that may be born of two flawed people; the nurse too expects

that at least they will kiss, once they are cured. But the idea repels them. They are puzzled about this themselves; both are young and said to be exceptionally good-looking, yet he would not have her nor she him, 'not with a million in each stocking'. They admire each other physically — but are slightly disgusted at the thought of even a kiss. Perhaps they feel it would be incestuous; they had been united by fear and suffering in a relationship which had nothing to do with sex and to which sex seemed impertinent. No explanation is offered. Kipling simply felt that it would be so, but he recognized that anyone who had not shared that horror would expect the opposite. That he had experienced something of what he tried to describe seems to me an inescapable conclusion.

Thus even before 1914 the world of Kipling's imagination was intermittently lonely and haunted by pain and terror. There might be healing but it was as unpredictable as pain. From 1915 onwards, his concern with pain and healing grew and his most particular interest was with the shock and strain of war, the point at which a man would break, the damage to brain and nerves that continued when war was over. The theme of getting the sufferer to face and understand his own hidden wound is stronger than ever. In 'The Woman in His Life' (1928), the cure begins when the patient is manoeuvred into buying a small black Aberdeen bitch puppy, to whom he becomes enslaved. ('Manoeuvred' is the nearest word I can find in conventional English, but I believe that in American dialect there is a verb 'to hornswoggle', which means to push someone into doing something by a mixture of bluff, deception, and coercion, perhaps rather as a cow might nudge her calf into a stall — between encircling horns, with not much choice. Some such word is often needed in writing about Kipling's stories.) The enslavement to something outside himself and his work starts the cure, but it is only when Marden is sent into the country for a rest cure and Dinah's collar gets caught by a root at the end of a tunnel in a sandstone quarry that the process is complete. It is near midnight when he finds her, and then he has to crawl along that tunnel and face the dread of being buried alive which had filled him with terror in the war. A minor theme in this story is one that runs right through Kipling, manipulation of events by a hidden figure behind the scenes, in this case the hero's wartime batman and peacetime valet, who 'hornswoggles' him into buying Dinah.

The main healing theme reappears in 'Fairy-Kist' (1927) in
which circumstantial evidence points to one Wollin as the
criminal in what looks like a sex murder. He had had a rough time
in the war and many months in hospital and he hears voices; his
housekeeper says he is 'fairy-kist'. He can see that the evidence,
though entirely coincidental, points to him and is sure that if he is
once put in the dock he will be sent to Broadmoor. Rather than
that, he will shoot himself, and he sits with a loaded revolver in a
cellar for a month, waiting for the moment when they come for
him. But the murder is proved to be an accident and the dreams
and voices to go back to a time in hospital, when he had thought
he was going mad and when the hospital was being bombed, but
a kind nurse used to read to him. The book from which she used
to read is identified and it accounts for the words of his voices and
the form of his dreams. It is too complicated a story to summarize, and marked by some returns to early faults. It begins, for
instance with a piece of mock-pomposity which recalls *Plain
Tales*. These are the opening words: 'The only important society
in existence today is the E.C.F. — the Eclectic *but* Comprehensive
Fraternity for the Perpetuation of Gratitude towards Lesser
Lights.' This proves to be a group of four or five elderly men of
varied tastes who meet periodically for talk over a good dinner.
Again, later in the story, one of the several narrators says that at a
crucial point Wollin's face was like: 'and he named a picture by an
artist called Goya' — a phrase which is either an insult to the reader
or the kind of self-conscious after-dinner joke that is quite out of
place at a serious point in the story. It turns back forty years and
recalls the complicated attitude of the strangely clever youth, who
was always saying: 'I don't want to seem too clever — but on the
other hand I don't want you to forget how clever I am!' But these
are trifling irritations; the serious concern of the story is breaking-
strain, and not only in Wollin's case. A minor character, a young
man who had quarrelled with the apparently murdered girl,
becomes obsessed by the thought that, if only he had gone back
to make it up, the accident need never have happened. 'He's been
tried too high — too high,' said one of the narrators, who is a
doctor. 'I had to sign his certificate a few weeks later. No! He
won't get better.' As prelude to the story is a poem, central to all
this period: 'The Mother's Son'. The speaker is in a Mental Home,
looking at his own reflection in the looking-glass and watching a
man go out of his mind.

And it was *not* disease or crime
Which got him landed there,
But because They laid on My Mother's Son
More than a man could bear.

Here the Kipling from below the threshold is writing about
They — cruel social forces which the stricken man fears and feels
unjust.

They broke his body and his mind
And yet They made him live ...

Yet the surface of Kipling's mind is still on the side of respecta-
bility and the Establishment.

The theme of breaking-strain and of healing by bringing a
wound to the surface recur in 'A Madonna of the Trenches', but
they are subsidiary to the main interest. That story I deal with in a
later chapter. Two more healing stories, both in the last collection,
are important. 'The Tender Achilles' (1929) is about a doctor who
is himself a patient; he is subjected to strain greater than he can
bear and cracks. Wilkett is a brilliant research man, in charge of
the bacteriology at St Peggotty's, a great teaching hospital. But
in the army and in war, every doctor had of course to be used to
the limit of his capacity without consideration of any special skill
or temperament. The story is told, like 'Mrs Bathurst', by a group
of narrators. Wilkett volunteered to go to the Front and for a long
time was at a casualty clearing-station, where there is intermittent
bombing and everything very rough-and-ready and a long line of
cases waiting for major operations. There will be head injuries
that mean cutting a piece out of the skull; there will be ab-
dominals; one of the narrators remembers a machine-gunner
with twenty-three perforations of the intestines. But whatever it
was, you had to make up your mind and operate at once; it was
fifteen minutes for a case and when at last you staggered away,
blind with fatigue, and lay where you dropped, the dressers would
wake you by waggling your foot because there was one more who
might be saved.

Wilkett had never been a good surgeon; he liked time to think,
and like every research man he was a perfectionist. Then, to cap
all, he was sent to a hospital for self-inflicted wounds — men who
had blown off their big toes and had to be patched up to face a
court-martial. 'Enough to send a tank up the pole,' someone

throws in. This was more than he could bear. After the war, he remembered his mistakes and thought he was a murderer. There was blood on everything he ate. He saw the head injuries — lines of heads waiting for operation. He refused to go back to his old post of bacteriologist at his hospital and lived in the country with his mother, who — you will not be surprised to learn — was a possessive woman who did not understand the importance of his work. His colleagues decide that he must be hornswoggled into coming back and engage in a highly improper — but thoroughly Kiplingish — conspiracy, never fully put into words. He has had a minor wound in his foot which had healed but has now broken out again, perhaps as part of his neurosis. One colleague pretends to think it is tubercular and persuades him to have a sample from it tested in his old department. There is a positive report and Wilkett is operated on by one of the narrators. Then he is told there had been a mistake; the slides had been changed and there need never have been an operation. He is very angry but the two biggest men in the hospital sit by his bed and talk to him till 'they had him apologizing at last for owning a foot at all'. Then the Head of the Hospital in his precise diction, sums up: 'if you had been at your post here after the War, Mis-ter Wil-kett, in-stead of relaxing your mind in rest cures, this lit-tle affair, which we have ag-reed to for-get, would never have ta-ken place.' Wilkett apologizes, obediently takes up his old appointment, and from that moment there are no more visions of heads accusing him of murder.

It is too technical a story to be a general favourite — though to me medical technicalities and rivalries between surgeons and physicians are more interesting than ships' engines — and I should find it hard to believe in the conspiracy if I had not come to see so clearly the Head of St Peggoty's — 'his likeness, in face and carriage, to the hawk-headed Egyptian god, the mobile pursed lips, and the stillness of the wonderful hands at his sides' — and to observe how rapidly everyone sprang to do what he said as soon as he 'began to dissect his words'. The casualty clearing-station, the fatigue, the strain of constant decision immediately put into effect, the lines of waiting stretchers, all these build up to something which carries conviction and which for that one man meant breaking strain.

But what is it that breaks? The outer crust or mask, the personality built up by training and discipline, the imposed mould, by virtue of which inchoate desires and impulses are harnessed for action—that is clearly the answer. What makes it crack and then allow the personality to dissolve into its component parts? Wilkett's colleagues say that in his case it was his 'bleeding vanity'—and perhaps they were partly right. Wilkett was a perfectionist; he expected too much of himself and thought he could put the world to rights; he was not content to be an ordinary mortal doing the best he could. He was a true research man. It is such men who suffer from Rahere's disease of Wanhope, or who are smitten with the sickness of Aurelian McGoggin, and both sicknesses come from pride, from too high a sense of self-importance, a failure in common sense, in humility, in a sense of proportion.

There is a refrain running through the story, introduced casually—or so one is at first misled into thinking—to illustrate the mannerisms of Sir James Belton, the Head of St Peggoty's: 'In our Pro-fession we are none of us Jee-ho-vahs. Strange as it may seem, not an-y of us are Jee-ho-vahs.' It is a catch-word, a joke, something he was expected to say—but it is the essence of the story just as: 'What else could he do?' is of *Rewards and Fairies*. A man must do his own thing—but he must do it humbly and obediently and not try to put the world right by himself; he must follow his own star, and if because of greed or pride he doesn't, he will find he 'has not lived and dare not die'. There is an unforgettable moment, when Sir James Belton is going home after a long evening listening to Wilkett's visions. He says on the doorstep that he 'can't afford to lose Wilkett's intellect for the sake of his bleeding vanity'. Then he sees a star, stares for half a minute at the driver who is to take him home and says: 'Oh, Lord! What *do* You expect for the money?' It worried the driver but Sir James 'was only questioning the general scheme of things ... '

This story is one to which I did not attach much importance until I tried to summarize it, but it grows as one reflects on it into a mirror of the importance of man's work in the universe. It is placed last but one in the last collection and it is sandwiched between two poems, the 'Hymn to Physical Pain' and 'The Penalty', both already quoted in this chapter. 'Dread Mother of Forgetfulness', the 'Hymn' begins, and it is sub-titled 'Mr C. R. Wilkett's version'. Does this mean that Wilkett induced his septic foot as a refuge from his mental torment? The poem clearly has a wider application than this story, but the narrower application to

Wilkett is more difficult; he forgets those rows of head injuries not because he is suffering physical pain but because he gets back to his proper work. 'The Penalty', on the other hand, is clear in its direct relevance to Wilkett and it is the wider application, and particularly the application to Kipling, that is more difficult. The title of the story refers to a family joke about the Achilles tendon, also to the operation on Wilkett's foot which gave him a false heel, also, I suppose, to that tenderness of conscience, proceeding from vanity and specialization, that had tripped Wilkett up by the heels.

'Unprofessional'—written later but placed before 'Achilles' in the last collection—is not less full of meaning. Harries, an astronomer, suddenly finds himself immensely rich; he gets in touch with three doctors—a surgeon, a pathologist and an administrator—whom he 'had tried and proved beneath glaring and hostile moons in No Man's Land.' He persuades them to drop everything else and join him in a partnership, based on a private clinic of which one of them has always dreamed. Each will follow his own bent, but with an open mind as to the ideas of the others and a readiness to co-operate. The governing idea is that men who look through microscopes should talk to men who look through telescopes; the atom becomes more and more like a universe and there are phenomena in both for which we cannot account. The astrology of the ancients—still, Harries might have added, regarded by hundreds of millions in Asia as affecting human life—was no doubt based on false theories, but is it really beyond belief that there should be 'tides' in the whirling planets and nebulae that have some correspondence with 'tides' in atoms and bacteria? All he asks is that, as they pore over their bacilli, the pathologists should take note of everything they see and keep a log. 'What' he asks, 'do you suppose is the good of Research?' 'God knows', replies the pathologist, 'Only—only it looks—sometimes—as if He were going to tell.' We see something of the working out in one case; the operation, for a cancer generally reckoned incurable, is taken when the 'tides' of this particular case, reckoned on the basis of minute observation, are at the flood. The patient makes a physical recovery—quite unexpected—but when the cheated grave should, by all normal calculations, have had its due, she tries to break her neck by dashing against a wall and has to be held down by force. A sharp moral shock breaks her out of her obsession and once over it—it is implied—she will be safe. But it is more a question-mark than a story. The painstaking detail of scientific research-work, the slow precise grind of daily observation, are brilliantly drawn, but what actually happened remains obscure, still more the possibility of some connexion between the universe and the individual. The impact on one woman of what the research team discover is still haphazard, a matter of chance in the echoing distances of eternity. This woman is saved, millions are not.

Put this beside Shaw's play *The Doctor's Dilemma* and you get an almost complete reversal of interest. 'Unprofessional' was written some twenty years later than the *Dilemma*, but they both have their roots in a period when people had the most extravagant hopes of science. Both turn on a scientific discovery which scientists today would disclaim. But to Shaw the scientific side of the discovery is little more than a chance for a quick laugh at the idea of 'buttering the phagocytes' and another at the fashionable physician who misunderstands the process. Shaw's interest is in using the discovery to put a moral dilemma in dramatic form. Only one man understands how to use the discovery, and he has only one bed in his clinic. Shall he use it to save a selfish scoundrel who is a brilliant artist or shall he save a humble but unsuccessful general practitioner and let the artist die? That he loves the artist's wife makes the dilemma one degree more sharp. The phagocytes are mere dramatic machinery. There are two lives and only one chance of survival; it might just as well be one place in a lifeboat. Kipling's interest by contrast is in the consequences for human existence of such possibilities. What are the implications for man's place in the universe? It leads to profound chasms of metaphysical paradox. The work of the research team, the chance — if it is a chance — that has given them the money to do it, their vision and imagination, have saved this woman in a way they hardly understand. But some mysterious demand seems to drag her away. The contradiction of 'In the Same Boat' reappears; much of it looks like blind chance, which human will can only occasionally influence — and yet her suffering was 'laid' on this woman, and the grave clamours for its due. *The Doctor's Dilemma* can appear on television half-a-century after it was written; 'Unprofessional' could not. Yet to me the one asks questions about man and the universe; the other in comparison is a light-hearted canter through the sunny uplands of the intellect.

This chapter has been about two different means of redressing the balance—vengeance and healing. Vengeance is a personal attempt to redress a moral balance upset by some shameless act outside the law. It is ultimately futile and will rebound upon the avenger. Healing is also an attempt to redress the balance upset by some force from beyond human understanding. But here the conclusion seems to be the reverse. However feeble and imperfect man's knowledge, he must follow his bent and do what he can; he must try to heal, even though we are none of us Jehovahs and his theories will soon be proved wrong.

> Through abysses unproven,
>   And gulfs beyond thought,
> Our portion is woven,
>   Our burden is brought.
> Yet they that prepare it
>   Whose Nature we share
> Make us who must bear it
>   Well able to bear.

That Kipling had written twenty years earlier, in 'An Astrologer's Song', which is a character piece, reflecting the confidence of the astrologer in his understanding of matters of which he really knew nothing. By 1930, Kipling had seen that men were not always able to bear the burdens laid on them, but that, feebly and with infinite humility, they must try to find out what they could. It is time to see if we can put his positive beliefs into any shape.

PART THREE
Retribution and Compassion

10
Belief

1. WHAT DO YOU EXPECT FOR THE MONEY?

It would be a mistake to look in Kipling for anything so explicit as
a creed. His beliefs – they must be spoken of in the plural – regard-
ing man's place in society and in the universe were flashes of
vision. Sometimes he put such a kingfisher-glimpse to a tune and
it appeared as verse; sometimes he wove it into a story. If he set
his intellect to work on these revelations, it was to find the best
means of displaying them as art; it was never to modify them, to
reconcile them with each other, to formulate them into a consistent whole. None the less, throughout his writings, from
beginning to end, obsessed though some of them often seem to be
with the externals and even the conventions of life, there is a
consciousness of death, of the smallness of man in the face of
eternity, of a vastness and power beyond man's comprehension.
At first the emphasis is on chance; the gods are blind, they strike
at random, as they struck at Holden and Ameera. Later, towards
the end, there is a growing suggestion of something still incomprehensible but certainly not chance; pain and evil have a place
within a wider purpose, a Mercy at which man can only glance
over his shoulder occasionally, sometimes in terrified awe, sometimes in an almost affectionate mockery.

In the early stories, the emphasis is on man's duty, his valiant
determination to do what he has to do in the face of death and
disease, even though there are moments when he sees that his
efforts are futile; it is only dirt digging in the dirt.

> Cities and Thrones and Powers
>   Stand in Time's eye
> Almost as long as flowers,
>   Which daily die ...

These moments grow more frequent until in the late stories the
preoccupation is with pain and love, revenge and mercy, with
breaking strain and the moment when the personality cracks into
disintegration. The unity which runs through all his work, from
beginning to end, can in the end best be defined by what it is not.

But before we attempt that definition, there are a few pre-
liminary points. At the House of Desolation, he had acquired a
horror of the narrow, negative, Evangelical religion of Aunty
Rosa – some of which is displayed in the Anglican chaplain of the
Mavericks in *Kim* and in Miss Moultrie of 'The House Surgeon' –

but he none the less learnt to know the Authorized Version of the Bible and the lovely cadences of Cranmer's Collects. He had been allowed to read nothing but the Bible on Sundays and the Collects he had been set to learn. These were lasting influences on his style. As to accepting what he read, the nearest he ever came to saying what he believed was during that brief and early love affair with Caroline Taylor. He wanted to satisfy her father's distress at his lack of orthodoxy and wrote to her: 'I believe in the existence of a personal God to whom we are personally responsible for wrongdoing—that it is our duty to follow and our peril to disobey the ten ethical laws laid down for us ... I disbelieve directly in eternal punishment ... I disbelieve in an eternal reward.' And at the end of the same letter, he writes: 'I believe in God the Father Almighty, maker of Heaven and Earth and in One filled with His spirit who did voluntarily die in the belief that the human race would be spiritually bettered thereby.' As Charles Carrington says, the words sound as though dragged out by an effort; this was as far as he could go. Carrington suggests that not too much should be made of this, and it should certainly not be regarded as representing what he would have said he believed in later years. None the less, all the evidence suggests that he continued all his life to believe in a personal moral responsibility to some kind of divine purpose. And his knowledge of the Bible often influenced his reactions to circumstance in ways he did not attempt to define or formulate. He was always aware of the majesty of the Hebrew vision in the Old Testament—the sanctity of the Law, the purpose of God for mankind, the balance that must be restored by punishment or sacrifice, the sense of man as somehow knitted into Family and People. Not less, and increasingly in his later years, he drew from the New Testament a belief that suffering on behalf of others might purify and ennoble, and, as we saw in the verses 'Cold Iron', he might use Christian symbols to make his point. That is not to claim that he was a secret Christian; even his St Wilfred is public school and Anglican rather than Christian. Kipling picked and chose his loyalties and admirations. 'The Miracle of Purun Bhagat', 'The Bridge-Builders', and much of *Kim* show Hinduism with sympathy and understanding, and there is a passage about a mosque in Egypt which seems to express the essence of Islam:

... a deserted mosque of pitted brick colonnades round a vast courtyard open to the pale sky. It was utterly empty except

for its proper spirit, and that caught one by the throat as one
entered. Christian churches may compromise with images
and side-chapels where the unworthy and abashed can traffic
with accessible saints. Islam has but one pulpit and one stark
affirmation—living or dying one only—and where men have
repeated that in red-hot belief through centuries, the air still
shakes to it.

He can also put himself into the place of a Roman subaltern who
had dedicated his life to Mithras and who protests that the
Christians have taken over the ritual and even the doctrine of that
soldier's faith.

Kipling's attitude to the Heavenly Powers was ultimately very
like his attitude at school. He had believed in the Headmaster and
the purpose of the school but did not think highly of the house
masters; he never doubted that there was some divine purpose—
often concealed beneath a flippant reference to Allah—but he was
sceptical about most human doctrines and interpretations of the
divine. Faithful to an Unknown God, he was agnostic about
formulations.

'No man was less of a materialist. No writer has been less able,
or less willing, to ascribe shape or nature to that which filled him
with awe,' wrote Miss Tompkins. She goes on, with admirable
perceptiveness, to point out that many of the stories seem to be
set in darkness, so that 'a stone's throw out on either hand' one
steps off a lighted stage into a blank, dark unknown. Of some
stories, such as 'At the End of the Passage' or 'Unprofessional',
that is clear enough, but in others—sometimes in quite unexpected stories—a sudden touch, a phrase or a paragraph, will
open up vistas of eternity. As Miss Tompkins observes, the last
four words of that very difficult story, 'The Dog Hervey', suddenly reveal that one of the participants had died without understanding what had happened, and 'I have written this tale to let
her know—wherever she may be.' In 'The Ship that Found
Herself'—which I regard as one of the less interesting tales from
the technical phase of the middle period—Miss Tompkins notices
an ironical remark which again opens chasms at the reader's feet.
The parts of the ship, Kipling writes, talk continuously, 'but their
conversation is not half as wise as our human talk, because they
are all, though they do not know it, bound down one to the other
in a black darkness, where they cannot tell what is happening near

them, nor what will overtake them next.' In the first illustration to 'The Crab that Played with the Sea', the Man, with his little daughter on his back, is talking to the Eldest Magician, who had set each animal to play at being itself—to Do its Own Thing. Just behind the man is a Maze, and when he has finished talking to the Magician, the Man will walk in that Maze 'because he has to'. 'All this picture' the caption concludes 'is Big Medicine and Strong Magic.'

A list of such heart-shaking moments could be extended almost indefinitely, but let me add only two. The first is the moment in 'Mrs Bathurst' when Vickery, having made to Pyecroft that strange remark that at least he had not been guilty of murder, added his last recorded word: '"The rest", he says, "is silence" an' he shook hands and went clicking into Simonstown station.' And the second comes in 'The Army of a Dream' (1904), a tale that to me is not very interesting and which any other man would have put in an article in *The Times*. It is a long discussion of an enormously improved army, in a country really keen on defending itself against Germany. But at the end, the narrator sees the men he has been talking to change before his eyes; it came upon him, 'with no horror, but a certain mild wonder' that they had died in the Boer War.

> Bayley, shifting slightly, revealed to me the three-day-old wound on his left side that had soaked the ground about him … Luttrell with a foolish tight-lipped smile lurched over all in one jointless piece. Only old Vee's honest face held steady for awhile against the darkness … Then his jaw dropped and the face stiffened, so that a fly made bold to explore the puffed and scornful nostril.

That note of horror at the physical manifestations of death had been strong in England three hundred years earlier, in Webster, for instance, and Donne, but it had hardly been heard in the England of Pope or of Tennyson. And it is here that it is possible to take a step towards defining Kipling's beliefs by what he was emphatically *not*. He never shared that generalized optimism about scientific progress and a materialist millennium that was so prevalent at the time and which for want of a better name I call Pelagianism. What Pelagius actually taught no one knows exactly, because all we have is St Augustine's refutation of him; but it appears that he believed man was perfectible by his own efforts.

He was British and there is surely something characteristically British about the idea. At any rate, it seems convenient to class under the name of his heresy all those simple and rather superficial souls who have supposed that men would be good if no one interfered with them and that happiness can be achieved on earth if only certain political and external obstacles are removed. For Rousseau, it was Kings and Priests; for Wells and Shaw, it was Capitalists; once the systems they stood for had gone, men would live together happily in universal brotherhood. Shaw, indeed, even suggested that old age and death could be overcome by man's intelligence and will.

In the middle period of Kipling's life, the unconscious creed of most middle-class Englishmen for most of the time was a Pelagian optimism, a vague belief in material progress under a benevolent state, an increasing reluctance to talk about death or acknowledge that 'sin' had any meaning or that crime was anything but the result of adverse circumstance. To all this, Kipling would have returned an emphatic no; death and birth were crude inescapable physical facts; pain and sorrow are real and most men encounter them. Man *is* responsible for his act. He is a bundle of desires which need to be trained and harnessed; the man who truly deserves the name of man is under discipline and master of himself, even though his self-command is something that has to be watched and jealously preserved. He is like the captain of a pirate ship, for whom mutiny is always close. But watchfulness is not enough; fate and metaphysical aid may sweep him away at any moment. Civilization, too, like the trained man, is a fragile creation, laboriously built up and easily destroyed; it has fallen into fragments when men grew idle and arrogant.

Up to a point, this is like Greek thought; the ideal man of Athens is beautiful-and-good, controlling his sensual desire and selfish ambition, an aristocrat by training. But Kipling's half-conscious debt to the Old Testament made him go further; the state would decay if it did not remember beneath Whose awful hand it was permitted to hold sway; man would inevitably be dismissed to the Mercy and would need mercy. His merit, it seems sometimes, would depend on the extent to which he had suffered and kept his integrity.

I spoke earlier in this section of looking at eternity with something not far from affectionate mockery. This is strongest in 'On the Gate' and 'Uncovenanted Mercies', discussed later in this chapter. But there is also an example — already referred to — of just this note in 'The Tender Achilles', when Sir James Belton, after catching a glimpse of a star, says: 'Oh Lord, what *do* You expect for the money?' He was contrasting the majesty of infinite distance, awe at immensity, wonder at beauty, with the fragility of human material.

> To the Heavens above us
>   O look and behold
> The Planets that love us
>   All harnessed in gold!
> What chariots, what horses,
>   Against us shall bide
> When the Stars in their courses
>   Do fight on our side?

He had that evening seen Wilkett all to pieces, out of control, no longer the disciplined research worker who could switch his brilliant imagination on to dark places like an electric torch; from the star, he turns his gaze on the uncomprehending driver, hardly seeing his face:

> Through abysses unproven
>   And gulfs beyond thought
> Our portion is woven,
>   Our burden is brought.

'Oh, Lord! What *do* You expect, with what You've given us?'

2. FORGIVENESS

It is hard to illustrate Kipling's beliefs because there are so many facets and such a wealth of points that might be made. But one story that displays a wider variety of themes than most is 'The Church that was at Antioch' (1929). Valens is a young Roman officer whose mother is disturbed by his adherence to the cult of Mithras, and she therefore pulls strings in Rome to get him transferred to Antioch, where his uncle is head of the police. Valens and his uncle Sergius, like all Kipling's Romans, are very English and have been, one feels, to a good public school; Sergius is the wise old Commissioner, Valens the dedicated young subaltern, eager to put the world to rights, very like the Brushwood Boy except that he has a girl whom he had bought in the market at Constantinople.

The two Romans look on Antioch much as a British officer in India looked on Lucknow; you had to know something of the difference between Sunni and Shi'a, as well as between Muslim and Hindu, if you were to keep them from flaring up in riot and cutting each other's throats. And Valens has to learn of the quarrels between Jewish Christians and Greek, all the problems of how far the old Jewish Law should be obeyed by new Christian converts. There are trouble-makers from Jerusalem eager to pin something on the Christians that will discredit them in Roman eyes. They find a Cilician with a grievance; Valens had killed his brother, who attacked him in a mountain pass when he was on his way to Antioch. They make an opportunity for this Cilician to kill Valens at a Christian gathering, but the bodyguard seize him in time and Valens lets him go when he hears of the brother, saying that now it is even-throws. Valens is a good officer, conscientious and sympathetic and only mildly contemptuous of the Christians because they have borrowed so much from Mithraism; both he and Sergius have a respect for Paul the local leader, and for that greater leader Peter, whom Paul brings from Jerusalem to settle their disputes. Peter thinks there might be advantage in having separate tables for those of Greek and Jewish origin; Paul will have none of it. Valens tells Paul that at the feasts in honour of Mithras they make no difference between peoples; 'we are all His children,' says Valens, and goes on when pressed: 'Men make laws, not Gods ... Gods do not make laws. They change men's hearts. The rest is the Spirit' — a saying that Paul excitedly claims as 'the utter Doctrine itself'.

So we have Valens and Paul each claiming the true doctrine and thinking the other has it in a borrowed or perverted form. And this theological exchange is set against a counterpoint between the politico-religious disputes — which have really nothing to do with religion — and the Roman determination to keep the peace; with them it is part of the technique of good government to keep the crowds moving, to steer them homeward at the right moment. Then develops a new theme, the contrast between Paul — voluble, well-educated, highly articulate, utterly dedicated — and Peter. Paul is clear that there can be only one answer to the question of Greek and Jew; no compromise is possible; God has made all men equal in the spirit. But Peter is dumb — a great clumsy man, whose

right hand has withered since he raised it to deny his Master, and
he is still obsessed with the memory of that denial. He is inconsistent, infirm of purpose; he has to be pushed and primed by Paul
until he is brought to the point. Then at last he speaks with a
force Paul cannot match and carries the day.

There is a minor theme, the girl Valens had bought; she does
not have much to say before the finale, but she comes like an
unaccompanied phrase on a flute, a few simple notes that we know
will recur. When Paul is struck down with fever, she brings a
cloak of jackal-skins to warm him and, later, when the Christians
have gone, she asks about Peter. Valens tells her that he believes
he once denied his God.

> She halted in the moonlight, the glossy jackal skins over
> her arm.
> 'Does he? My God bought me from the dealers like a
> horse. Too much, too, he paid. Didn't he? 'Fess, thou?'

She stands for a moment, alive, laughing and adoring; the glossy
jackal-skins in the moonlight bring her sharp to the eye.

Next day was the great meeting when Peter spoke; he won the
day, the Romans gently dispersed the crowds to their homes. Paul
and Peter relaxed, 'now that the day's burden is lifted,' and Valens
asks them to his uncle's house. As they stroll there, an impudent
boy lures the bodyguard away and an assassin runs in to stab
Valens under the ribs. It was the same Cilician whom he had
spared before. As he lies dying, Valens begs his uncle: 'Don't be
too hard on them ... They get worked up ... They don't know
what they are doing ... Promise!' Peter and Paul recognize the
Word from the Cross and Paul suggests that they should baptize
the dying Roman.

> Painfully, that other raised the palsied hand that he had
> once held up ... to deny a charge.
> 'Quiet!' said he. 'Think you that one who has spoken
> Those Words needs such as we are to certify him to any God?'
> Paul cowered before the unknown colleague, vast and
> commanding, revealed after all these years.

In the closing bars, the minor theme is heard again. The girl
has been trying to warm Valens with the furs and with the warmth
of her body. Now 'the brow beneath her lips was chilling, even as

she called on her God who had bought her at a price that he should not die but live.'

All the themes of the story thus meet in the finale. It proclaims as a supreme virtue the forgiveness of wrong, planned and carried out deliberately, but in the same breath it denies that this virtue is exclusively Christian. But, as in the verses 'Cold Iron' and in 'The Gardener', it uses Christian symbols without hesitation.

3. UNTIMELY

If one aspect of Kipling's belief can best be expressed in negative terms, another, its direct counterpart, is positive though just as difficult to put in a single word. He was never a Pelagian; he was on the contrary always a disciple of Bishop Blougram. You will remember that King in *Stalky*—and Crofts in real life—had thrown Browning's *Men and Women* at Kipling's head, and King often addressed Beetle as Master Gigadibs; no doubt the form sniggered at this as a reference to Kipling's nickname of Giglamps or Gigger. But King (or Crofts) meant him to read Browning, and he did. Bishop Blougram is pictured sitting over his wine after dinner—when 'body gets its sop and holds its noise'— rolling out his mind to 'Gigadibs the literary man'. The essence of his long discourse is that man must fit himself to a given world; if, on the contrary, he selects for himself some ideal system of belief or enjoyment and expects the world to conform, he is liable to be sadly disappointed. In one of the many metaphors with which Blougram illustrates the theme, he pictures two men going on a six-months sea-voyage. One knows the cabin is only six feet square and prepares accordingly 'Neat ship-shape fixings and contrivances'. But the other despises so petty an outlook and brings a Correggio, a marble bath and a piano-forte. Of course he can't bring these splendours into the ship and so he has nothing, and later peeps enviously from his bare boards at the other's 'snug and well appointed berth'—but none the less despises him because he hasn't his artist-nature. Gigadibs—who really ought to have been a character in Kipling—is converted, sails for Australia and:

> By this time he has tested his first plough
> And studied his last chapter of St John.

Gigadibs seems unlikely to have made a good settler, and there was no need for him to have been converted to so robust a denial of intellectual interests; Blougram had in fact preached only that a man should find a niche in the world as it is, not as he would have it be. He had not insisted that he must toil with his hands. Kipling, like Gigadibs, sometimes expresses Blougram's doctrine in a crudely muscular form, but he is no more consistent in this than in anything else. It has been said that the verses called 'The Sons of Martha' (1919) contain the essence of Kipling, and they do express one aspect of his Blougramism:

> The Sons of Mary seldom bother, for they have inherited that good part;
> But the Sons of Martha favour their Mother of the careful soul and the troubled heart.
> And because she lost her temper once, and because she was rude to the Lord her Guest,
> Her Sons must wait upon Mary's Sons, world without end, reprieve or rest.
>
> It is their care in all the ages to take the buffet and cushion the shock.
> It is their care that the gear engages; it is their care that the switches lock.
> It is their care that the wheels run truly; it is their care to embark and entrain,
> Tally, transport and deliver duly the Sons of Mary by land and main.

A polished set of verses, certainly — the long and seemingly casual line broken by internal rhyme to mark the caesura — and the message too is characteristic of Kipling. But it would be misleading to suppose that this is the essence of his belief. In his verse even more than in his prose, he was apt to take one idea, one mood, one metaphor, and follow where it led. Here, the sons of Martha become by the end almost entirely manual workers and the sons of Mary their rich employers; it would have been no use cross-examining him to find out whether he would have classed a research worker in pathology or a writer of tales as a son of Martha or of Mary; he would have evaded reply or simply said that was how he felt at the time he wrote the verses.

There is another aspect of Blougramism at which Kipling hints several times. Browning put into Blougram's mouth:

9

Pure faith indeed — you know not what you ask!
Naked belief in God the Omnipotent,
Omniscient, Omnipresent, sears too much
The sense of conscious creatures to be borne ...
... Some think, Creation's meant to show Him forth:
I say, it's meant to hide Him all it can,
And that's what all the blessed evil's for.

Kipling was at one with Blougram on this. His prayer was:

A veil 'twixt us and thee, dread Lord,
A veil 'twixt us and thee ...

Perhaps his most explicit statement of this kind of view comes once again in a conversation with Rider Haggard, quoted by Miss Tompkins:

I [Haggard] told him that I did believe that as a result of much spiritual labour there is born in one a knowledge of the nearness and consolation of God. He replied that occasionally this had happened to him also, but the difficulty was to 'hold' the mystic sense of the communion — that it passes ... Rudyard's explanation is that it is meant to be so; that God does not mean we should get too near lest we should become unfitted for our work in the world.

The gospel of Blougram was something on which he pondered a good deal, and one aspect of it is at the heart of one of his most subtle and complex stories, 'The Eye of Allah' (1926). He had touched before, in 'Marklake Witches' (1910) on the theme of a discovery made before the world was ready for it. In the later story, the dramatic effect is considerably sharpened; the stethoscope of the early story would surely have been hit on by someone else within a few years if its first inventor had perished, but the microscope may well have been kept out of Europe for four centuries by obscurantism. To put the point dramatically was not easy, and in *Something of Myself* Kipling has recorded that again and again this story went dead under his hand. He could not see why, but put it away and waited until his 'Daemon' said to him: 'Treat it as an illuminated manuscript.' What this means in more matter-of-fact terms is that he suddenly perceived that detail would make it live. That is one reason why it is impossible to give the flavour without copious quotation, and impossible by any means to do justice to its full richness.

The central figure is John of Burgos, who is an illuminator of manuscripts. The scene is an English monastery—Benedictine, and we are in the thirteenth century, when there were still large tracts of Spain held by the Moors. John is at work on his Great Luke, which will be his masterpiece. When the story opens, John is about to leave once more for Spain, and the specialists in the various departments of the monastery ask him to get them drugs for the hospital and colours for the scriptorium; Moorish culture is strong in the South of Spain and there is much there that Europe does not know. As he takes his leave, we learn, in hints half spoken, something of his work and something of another reason for going to Spain so often:

> ... the first words of the Magnificat were built up in gold washed with red-lac for a background to the Virgin's hardly yet fired halo. She was shown, hands joined in wonder, at a lattice of infinitely intricate arabesque, round the edges of which sprays of orange-bloom seemed to load the blue hot air that carried back over the minute parched landscape in the middle distance.
>
> 'You've made her all Jewess,' said the Sub-Cantor, studying the olive-flushed cheek and the eyes charged with foreknowledge.
>
> 'What else was Our Lady?'

But it was not only to see that Jewish girl, nor only for colours and drugs, that he went. He wanted devils—for Luke has many scenes of devils dispossessed and John was sick of church devils, who are only 'apes and goats and poultry conjoined'. What kind of devils would they be who came out of Mary Magdalene? She-devils, surely; and the devil who came out of the dumb man would be faceless as a leper.

He was back, twenty months later, with much of what he had been asked to bring. He takes a present to the Abbot's lady, whose sickness nothing seems to cure, and to her he tells that she who had been his model had died in his arms, and the child with her. Later, the Abbot—who is more doctor than monk and had learned wisdom from the Saracens as a prisoner in Cairo after a Crusade—says to John, as they store the new drugs: ' ... for pain of the soul there is, outside God's Grace, but one drug; and that is a man's craft, learning, or other helpful motion of his own mind.'

It was late in the summer that John was asked to dinner by the Abbott, to meet some learned doctors of medicine and to show them some pages from his Great Luke. There is one noted physician from Italy, Roger of Salerno, and a Friar from Oxford, Roger Bacon. Their talk is mostly of medicine and of the obstacles to any true advance which the Church puts in their way. The Infirmarian of the Monastery has come to wonder whether 'certain small animals which the eye cannot follow may not enter the body by the nose and mouth, and set up grave diseases.' But neither reason nor experiment are permitted; the test for everything is whether it is to be found in Scripture. They are on the edge of a wrangle when the Abbot tactfully asks John of Burgos to show them his devils. 'The Magdalene was drawn in palest, almost transparent, grisaille, against a raging, swaying background of woman-faced devils, each broke to and by her special sin, and each, one could see, frenziedly straining against the Power that compelled her.'

They question John and he explains that she is so pale because 'evil has come out of her — she'd take any colour now ... like light through glass'. And the seven devils who had been expelled:

> ... melted into convoluted flower or flame-like bodies, ranging in colour from phosphorescent green to the black purple of outworn iniquity, whose hearts could be traced beating through their substance. But, for sign of hope and the sane workings of life, to be regained, the deep border was of conventionalized spring flowers and birds, all crowned by a kingfisher in haste, atilt through a clump of yellow iris.

Then they turned to the Gadarene swine:

> Here were devils dishoused, in dread of being abolished to the Void, huddling and hurtling together to force lodgment by every opening into the brute bodies offered. Some of the swine fought the invasion, foaming and jerking; some were surrendering to it, sleepily, as to a luxurious back-scratching; others wholly possessed, whirled off in bucking droves for the lake beneath. In one corner the freed man stretched out his limbs all restored to his control, and Our Lord, seated, looked at him as questioning what he would make of his deliverance ...

This is the general scene. But they look more closely at the beings dishoused from the man possessed and see:

Some devils were mere lumps, with lobes and protuberances—a hint of a fiend's face peering through jelly-like walls. And there was a family of impatient, globular devillings who had burst open the belly of their smirking parent, and were revolving desperately toward their prey. Others patterned themselves into rods, chains and ladders, single or conjoined, round the throat and jaws of a shrieking sow, from whose ear emerged the lashing, glassy tail of a devil that had made good his refuge. And there were granulated and conglomerate devils, mixed up with the foam and slaver where the attack was fiercest. Thence the eye carried on to the insanely active backs of the downward-racing swine, the swincherd's aghast face, and his dog's terror.

The border to the picture was hardly less strange:

... a diaper of irregular but balanced compartments or cellules, where sat, swam or weltered, devils in blank, so to say—things as yet uninspired by Evil—indifferent, but lawlessly outside imagination. Their shapes resembled, again, ladders, chains, scourges, diamonds, aborted buds, or gravid phosphorescent globes—some well-nigh starlike.

These could only have been seen under the influence of drugs, says one of the doctors, but the Infirmarian of the monastery remembers that John had once shown him a snow-flake through a crystal that made things seem larger. Could it be that he had actually seen such shapes as these? John admits it and shows them a simple microscope, like a compass for drawing circles, with a lens on one arm, a screw to adjust the distance, and a mirror to reflect light on the object. All he needs is a drop of rainwater from the roof, so they go on to the leads and he shows them a new world in a drop of water. Roger of Salerno and Roger Bacon cry out at the possibilities of research, experiment and discovery; such creatures as they see in the water must rage in the blood too. The Infirmarian falls on his knees to thank God that his dream of little creatures was not a presumptuous sin but the truth. But the Abbot—though as you remember he was more doctor than monk and though his own Lady is dying of cancer—sees further than the others. He had seen such a device—the Eye of Allah they called it—among the Saracens when he was a prisoner in Cairo. 'It was shown to me' he said 'in Cairo, that man stands ever between two Infinities—of greatness and littleness. Therefore, there is no end—either to life—or—' but at this point he is interrupted. The doctors break out again into speculation about the possibilities, but at last the Abbot quiets them, resuming the ring that is the sign of his authority. He tells them how men will see it; John, they will say, comes back from the Moors and shows 'a hell of devils contending in the compass of one drop of water. Magic past clearance! You can hear the faggots crackle.' He, too, he says, had dreamed like the Infirmarian, but with fuller knowledge, and he had put the dream away. 'This birth, my sons, is untimely. It will be but the mother of more death, more torture, more division and greater darkness in this dark age.' 'The choice,' he says, 'lies between two sins. To deny the world a Light which is under our hand, or to enlighten the world before her time.' He takes the device from John and destroys it, taking on his conscience the Choice.

As prelude to this story is printed a short poem of fourteen lines, 'Untimely'. It does not conform to the conventional shape of a sonnet, the rhymes being arranged in a scheme so complex and unusual that they may escape notice at first reading, and the beats to a line being varied. In a sense it is a sonnet reversed, the opening theme being stated in six lines instead of eight, while a second theme comes in a central section of five lines and the third theme is expressed in a longer metre in the last three lines. It states the main theme of 'The Eye of Allah' and it should be read in full, preferably aloud, slowly and with a heavy beat. It ends:

> Heaven delivers on earth the Hour that cannot be thwarted,
> Neither advanced, at the price of a world or a soul, and its
>   Prophet
> Comes through the blood of the vanguards who dreamed—
>   too soon—it had sounded.

But that, though it is the main theme, is only one of many in a story that is in danger of being too rich. There is also a variation on the most frequent of all Kipling themes—man going on with his craft or art or duty against the background of death and personal sorrow, both for the artist John and for the Abbot. And for almost everyone in the story there is a conflict between the single-hearted pursuit of his special craft and the pressures of the world, or the church, or both. There is the parallel between devilkins and animalcula, possession by evil and disease – and no one who has read the Kipling stories about shell-shock and breaking-strain could fail to link these with the demoniac possession of Luke. But sanity and healing run through the story like the kingfisher atilt through the irises and the freed man stretching his limbs; there is a vision from the roof of the Abbey of: 'three English counties laid out in evening sunshine around them; church upon church, monastery upon monastery ... and the bulk of a vast cathedral moored on the edge of the banked shoals of sunset.' There is the sound of choir practice in the Abbey church coming up to the dinner guests as they walk along the triforium; there is the Abbott's dining-room, when they come back to find that the 'fire had been comforted and the dates, raisins, ginger, figs, and cinnamon-scented sweetmeats set out, with the choicer wines, on the after-table.' For all the doubts and stress and pain, it is a world in which man can make his cabin snug.

But Blougram, though he had made himself as comfortable as he could, had not been complacent. He had asked whether anyone could make up his mind to be wholly and consistently materialist. Such a man might try to banish the unknown, but:

> Just when we are safest, there's a sunset touch,
> A fancy from a flower-bell, someone's death,
> A chorus-ending from Euripides ...

and rigid disbelief is shaken again by doubt. The Abbot knew that man was poised between two infinities, the unseeably tiny and the immensities of space, and when he was interrupted he was going on to the parallel thought of man's life on earth poised between two infinities in the future and the past: 'A stone's throw out on either hand ... '

With all this richness, the central message is simple and it is pure Blougramism. If the world is not yet ready for a truth or a discovery, it may be better to jettison the discovery than to try to change a world that is far too big and complicated for one man to alter. No Correggio should be marked: 'Wanted on the Voyage'.

He had made a similar point, not so fully developed, long ago in the early middle period, in a story called: 'A Matter of Fact' (1893): 'Truth is a naked lady, and if by accident she is drawn up from the bottom of the sea, it behoves a gentleman either to give

her a print petticoat or to turn his face to the wall and vow that
he did not see.'

4. A VISION OF HEAVEN

Picture, then, Rudyard Kipling in his sixties, often in pain, eating
sparely because of his pain, essentially lonely, firmly opposed to
any easy optimism that denies the reality of death, defeat, and
evil, determined—as a counter to that recognition—to live the
rest of his life as best he could in the world of things as they are.
He and his wife planned together their journeys in search of sunshine—but while Rudyard was advised to try sea voyages, she
found the sea exhausting. The rheumatism which caused her such
pain was to some extent relieved at spas, and they went to Vernet-
les-Bains and Bath. Her eyesight also began to fail, and it was
found that she was diabetic. There was no one at home to look
after her, but with indomitable courage she continued to look
after Rudyard when she could. Twice they went to Egypt for
warmth, and in 1930 they went to the West Indies, where Carrie
went down with appendicitis. He would not take her to New
York, where the memories would kill her; he had to arrange for a
journey to England by way of Canada.

In these last years, travel 'nearly always ended in illness for one
of them,' Carrington notes, 'since the changes of diet—on motor
tours which he so much enjoyed—usually upset his digestion.'
He had loved France. Something in him responded to the French
spirit, and in 1913 he had written:

> Broke to every known mischance, lifted over all
> By the light sane joy of life, the buckler of the Gaul;
> Furious in luxury, merciless in toil,
> Terrible with strength renewed from her tireless soil;
> Strictest judge of her own worth, gentlest of man's mind,
> First to face the Truth and last to leave old Truths behind—
> France, beloved of every soul that loves or serves its kind!

Some might question the judgment that France is the 'strictest
judge of her own worth' but in the middle period it had not been
Kipling's way to understate his case, particularly in verse, and the
French spirit appealed to him because it was not Pelagian, because
it was firmly Blougramist, and because (in spite of superficial
logic) it was 'in touch with the deepest layers of human conscious-

ness' in much the same way as Maurois had said that Kipling was. And with that intellectual assent went an almost physical delight in travel in France, which is expressed in the 'Song of Seventy Horses', companion verses to 'The Miracle of St Jubanus' (1932). 'Once again,' it begins, 'the Steamer at Calais', and it pictures the car, with its seventy horses, being unloaded and driven away — and wherever it goes, to whatever region of France:

> 'It is enough — it is France!'

> Whether the broken, honey-hued, honey-combed limestone
> Cream under white-hot sun; the rosemary bee-bloom
> Sleepily noisy at noon and, somewhere to Southward,
> Sleepily noisy, the Sea.
> (Yes, it is warm here, my horses!) It is enough — it is France!

These pleasures became rare and difficult to arrange. That is the lot of many elderly folk, but it must be supposed that this was an influence that turned his thoughts more and more in the direction they were taking in his later years. One more 'lateral escape from the self' was closing down. They were both often ill, they were both often in pain. Even if, as I think, there were areas of Rudyard's thought and feeling which were never discussed between them, even if in these matters he felt increasingly lonely, one may picture on another level a tenderness arising from shared sorrow and shared experience and from the knowledge of the other's pain.

However that may be, his thoughts turned increasingly to death and to the survival of the spirit. There are two late stories which go together and both explicitly picture a future life. They might be called a Vision of Heaven and a Vision of Hell. They are not, of course, for a moment to be regarded as describing what Kipling seriously supposed a future life would be like. Indeed, the earlier 'On the Gate' — published in 1926 but subheaded 'A Tale of '16' — begins as a kind of bitter joke. Can the normal arrangements at Heaven's Gate possibly cope with the sudden influx of souls wrenched from their bodies in War? There will have to be temporary staff who don't know the rules — won't they relax their standards a bit, just like temporary civil servants on earth? On that basic idea, Kipling erects a gloriously comic structure in which the traditional hierarchy of Heaven — Archangels, Saints, Seraphim, Powers, Dominions and Thrones, complete with wings and haloes — are set against a background of dockets,

9*

typewriters and forms in triplicate, and display the departmental jealousies, the anxiety about precedent and rule, that we have learnt to expect in Whitehall. But behind the comedy—which to me is funny while 'My Sunday at Home' is not—runs something very different, a sense of the agony men and women are enduring and a commitment on the part of St Peter—who here represents the Headmaster, never seen or mentioned—to cut across rules and extend mercy. Peter, incidentally, is not much like the Peter of 'The Church at Antioch'.

The opening is gravely ironic. Life has been so much prolonged by scientific means that there is normally good warning before death occurs. Heaven is consequently in a state of unreadiness for War and we meet Death, complaining of the inefficiency of temporary staff to St Peter, who with all the help he can get is on the Gate twenty-two hours of the twenty-four. But their talk is interrupted by 'a prim-lipped Seraph' with an expulsion-form for signature. It is for a man who *will* keep on saying there is no God. 'Pass him in at once! Tell off someone to argue with him … ' is Peter's instant reaction. Then there is a hospital-nurse whose war service is excellent but whose civilian record is contained in a 'vivid scarlet docket'. Peter—who must have been very trying to his subordinates—marks it Q.M.A., which is not a department but a ruling and stands for *Quia Multum Amavit*. 'A most useful ruling. I've stretched it to … ' The phrase dies away unfinished—a characteristic of Kipling's conversations from his earliest days; it is the way people do talk and it sets the reader's imagination to work. Then Peter finds that she had died of 'Heart-failure after neglected pleurisy following overwork.' 'Good!' St Peter rubbed his hands. 'That brings her under the higher allowance—G.L.H. scale—'Greater love hath no man—'

Death invites Peter to join him in an inter-departmental inspection and he leaves the Gate in charge of the Seraph, with a Board of Admission which includes St Christopher, who, 'of course, will pass anything that looks wet and muddy.' And Peter adds to the seraph: ' … oh, my child, *you* don't know what it is to need forgiveness. Be gentle with 'em—be very gentle with 'em!'

'Swiftly as a falling shaft of light the Seraph kissed the sandalled feet and was away.'

Read that quickly, as I did at first, and you will miss an implication, which Kipling would have refused to call theological, but which does, none the less, open vistas of enormous theological significance. Peter has been human, he has been tempted, he has failed through lack of courage and has redeemed himself. The Seraph, created stainless, ranks lower in the hierarchy. He kisses the sandalled feet—though he has no need of sandals himself. Heaven needs human beings for the officer ranks—and this implies a good deal about the nature of the commanding officer. Peter and Mary Magdalene and even Judas are very important to Kipling—and this implies a complete farewell to Parlour Buddhism or the one red-hot affirmation of Islam, in which repentant sinners do not hold so important a place.

Death and St Peter walk over to the office of Normal Civil Death; the head of it is a pompous civil servant who is at first graciously condescending to his two visitors, but when asked how his office is working becomes at once the Departmental Head with a grievance. ' "Thanks to this abominable war," he began testily,' his department 'had to spend all its time fighting for mere existence.' There is a woman dying in Worcestershire in whom 'We' are all interested, but her record is in the basement, which is 'given up to people over whom We exercise no departmental control.' He regards 'this recent outbreak of unregulated mortality' as an irritating irrelevance. It is with relief that Death and St Peter escape from him to listen to the chatter of the clerks in the outer office, editing dying speeches to suit the conventional outlook of their chief. One who shows a touch of originality proves on questioning to be a volunteer who 'had slipped in from the Lower Establishment' and, sure enough, when encouraged to shake off the conventional uniform of the department, there he stood, 'an unmistakable, curly-haired, bat-winged, faun-eared Imp of the Pit'. But 'where his wings joined his shoulders, there was a patch of delicate dove-coloured feathering that gave promise to spread all up the pinion—'so they gave him a chance and later he is sent to Earth on a difficult mission. He is so eager to prove himself that, 'scarcely pausing to salute, he poised and dived, and the papers on the desk spun beneath the draught of his furious vans'.

It is hardly a story. The centre of it is a succession of cases, linked only by Heaven's desire to cut through the red tape and save the individual, by the brilliance of the décor and by such phrases as: 'The waiting Seraphs stiffened to attention with a click of tense quills.' But it rises to a climax with the last case, a very bad one. They are waiting, listening to the S.O.S. signals, 'sparking furiously' on a recorder. The signals stop 'with an emphatic thump' and a Love in Armour whispers to Peter that it is a firing-party—he is deserter, spy and murderer. Peter gathers his robes about him and makes for the Gate to meet him.

Here convoys are arriving from France and, on the great plain beyond the Gate, the Lower Establishment are out in force. It is like Victoria station in the war—voluble and insinuating spirits try to lure the soldiers to all kinds of disreputable destinations while the Heavenly pickets try to edge or persuade them towards the Gate. Perhaps the best of Heaven's pickets is Judas, worming through the crowd like an Armenian carpet-seller or a peddler of postcards at Port Said: 'Yes', he would cry, 'I am everything they say, but if I'm here it must be a moral cert for you, gents. This way, please. Many mansions, gentlemen! Goo-ood billets! Don't you notice these low people, Sar!'

At last, the murderer, spy and deserter who had faced the firing-party is there. It had been everyone else's fault, not his, and everyone had always been against him. Even St Peter can at first think of no ruling under which he can be given hope until some-one suggests a verse from the Second Book of Samuel, the four-teenth chapter and the fourteenth verse, which reads: 'For we must needs die and are as water spilt on the ground, which cannot be gathered up again: neither doth God respect any person: yet doth he devise means, that his banished be not expelled from him.'

Peter accepts this as covering the case and scribbles an order on his pass; he is marched off by an escort to the Lower Establish-ment where: 'You'll have a thin time of it but they won't keep you a day longer than I've put down.' The pickets and the convoy march off for the Gate, and:

> the Saint and Death stayed behind to rest awhile. It was a heavenly evening. They could hear the whistle of the low-flighting Cherubim, clear and sharp, under the diviner note of some released Seraph's wings, where, his errand accomp-lished, he plunged three or four stars deep into the cool Baths of Hercules; the steady dynamo-like hum of the nearer planets on their axes; and, as the hush deepened, the surprised little sigh of some new-born sun, a universe of universes away.

It is certainly a more amusing heaven than that revealed to John on Patmos and if, as I have said, it is not exactly a story, 'On the Gate' has many engaging touches. The prim-lipped Seraph who bothers Peter at the beginning is, says Peter: 'The usual type nowadays ... A young Power in charge of some half-baked Universe. Never having dealt with life yet, he's somewhat nebulous.' And there is an old lady 'firmly clutching a mottle-nosed, middle-aged Major by the belt ... in that terrible mother-grip no Power has yet been able to unlock.' Peter lets him in under the ruling known departmentally as I.W. — the Importunate Widow. I think there are rather too many distinguished figures among the pickets — Joan of Arc, John Bunyan, Bradlaugh (famous in Victoria's reign for his avowed atheism) and Shakespeare, who reminds Peter of the ruling in Samuel. In the references to some of these people, there is a hint of that note so familiar in the early stories: 'See how clever I am! Are you clever enough to understand me?' And of course it is an absurdity — even within the terms of the fable — that the Peter here depicted should not have that verse from Samuel at his fingertips, since he could stretch it to cover everything. I cannot claim that 'On the Gate' is artistically of anything like the quality of 'The Gardener'. But it is funny and I do find phrases in it heart-shaking with that sudden quality of freshness that is special to Kipling. Few stories show more clearly his development towards tolerance and understanding; consider with what rancour such a character as Normal Civil Death would have been portrayed in the worst of the middle period, whereas here he is regarded with tolerant amusement. And the tale is central to an understanding of Kipling's beliefs, which are not so far different from those he had stated to Caroline Taylor. Man is responsible for his acts — but Compassion is infinite and Mercy is incomprehensible but vast. Even more important, to have been tempted and to have failed and to have recovered puts the Saint above the Seraph and suggests some meaning in life and pain even, perhaps, Heaven's need for man's co-operation. Also, it introduces a set of verses which I find one of his most complete achievements in that particular vein. It uses the language of the Psalms in the Authorized Version and expresses Kipling's Blougramism more completely than 'The Sons of Martha' because it adds a sense of wonder and awe. The pause in the long line is stamped home by an internal rhyme, which I think should be emphasized. 'The Supports' should be read in full, but let us recall some fragments. It is sub-titled: 'The Song of the Waiting Seraphs', and opens with the full Chorus. Other verses are sung separately by specialized bands of Seraphs. The Services and Loves sing:

> Heart may fail and strength outwear, and Purpose turn
>   to Loathing,
> But the everyday affair of business, meals, and clothing,
> Builds a bulkhead 'twixt Despair and the Edge of Nothing.

Before the final full Chorus, the Services, Patiences, Faiths, Hopes and Loves sing:

> He Who used the clay that clings on our boots to make us,
> Shall not suffer earthly things to remove or shake us ...

And finally the full chorus — with every stop out, the full orchestration, every head flung back:

> For He Who makes the Mountains smoke and rives the
>   Hills asunder
>   And, to-morrow, leads the grass —
>   Mere unconquerable grass —
> Where the fuming crater was, to heal and hide it under,
>   He shall not — He shall not —
> Shall not lay on us the yoke of too long Fear and Wonder!

5. DISMISSED TO THE MERCY

'Uncovenanted Mercies' is the last tale in the last published collection, and I have no doubt that it is placed there deliberately. In one sense, it is more of a story than 'On the Gate', since its main concern is with two human beings, but it is darker and twistier by a good deal than 'On the Gate'. The background is similar. Again, we are in supernatural regions — this time more often in Hell than in Heaven — which are run by a hierarchy of Celestial Beings on departmental lines. Most of the story is conveyed through a colloquy between Gabriel, who is in charge of all Guardian Spirits, Azrael the Angel of Death, and Satan, who is a member of the Hierarchy, on equal terms with his colleagues, wearing a halo as they do. He is the Satan of the Book of Job, not of *Paradise Lost*, a servant of the Mercy, whose task it is to test men and prove them. It is one part of his duties to recondition human souls for re-issue as Guardian Spirits, and this is an essential part of the story. He has to work closely with Gabriel, but complains that everything comes back to him in the end. Azrael's part in the discussion is less; his function, he says, is purely executive; he gets his orders to Dismiss to the Mercy and carries them out.

There is not much to laugh at in this story except the Archangel of the English, who is more English than his people, a civil servant of a different kind from Normal Civil Death, vaguely optimistic, a believer in progress, like the broadest-minded of Broad Church bishops, a rank Pelagian, suggesting—hands joined 'across a stomach that insisted a little'—that, now that his People's standards of living have risen, Azrael should make death a little less coarse, or, as he puts it: 'mitigate the crudity of certain vital phenomena ... ' He believes that 'unhappy people can't make other people happy, can they? ... ' and he wants to give the two people with whom the story is concerned 'full advantages for self-expression and realization' which will include 'impeccable surroundings, wealth, culture, felicity'. But the others do not think that cosseting gets the best out of people and Azrael says he has seen wonderful work done, 'with my sword practically at their throats'. Eventually, the other three make their excuses and leave the Archangel with relief, launching 'into the Void that lay flush with the Office windows'.

But the story itself is sombre. There are two human beings, a man and a woman, on whose foreheads are written Orders for Life, which are identical except for the names: 'If So-and-So shall meet So-and-So, their state at the last shall be such as even Evil itself shall pity.' Now by an error in Gabriel's department, these two have been allotted as Guardian Spirits two reconditioned and re-issued souls who on earth had met and loved—and suffered in Hell for their love. And—by pure chance, the Guardian Spirits say—the two do meet, under the clock at a great London railway terminus which is never named. It was here that their Guardian Spirits too had first met when they were on earth. From that moment on, the sequence of events is obscure, which is perhaps natural since we are moving in and out of time and infinity. But the two humans appear to have met with some worldly success— as the Archangel of the English had intended. The woman wore tiaras and diamonds, the man orders and decorations; they went to the opera. But the Archangel found them disappointing and ceased to take interest in them. At that stage, it appears that Satan took over and that for some years the man was tested as Job had been; he was poor and ashamed, living on charity, suffering from an incurable disease. He was down and out—and 'in *our* humble judgment', Satan reported to the other two, 'his last five years' realization-output was worth all his constructive efforts.' We hear less of the woman, but eventually both 'were filed', which is the departmental way of saying 'died'. Both are in Satan's hands; she has been in one of his shops, on test for breaking-strain, and at the moment of the story's main action, the man too is about to undergo a final test.

Satan brings Gabriel and Azrael to a replica of that London railway terminal where the two couples in turn had met. Hell had long ago given up that old motto about abandoning hope; hope deferred, they found, was the most potent torment of all. It was effective too to let people think they were escaping. Hell's terminus was just like the one in London, 'as it would appear to men and women at the end of a hot, stale, sticky petrol-scented summer afternoon under summer-time — twenty past six o'clock standing for twenty past seven.' Here the most faithful of those who have promised to meet in eternity wait endlessly for each other; train after train rolls in but the beloved is never on it. The Three see the man for whom they are looking, down at heel, disreputable, blurred of speech; they see him handed a telegram that makes him collapse into unconsciousness; they follow him to a first-aid room, 'with a porcelain wash-stand beneath the glass shelf of bottles, its oxygen cylinders tucked under the leatherette couch, and its heart-lowering smell of spent anaesthetics.' A doctor brings him round and tells him that, if he will give permission, memory can be taken away and he will be saved that much pain. But he will not give the authority and the doctor's face lights up; he has passed the test. He is sent away; the Three wait and their waiting is very terrible because it shares in the terrible waiting of Hell. They waited:

> till the agony of waiting that shuffled and mumbled outside crept in and laid hold; dimming, first the lustre of their pinions; bowing, next, their shoulders as the motes in the never-shifted sunbeam filtered through it and settled on them, masking, finally, the radiance of Robe, Sword and very Halo, till only their eyes had light.
>
> The groan broke first from Azrael's lips. 'How long?' he muttered. 'How long?' But Satan sat dumb and hooded under cover of his wings.

At last the woman too comes, accompanied by a nurse. She is

hysterical, but the nurse calms her and shows the Three the Order for Life written on her brow. Then the nurse, looking Satan straight in the eyes, commands him to go. And the Three are ignominiously turned out, just as the man comes back and the woman greets him: 'What does it matter now, dear?' Of the Three, two are a little ruffled, Satan 'somewhat apologetic'. Their expulsion was his invention, he said—'But, my Brothers'—the Prince of Darkness smiled—'did you *really* think that we were needed there much longer?'

I cannot pretend to understand with certainty the last two or three pages of this story. The doctor was the Guardian Spirit of the man, acting also as inquisitor under Satan's authority; the nurse was the woman's Guardian Spirit. Satan has clearly felt pity, as their Orders for Life foretold, and has apparently agreed that, now that both have passed the test for breaking strain, they shall meet—but for how long? It is Azrael's task to dismiss to the Mercy and also to separate the Spirit from the Flesh, and at first one is inclined to think both these phrases refer to the same event, namely, what on earth is known as death. But Azrael says just before the end of the story that he has orders to dismiss to the Mercy, and already both these two have been 'filed' for some time. One begins to suspect that 'dismissing to the Mercy' is a final stage, when the soul has been winnowed and tried long enough in the fires of Purgatory. But it is probably as much a mistake to try to build a rational theology on this vision as on that other at Patmos. It is a glimpse of certain truths, and what comes through clearly is the reality of suffering and death, a faith in the power of the human spirit to profit by pain, a faith in ultimate, if very distant and often incomprehensible Mercy.

There is a moment when the Three first leave the Archangel of the English and decide to visit Satan:

> The Three nose-dived at that point where Infinity returns upon itself, till they folded their wings beneath the foundations of Time and Space, whose double weight bore down on them through the absolute Zeroes of Night and Silence … The glare of the halo [Satan] wore in His Own Place fought against the Horror of Great Darkness.
>
> 'Have we gone beyond the Mercy?' Azrael whispered, appalled at the little light it won.

They had not.

PART THREE
Retribution and Compassion

II

Pain and Love

I. THE LAST PERIOD

Kipling's last period, that is from the First World War till his death in 1936, is one whole, whether one is thinking of his life or his writings. There were few external events that he himself thought important; all that happened was within. His daughter wrote that when she married and went away in 1924, 'something like despair filled him as he looked forward to life at Bateman's without his only remaining child.' He continued to refuse all official honours — not only the Laureateship or any title but also the Companionship of Honour and the Order of Merit, twice offered; even membership of the British Academy. He went, dutifully, to receive doctorates from universities and seems to have been pleased by French degrees, particularly at the Sorbonne; he did not refuse when he was elected to the Institut de France. His popularity with his public continued; his books sold and many of his readers were devotees. He dealt every day with that voluminous mail — or at least as much of it as his wife thought he should see, for example letters from young writers to whom he was unfailingly kind. Letters and telegrams rose to a peak on his birthday. But his attitude was that which he had expressed to Rider Haggard: 'What is it all worth?' It was a weariness of the flesh. The zest had gone. 'When my mother thought he needed a new suit, he went obediently to his tailor,' wrote his daughter — and that somehow expresses the external part of his life.

But his mind was active. This was not true of the surface of his mind, those parts which were concerned with politics; they really did not move, except further to the right. In his middle period, he had perceived, with prophetic insight, that a turning-point had been reached, perhaps with the Liberal Government of 1906, which meant extreme danger to all he valued, a long slow-moving process of social change towards a society far more permissive, more merciful perhaps, but far less convinced that man is responsible for his actions and must fight for his independence — a process by no means complete forty years after his death. But though he rightly saw this, as few of his contemporaries did, his remedy was not to guide change but to hold on grimly to everything, just as it was. He particularly deplored any loosening of imperial ties — and if he had had his way Britain would have been faced after the Second World War with the kind of situation France faced in Indo-China and Algeria. His cousin Stanley

Baldwin, he said, was a socialist at heart, and the language Kipling used of some of Baldwin's colleagues in the Coalition Government was (says Carrington) unprintable.

It was beneath the surface that his mind was working, and on lines that might not have been expected. We have seen it in the stories looked at in the last two chapters, but it comes out also in odd remarks that have been preserved by Carrington. 'He said he would not be surprised if in a few years the monastic life was revived—men were seeking relief from the burdens of a hard world and turning more and more to spiritual matters.' He wrote to a friend, a little before his seventieth birthday: 'You have my acutest sympathy over what you call the "nuisance" of growing old. A train has to stop at some station or other. I only wish it wasn't such an ugly and lonesome place, don't you?' But on the actual birthday, he wrote to Edith Macdonald, his mother's only surviving sister, thanking her affectionately for her birthday letter to him and adding: 'He who put us into this life does not abandon His work for *any* reason or default at the end of it. That is all I have come to learn out of my life. So there is *no* fear.' It was only three weeks later, on January 18th, 1936, that he died.

Mention has already been made of that early cartoon of Max Beerbohm's which shows Kipling out for the day with his girl, Britannia. There is enough truth in that to be funny; he *had* shouted about patriotism, committing just the offence which Stalky found so distasteful in the jelly-bellied flag-flapper. There is also a much later Beerbohm cartoon in which the aged Kipling sits propped up in a doctor's gown, wreathed with laurels, his hand resting on the globe—a grey stuffed lay-figure—confronted by the young Kipling in a white tropical suit—brash, vulgar, vigorous—hissing with a prurient grin: 'I say! Have you heard the latest about Mrs Hauksbee?' That seems to me more cruel than the other and to have so little truth as not to be funny. It is meant, I suppose, to indicate that the young Kipling, distasteful though Beerbohm found him, at least had vigour, while the old Kipling was interested in nothing but his past success and the outward signs of it. And this is the opposite of the truth. He was not very interested in the signs of success; his mind was far from stagnant and he was doing his best work.

Debits and Credits (1926) must stand at the head of the collections; it contains five out of the eight stories I regard as in the first flight—'The Bull that Thought' and 'The Eye of Allah' as well as the three to be dealt with later in this chapter—not to mention 'The Janeites' and 'On the Gate'. *Limits and Renewals* (1932), the last collection, starts with the superb 'Dayspring', ends with 'Uncovenanted Mercies', and includes the two stories about St Paul as well as 'Unprofessional' and 'The Tender Achilles'. There are trivialities from an earlier period, but it is impossible to say that creative force has run out. Nor can one divide the late period and trace the growth of his ideas chronologically. This is partly owing to Kipling's habit of keeping stories by him for years, partly to the intuitive habit of his mind, which advanced by feeling rather than by reasoning. He did not always himself recognize the conclusions he had reached. He saw, heard and smelt life rather than sitting down to think about it. But during this last period of his life, though not at any precisely recognizable moment, he did go beyond the convictions about man's place in the universe which have, I hope, emerged from what has been said already, and go to something more positive, which it is the purpose of this chapter to illustrate by three stories.

2. THE BRUTALITY OF ART

The three stories which I mean to look at in this, the last chapter of evidence, are I think the best, and are certainly to me the most moving. They are a long step from the vision of archangels and seraphim we have just left, the flights from universe to universe through frozen space; they concern two or three central figures and in each there is an intense and all-demanding love, which brings with it much pain. Explicitly in 'The Wish House', pain is deliberately accepted by the lover in order to save the beloved from pain; implicitly in 'A Madonna' and 'The Gardener', pain is accepted as inseparable from this particular love and I think it is regarded as enriching it.

It so happens that the stories I have chosen as the best of the late Kipling all include elements of what is commonly called the supernatural—things not to be explained in terms of material truth. That is not why they are chosen; I choose them because I find them moving. The 'supernatural' element is in part equipment for making an artistic point and to me is no more a hindrance than the ghost in Hamlet or the appearance of Artemis or Aphrodite in a play by Euripides. But that is not the whole story. Kipling had always thought a great deal about death; his time in

India had forced it upon him. He had been young then, and for the young, death is something that happens to other people. As he grew old, and as pain became more and more part of his life, Kipling thought more and more often of death as something that would happen to himself. He was vividly conscious of something in himself that appeared to be separable from the body; he wrote several times of floating away from the body and looking down on it. And, though he firmly rejected 'spiritualism' as it was understood and practised in the 'twenties, he supposed there would be some continuance of the individual spirit after death. He was never a man for definitions, and in this life he was not sure where the boundary lay.

There are two late stories of high quality on which I do not propose to spend long. 'The Bull that Thought' is superb entertainment. It is about a bull endowed with almost human intelligence and supreme artistry in the one art open to him – the art of which the other half is that of the matador, who with graceful judgment of the exact inch and second must draw the bull's deadly horns as close to his body as he can. But imagine a bull who sees through the device of the cloak and can read the mind of the man, who takes the initiative from the man and holds it! Apis is an artist of top rank, a Michelangelo, a Beethoven among bulls; he understands what he is doing and knows that an audience demands variety. He is also a humourist, and a murderer of any bull who presumes to be a rival, but a fastidious murderer who cleans his horns in the earth after disembowelling his victim. When he goes into a Spanish bull-ring, he kills several men and horses before at last he makes his triumphal exit as no bull has ever done before – the idol of the crowd! You can read it as a bull-fighting story with a difference, and be carried along to the crescendo of excitement when Apis puts on his final stupendous act with a matador with whom he has reached an understanding. And there can be no doubt also that you are meant to go further than this; the references to the artistry are explicit and deliberate. Apis displays: 'a breadth of technique that comes of reasoned art and, above all, the passion that arrives after experience'; he studies the troupe of bull-fighters 'with the gravity of an equal in intellect and the remote and merciless resolution of a master in his art'. In the final scene, he 'despaired in statuesque abandon and thence flashed into fresh paroxysms of wrath – but always with the detachment of the true artist who knows he is but the vessel of an emotion whence others, not he, must drink.' The story is a superb display of technique as a writer; it is also saying something about art—that the artist must be ruthless, that he may have to be cruel, that he is born but must perfect his technique by labour, that he must have passion and inspiration. But I think the symbolism can be pursued too far; I am not convinced that symbolic importance should be attached to the champagne in the story nor to the motor-car—as some have suggested—and, if the artist must be ruthless about his time and about the demands made on him by other people, it is surely seldom that he need hook anyone under the heart and toss him to the barrier. Apis was a little extreme. The manner of the telling persuades me that the story is not to be taken too seriously. It is primarily entertainment.

The other story on which I do not propose to dwell is 'The Janeites', though it has been much admired. More perhaps than any other, it illustrates Kipling's passion for belonging to a group from which others are excluded. It begins in a Masonic Lodge; this is the first secret society. Once we are inside this, the talk flows on and we are aware of a second fellowship of men who have been through the war; within that again is a third inner lodge, of which the passwords are taken from the works of Jane Austen. The scene of the story proper, the inner story, is a battery in France; the enemy are searching for it with their heavy guns. The officers and the servants in the mess take their minds off what is likely to happen by making a parlour game of these quotations. Personally, I am irritated by the characters' habit of referring to Miss Austen as though she were a popular barmaid. And this third or inmost secret society is trivial compared with the second. It takes on a life of its own, and the light facetious note does not accentuate the horror—as it might—but jars with it when the enemy's shells do at last find the battery.

But let us turn to the three I have chosen. The first is 'A Madonna of the Trenches'.

3. IF THE DEAD RISE NOT ...

Once again the opening scene is a Masonic Lodge, one that has made a special point of welcoming men who have been in France; it has had much experience of shock and lost memory. A young visitor from a Lodge in South London suddenly gives way to hysteria and rushes out of a ceremony. He is closely followed by

Keede, who is both an official of the Lodge and a doctor, and by the narrator. These two take the hysterical youngster into a side-room, where Keede gives him sal volatile and talks to him. It happened that Keede had been medical officer to the battalion in which this boy, Strangwick, had been a messenger, and he had had him in his hands before. He had never been satisfied that he had got to the bottom of Strangwick's trouble; something had pushed him past the breaking-point but Keede had been convinced that he was lying about what it had been—though the reason he gave was gruesome enough to disturb anyone. There was a section of the line taken over from the French where the dead had been used to face the trench and keep the mud back. When you walked along that trench in frosty weather the corpses creaked. That, said Strangwick, was what was on his mind. But Keede did not believe him.

Keede gave him a dose of another drug and went on talking about that stretch of trench—Butcher's Row, they had called it—and he brought in to the talk an elderly platoon sergeant. Godsoe was his name, an excellent platoon sergeant and the last man you'd expect to be careless; he had died just when he was due to go on leave. He had gone into a dug-out in Butcher's Row before he started on his leave, perhaps to warm himself; he didn't turn up for the leave party and was found next day between two braziers of burnt-out charcoal; the door of the dug-out must have swung to. And three days after that, on January 24th, 1918—it was Strangwick who remembered the date—he was brought to Keede 'clean out of his head'. He went on about the corpses in Butcher's Row but there was something else on his mind. Now at last, two years later, relaxed by the drug and under Keede's pressure, he begins to say what it was.

Godsoe was a friend of the family. Strangwick and his sister called him Uncle John, but he was not really a relation, just a close friend of the family. Dad and Ma, and Ma's sister Auntie Armine and her husband, and Uncle John and his wife had always been friends; the children had been in and out of their houses like rabbits. Uncle John was a retired sergeant, too old really for the army, but he had managed to get back. He had got Strangwick into his platoon and wrote to his mother about him; his mother's eyes had gone bad and she couldn't read so Auntie Armine came round to read the letters. Bella was her real name but they called her by her surname because it seemed to suit her;

she seemed like something slow-moving and in armour. She'd
nursed them through measles, they knew all about her. No one
had ever suspected anything. And then this!

Strangwick had been on leave for Christmas and when he went
to say good-bye to his aunt she had given him a message for his
Uncle John. She expected to be through with her little trouble by
the 21st of January and she'd be dying to see him as soon as
possible after that. She insisted on the exact words and wrote
them down. He thought nothing of it and gave the message.
When he read it, Uncle John looked different all of a sudden, as
though he'd been shaved. He said it suited him; his leave began
on the 21st. Strangwick forgot this till the 21st, when it was his
duty to go round and tell the men who were going on leave. He
went down Butcher's Row— it was no longer in use—and for a
moment thought he saw Auntie Armine by the entrance to the
dug-out. And he thought how truly comic it would be if she really
were there in the trenches. But when he came closer he saw it was
only some rags. Then he met Uncle John, who was freshly
shaved, ready for his leave, quite the dandy; he took two braziers
of charcoal and went with him to the door of the dug-out. And
there she was, 'this time quite plain, and he saw the look on her
face and the look on his. He said: "Why, Bella, this must be only
the second time we've been alone together in all these years."
And then he lighted the braziers and invited her inside; he went
in as though to a tea-party in the parlour. And she stooped and
went into the dug-out—with that look on her face. Strangwick
heard him wedge the door shut from inside. He felt very strange,
a long way inside himself and not rightly on the spot. He said
nothing to anyone and managed to survive the cross-examining
next morning. Someone had knocked away the wedges before any
officer saw Godsoe; there was nothing to show it wasn't an
accident. Strangwick managed to keep going till the telegram
came to say that Auntie Armine had died on the morning of the
21st. That cut everything away; he couldn't any longer think it
was hallucination. The dead did rise. Seeing his Uncle John and
her—'she dead since morning time and he killing himself before
my living eyes so as to carry on with her for all Eternity'—put an
end to everything, all he believed, all he'd planned. There was a
girl with whom he'd been looking in shop windows—but now he
knew what the real thing meant; it was for ever, and he wasn't
going to put up with a second-best. He would wait till he saw

that look on a face again. He knew now that the real thing only
begins at death.

When he had told his story, Strangwick fell asleep. Keede and
the narrator found the man who had introduced Strangwick. His
name was Armine; he was disappointed that his nephew wouldn't
marry the young lady with whom he had had an understanding.
She would have made him a good little wife.

As with 'They', there is little point in arguing about just what
Kipling believed, nor how Auntie Armine knew the exact date
when she would die nor how John Godsoe knew she would come
to that dug-out. What is important is the total effect of the story.
Here of course a summary cannot do justice to the original,
particularly in view of Kipling's late method. The 'I' has dropped
into the background; he is only a witness; it is Keede who draws
out the story — tooth by tooth — helped by his drug, but more by
his guess that there had been something funny about Godsoe's
death and that the dates suggested a link with Strangwick's
trouble. Was Keede pretending or did he really think it might be
murder? I am confident that he was pretending, in order to shock
the truth out of Strangwick, but the narrator was deceived (and
at least one critic).

The story builds up in little dabs of paint and spurts of light —
filled in with reminiscent detail. Death is close all the time; not
only are the *poilus* 'laid in six deep in Butcher's Row', but Strangwick finds his way by such landmarks as the two Zouave skeletons
near the old sugar boiler, and the corner where the four dead
Warwicks are heaped up; he has to go out of his way on that fatal
night because a support trench was blocked by dead and wounded
going back. Duckboards with slats missing, rags of gas screen
flapping in the wind, Strangwick's bits of army jargon and South
London genteelism, all underline the horror that overwhelms
him. What he keeps saying is that if the dead rise again he has
nothing to hold on to; buying bits of furniture and settling down
with a girl who didn't mean much to him just isn't enough. But
there is a note too of Hamlet's outrage at his mother's incest; my
own aunt, and she nearer fifty than forty — no one would have
guessed it. He had been her favourite, you see.

There are also certain resonant phrases which Strangwick
keeps harking back to. He had got them from Godsoe. One is
from the Burial Service: 'If, after the manner of men, I have
fought with beasts at Ephesus, what advantageth it me if the dead

rise not?' In Godsoe's mouth, this must mean that he has suffered
for years, and fought in secret for patience, waiting for this tryst
after death. Strangwick gets it a little wrong and makes it 'beasts
of officers', but clearly he understands the general meaning, which
is essential to the story. And so with the other phrases he had
heard from Godsoe, which he thought came from a hymn. They
come in fact from Swinburne—whom one would not have
expected to find on Godsoe's bookshelves—about 'the lords
above' showing man 'marvellous mercy and infinite love'—but
'not twice in the world shall the Gods do thus.' Kipling's characters, like Kipling, have a way of biting on a phrase and chewing
it over and over obsessionally. And his own phrases often have a
quality that makes one treat them in the same way.

A rendezvous after death! Did Godsoe have to wait in the
terrible Terminus of 'Uncovenanted Mercies'? I think not. In
this story, above and behind Strangwick and his troubles there
emerge the writer's conviction that there is a life after death in
which personal relations are renewed, and his belief that there is
the possibility of the kind of love between man and woman that
Dante wrote of, instantaneous and eternal. And also, I think, a
strong implication, made explicit in the next story, that pain and
patient endurance are in some mysterious way taken into the
reckoning.

4. THE WISH HOUSE

Nothing could be more different than the setting of 'The Wish
House'. It is told in the course of conversation between two
elderly Sussex women, who had been brought up together in the
country long ago. Grace Ashcroft had been a cook in London;
now she is pensioned and her friend Liz Fettley has come to see
her. Their talk flows on over tea-cups and a lavish meal; piece by
piece the story of a whole life emerges. A grandson runs in to
claim a picnic basket Mrs Ashcroft has been making for him.
Something in the turn of his head reminds Mrs Fettley of someone—now who was it? And then she remembers a haymaking
long ago and the angry outburst of a jealous woman who said
Grace was stealing her man. And *he* had been dead seven and
twenty years. But it showed in the boy. One confidence leads to
another, and Mrs Fettley tells of the one true love of her life; they
had read his death-notice to her out of the paper, last month, but

she could say and show nothing. And Mrs Fettley's tale—of which we hear no details—leads to the real story, which is Grace Ashcroft's. It comes out, slowly, like something sticky with lumps in it being strained through muslin. Grace tells it in answer to the story she has just heard; she is in pain with her sick leg and Mrs Fettley, who knows some of the people, helps it on by comment and question. There is no long uninterrupted narrative.

It began after her husband was dead. She had set a heap by him once but that had long been over; a violent man whose eye had roved, as hers had. He had told her on his deathbed that she would suffer as she had made him suffer. He had said he was death-wise and could see what was coming to her. He had been right. She went back to her situation in London when he was buried; they were glad to have her because she understood their ways. Then towards autumn, when they were travelling in France, she went back to the country and took on odd farm work. She had her wages from London and it was more for fresh air and change she worked. But there she met her master; *she* had always owned *them* before but this was different. It was Harry Mockler. She persuaded him to take a job she found for him near her in London; she paid the fare. They were happy for a time and then she saw that he was tired of it and wanted to get away home. She didn't try to keep him, once she was sure, but just walked off to her own sufferings. And she did suffer, as her husband had said she would.

One part of it was headaches which she'd never had in her life before. Once when she was sitting with her apron over her head, half mad with headache, the charwoman's little girl came in. She was crazy-fond of Mrs Ashcroft, who knew it would pass and didn't encourage her but hadn't the heart to beat her off. Sophy said she could take the headache away and slipped away to do it. Ten minutes later the headache took off as if it had been kicked. And then Sophy came back, quiet as a mouse, her eyes deep in her head and her face drawn, all sticky-lipped. She had got the headache now and it would last till Mrs Ashcroft's headache would have gone in the normal course. She had found out how to do it from a gypsy girl she had played with at the livery stable. You had to know where there was a Wish House—and there was one a few streets off. You had to ring the bell and wish your wish through the letter-box; you would hear the Token that lived inside come up from the basement and you must ask it to take the trouble from someone you loved. You could ask nothing for yourself.

In the autumn of that year, Grace went home and she saw Harry Mockler again. He was all shrunk and wizened; he had cut his foot with a spade when cleaning out an old pond; there was poison in his blood and the doctor didn't think he'd last the winter; he thought the same himself. So Grace made up her mind to go to the Wish House. It was a mean little basement-kitchen house, in a row of twenty or thirty, the paint off the front door, a tiny garden in front, all neglected. No one lived there. She rang the bell and it pealed loud in the empty house. She heard a chair pushed back and feet on the kitchen stairs, like a heavy woman in slippers. Then she said through the letter-box: 'Let me take everything bad that's in store for my man, Harry Mockler, for love's sake.' Whatever was on the other side of the door let its breath out, as though it had held it to listen, and then the steps went back.

Next day she knocked her leg just above the ankle; Harry got better that winter and by the spring she had a nasty little weeping boil on her shin. And from that day on, for years and years, when Harry had any trouble, the sick leg would be worse—she could make it worse by standing, which the doctor had told her not to do—and then Harry would get better. He got his good from her without knowing it—for years and years. Now the sore place had turned; she knew it was cancer, though the nurse didn't know she knew. She didn't think she had a year. Then Mrs Fettley told her own trouble; she wasn't sure she'd be able to come again within the year without a little dog to lead her. The district Nurse came in, brisk, business-like and slightly disapproving, all the bottles in her bag clicking. Mrs Fettley stooped to kiss Grace good-bye and she murmured for the last time: 'It do count, don't it—de pain?'

The central ideas of this story are in themselves simple and very ancient. They are that the love of a woman for a man can dominate her completely and that someone who loves sufficiently can bear the burden of suffering for someone else. The substitution idea is as old as Homer and the Bible; it is to be found all over the world. It is more advanced than the idea of the scapegoat —a beast with no understanding on which the sins of a whole people can be fastened by magical means. The sacrifice of sub-

stitution can only take place where there is love and where the
victim himself accepts the burden; it is at the heart of the Christian
doctrine of the Atonement and it was believed by the Early
Church to explain the ability of martyrs to endure suffering. It was
not they who suffered but Another in them. This would not be
original if presented intellectually in the form of theology or
anthropology, but it takes on many new dimensions and flashes
with new light when it is treated as part of a woman's life.

Grace Ashcroft is a woman of power, strong in her sexuality,
in her country wisdom, in her sizing up of people. She had never
had headaches and had healed clean; 'chop me all over with a
spade and I'd heal clean like turf,' she had said. She had owned her
lovers and disregarded her husband, who had once nearly killed
a man; she had said we only go through this world once and
therefore she would owe her belly nothing. She had not cried in
childbirth. She had incurred the anger of the pagan gods, who as
everyone knows, resent cocksure self-confidence more than anything else. That this was in Kipling's mind is clear from the verses
'Late Came the God' which stand at the head of this story.

> Late came the God, having sent his fore-runners
> who were not regarded —
> Late but in wrath;
> Saying: The wrong shall be paid, the contempt
> be rewarded ...

But the poem must be read in full. It is one that I would put
among my first choice of all Kipling's poems. It is too condensed
to fit the story exactly but it clearly refers to Grace Ashcroft. 'So
she lived, while her body corrupted upon her ... ' She lived, but
'she served by the light of her Vision ... ' The god struck but she
accepted the blow and her sacrifice was an act of her own will.
'These things she did in Love's honour ... ' But, I repeat, the
poem must be read in full.

Grace Ashcroft's sacrifice is based on something much more
positive than the stoic pagan endurance which had once seemed
Kipling's creed. She never suggests that she has any formal
religious belief, but the St Peter who appears in 'On the Gate'
would certainly have ruled that she was made of the same stuff as
the martyrs and marked her docket Q.M.A.

No one need boggle at the Wish House itself. Grace believed
in The Token that came upstairs and so did Mrs Fettley. But a

reader may acknowledge the redemptive power of suffering and —
going one stage further — the possibility of accepting suffering on
behalf of someone else, even if he thinks that the gypsy child's
charm does not have much to do with bringing it about. What the
story is saying is that someone who loves enough can accept
suffering for someone else. It is its strength that it draws on so
rich a mixture of beliefs and symbols and on such a depth of
earthy wisdom.

5 . THE GARDENER

'The Gardener' is written with a sustained irony for which I can
think of no parallel. It is the kind of irony used in Greek drama,
when the actor speaks words foretelling the death which the
audience knows will be his. They — the audience in the theatre —
are familiar with the legend on which the play is based and they
draw breath sharply when Agamemnon or Oedipus says those
fatal words. But the character in the play does not know what
will happen, nor do the persons on the stage who make his first,
direct audience. They are not in the secret; they understand him
differently. In 'The Gardener' too there are two audiences who
understand the words in different senses. One is reading the story
for the first time and is not in the secret. Such a reader perceives a
sequence of events which he understands as a casual observer
might, a distant relation perhaps who has come over for the day
and accepts without question all he is told. But the last words of
the story take him aback. Suddenly he perceives what he ought to
have known from the start. Now he reads the whole again, knowing the secret; this time he has joined the second audience and
almost every phrase strikes him in the light of what he has now
learnt. On a third reading, he may see the whole with new depth
and meaning, but there will still be questions to ask. It is impossible to convey this effect by a summary; the story must be
read as it was written. But it has been misunderstood, and to
understand it is essential to my main purpose; let us therefore
state the outlines as they would appear at first reading. The
reader comes to the story new, but he knows of the death of
Kipling's son, and is likely to read the story in the light of that
loss.

Helen Turrell had brought up her brother's son in the country
village where her parents had lived. They were both dead and she

was thirty-five and independent—that is, unmarried and comfortably off—when the news came of her brother's death in India. He had always been something of a black sheep and had recently become entangled with the daughter of a non-commissioned officer; the child was born soon after his death. Helen was in the South of France when the news came—there had been some suspicion of trouble with her lungs—but she decided to accept responsibility for her brother's son. She arranged everything and went to Marseilles to meet the baby with the nurse she had engaged for him by cable. She was delayed a little by the child's illness—the nurse was careless and had to be dismissed—but at last she brought him triumphantly home. All this she explained to her friends in full. She believed in being frank and did not try to conceal her brother's wrong-doing.

Michael was brought up just like any other English boy of that class and did well at his prep school and public school. He came to suspect that he was illegitimate but consoled himself with the thought that bastards had done well in history; on the surface at least he did not let it worry him. Since Helen was all he had, and he was all she had, there was a very special bond between them. The war came just when he was about to go up to Oxford, with the prospect of a promising career. He was given a commission in a new battalion, which for some time was used for coast defence and the like. Then suddenly it was sent to France. Here too it had a quiet time at first. But, just when Michael had written to Helen that there was nothing special doing, 'a shell-splinter dropping out of a wet dawn killed him at once. The next shell uprooted and laid down over the body what had been the foundation of a barn wall, so neatly that none but an expert would have guessed that anything unpleasant had happened.'

He was reported missing. Numbed by shock, Helen kept repeating to herself: 'Missing always means dead.' None the less, she 'did and wrote and signed everything that was suggested or put before her' as a means of finding him if he was a prisoner. But he was not. A time came when she could say his name. But it was not till a year after the Armistice that she could take the hand of the young who had come back and were alive 'and almost sincerely wish them well'. Then there came news that his body had been found, identified and reburied in a war cemetery, and she was told the row and number. It seemed to be expected that she should want to go and see her grave; and 'in the agony of being waked

10

up to some sort of second life', she obediently did as was expected of her. She felt as though she were a shell, going through a factory, as she had once seen one go, being shaped and polished into a dead finished product. She found an official in 'a board and tar-paper shed on the skirts of a razed city full of whirling lime-dust and blown papers.' He told her how to find the cemetery; there was a hysterical woman from Lancashire who did not know under what name her son had enlisted but Helen managed to escape from her. The nightmare went on; there was a Mrs Scarsworth, garrulous and informative, who had no grave of her own but came often on behalf of friends. She had a list of graves and took photographs to show them. They found it helped. She rattled on and Helen 'almost lifted her hands to keep her off'. She insisted on sharing a table at dinner and went on and on about the people on her list. It was small talk, of no consequence, dreadful to Helen. But hardly had she escaped to her bedroom before Mrs Scarsworth forced her way in again. She must tell someone the truth; the commissions for other people were an excuse and there *was* one grave that she came to see on her own account—but it oughtn't to be hers. It was the one real thing that had ever happened to her in her life and she had to pretend he was nothing to her. Years of lying and pretence! She had been to his grave eight times; this would be the ninth and she *must* tell someone ... 'Helen could not speak, and the woman went out; but it was a long time before Helen was able to sleep.'

Next day she found the cemetery but was not prepared for what she saw—'a merciless sea of black crosses ... a waist-high wilderness as of weeds stricken dead, rushing at her.' She did not know how to find the grave and went towards a man who was 'firming a young plant in the soft earth'. He asked who she was looking for.

' "Lieutenant Michael Turrell—my nephew," said Helen slowly and word for word, as she had many thousands of times in her life.'

He 'looked at her with infinite compassion ... "Come with me" he said "and I will show you where your son lies ... ' "

When she left the cemetery, she looked back and saw him again, 'and she went away, supposing him to be the gardener.'

This story had not yet been written when I was in my boyhood phase of enthusiasm for Kipling, and it was quite recently that I first read it. Until the last two or three paragraphs, I took it at its face value and read it as in part an attempt to understand the love an unmarried woman could feel for a boy she had brought up — and thus to be compared with 'Mary Postgate' — and in part Kipling's release of something of what he had felt at his son's loss. It was moving on that level. That Helen was Michael's mother did not occur to me till the last page. Then, on second reading, it seemed impossible that I could have been so obtuse; everything fell into place. It took a third reading to get to grips with the theme of truth and concealment which is central to the story. The grave irony of the opening paragraphs stresses what everyone in the village knew; they knew what they had been told about George Turrell's death and Helen's rescue of the boy, her determination to do her duty and her frankness in telling them that her brother's life had been unsatisfactory. It is only slowly that it dawns on the second audience of more persevering and discriminating readers that the village has all along known perfectly well that Helen was really Michael's unmarried mother. They approve of the way she has handled the situation, being as frank as she can about as much as she can.

Michael too is in the secret, though he does not say so even to Helen, and is not sure what it is that he knows. When he is about six, he asks why he may not call her 'Mummy'. She explains that an aunt is different, but says he may, as a special pet-name between themselves, call her 'Mummy' at bed-time. But later she tells her friends. Michael finds out that she has told and is in a rage with her. She had broken a bond between them. 'It is always best to tell the truth,' she says, but he replies that when the truth is ugly he doesn't 'think it's nice'. On first reading, without spending much thought on this incident, I thought Michael was angry only because they had made a pact which Helen had broken. But that will not do in the light of that saying; if he thought the truth was ugly, he must really have known that Helen was his mother. They were being truthful at bed-time, and at bed-time only, and that should be kept secret from the world. But no child of six could have put that in words for himself. I think that the whole incident can only be explained in the light of something that might easily not occur to anyone who had not lived in Edwardian England. There would have been maids in the house, probably a cook, a parlour-maid and a nurse-maid, and very likely also someone from the village who came in to scrub floors twice a week. There would have been a gardener. Helen must have reflected, after making that agreement with Michael, that maids have ears and that what is said at bed-time cannot be kept a secret for ever. It will be all over the village. So she will tell her friends and then no one will think anything of it. It is from the maids that Michael first learns that there is something he does not understand in his relationship with Helen. There would be gossip in the kitchen over a cup of tea in the middle of the morning, and it is easy to overlook a little boy who is keeping quiet. He must also have heard someone say something about it being better not to tell the truth when it is ugly. That must also have been how Michael learnt that Helen had told something which they had agreed to keep to themselves — something which he obscurely felt was true and important although they had agreed to pretend they were only pretending. In short, Michael agrees with the village in being tolerant about a fact so long as it isn't dragged into the open. And this, surely, is Kipling's belief too. He had been frozen and numbed by his own grief and is filled with pity at the thought of someone like Helen, whose case must be even worse because she cannot tell. That had made grief worse for Holden long ago, in 'Without Benefit of Clergy'.

In France Helen meets two other women in similar trouble. The hysterical woman from Lancashire is altogether repellent to Helen because she has not been trained in the same stoical code. With her there can be no contact at all. Mrs Scarsworth with her chatter about corner-seats and comfort in the hotel is at first an intrusion of another kind; to answer her facile remarks on the same level is a strain Helen finds intolerable. It is another thing when Mrs Scarsworth confesses that she too is masking a deep emotion by pretence. Helen asks her for how many years, and it is surely clear — though we are not told so — that, when she gets the answer, Helen is thinking that she has had to keep it up twice as long. As Mrs Scarsworth went on, Helen reached forward, caught her hands, bowed her head over them and murmured: 'Oh, my dear! My dear!' She is speechless with compassion and in tears; after twenty years of silence she cannot find words to show her response, but it is overwhelming. Her gestures leave me in no doubt that pity and sympathy are what she feels; Mrs Scarsworth, however, appears to think that, because her head is averted, she is shocked.

At least one critic, Dr Elliott Gilbert, has made the same mistake; but then he thinks that the whole story is directed against 'the village', whom he regards as a symbol for a stifling conventional morality, of which he supposes Kipling to disapprove. But this is wrong, both in history and psychology. It misunderstands Kipling and it misunderstands the English village of that time. It underestimates the strength of moral convention in early twentieth-century rural England; when he implies that Helen should boldly have proclaimed the whole truth, Dr Gilbert must really be thinking in terms of half a century later. She would have outlawed herself and Michael. We live in the 1970s in a permissive world with many Freudian assumptions. Kipling did not. In his world, sex outside marriage was a sin, an extreme self-indulgence, but, if accompanied by love, it was a part of the Christian tradition — though a part often forgotten — that it would eventually be forgiven as Mary Magdalene's was. The village were prepared to forgive — provided the sin was not rammed down their throats. They expected Helen, who was gentry, to set them an example — and Helen knew that too.

Kipling did not regard the conventional morality of his day as something to be fought, but as a fact of the life he knew. He could feel pity for a woman who suffered under the system without contemplating any change in it. He admired what he thought a peculiarly English habit, of hardly discussing, except by the most oblique reference, things that were better left undisturbed. This was something he had only come to understand in Sussex. It recurs constantly in the Puck stories, in 'An Habitation Enforced', in 'Friendly Brook'. To suppose that Helen and 'the village' are condemned for observing this rule of English country society is to misunderstand Kipling entirely. When he says, in the opening words of this story: 'Everyone in the village knew ... ' he means that everyone had tacitly agreed that this was how the matter should be regarded; everyone also knew that something quite different lay beneath; finally, all were agreed that it was the inescapable nature of life and society that things should be like that. 'Truth is a naked lady ... ' Helen accepted this and Kipling did not condemn her for her acceptance nor regard hers as a starved impoverished nature. He admired her stoicism and gave her all his pity. But it was an extra weight in her burden that when the chance to talk comes, she could not take it. Long habit had made it impossible.

The poem that goes with the story, 'The Burden', refers directly to Helen Turrell, and what it expresses is pity for her suffering and a comparison with Mary Magdalene, who was forgiven much because she loved much:

> One grief on me is laid
>   Each day of every year,
> Wherein no soul can aid,
>   Whereof no soul can hear:

The first three verses are spoken by Helen and, with a slight variation, the last two lines of each verse, addressed to Mary Magdalene, are the same. But the last verse — printed in italics, a device Kipling often used to represent a different voice — is spoken by Mary Magdalene herself, and I think we are meant to understand that Helen too has for one brief hour undergone a similar experience:

> One grave to me was given —
>   To guard till Judgment Day —
> But God looked down from Heaven
>   And rolled the stone away!

For one short hour — out of all her years — the stone had been rolled away from Helen's grave too, and in some deep unexplained way her burden was lifted, she knew herself to be close to Michael, to be able to tell all, to be understood, to be forgiven, to be free and happy.

The Gardener himself comes to the new reader as a shock at least as great as his use of the word 'son' to Helen. There can be no doubt that we are meant to identify him with the risen Jesus who appeared to Mary Magdalene by the empty tomb on Easter morning. The words from St John's gospel and the accompanying poem make this clear. My own view is that he is not an apparition, but that for this brief interval, 'One day of all my years — One hour of that one day —' the human figure of a gardener became an Incarnation of Divine compassion and understanding. As in the verses 'Cold Iron', Kipling was ready to use Christian imagery to express Christian ideas, but not in a way that can be clearly intellectualized. It is at first surprising that Helen went away still supposing him to be no more than the gardener. The poem is explicit that for an hour the stone was rolled away; for that hour she stood by her grave alone with the truth. But she did not recognize the agency by which that hour had been granted, just as she could not speak to Mrs Scarsworth. Something in her had been frozen.

There is nothing in the story about the identity of Michael's real father, nor of what Helen felt about him. It has been suggested to me verbally by Charles Carrington that he was incestuously begotten and that George Turrell was in fact his father. But this seems quite out of keeping with Helen's character. It seems to me more probable that in the first flush of freedom after her parents' death she met a man of her own class who regarded a lonely woman as a challenge to his power to charm, deceived her as to his intentions and either deserted her or disillusioned her so completely that she shut him out of her mind. All her references to Michael's likeness to George are meant to explain the likeness to herself or her father; his mouth was 'better cut than the family type'. But this is surmise and it is not important; what is important is that she concentrated all her love on Michael, that Kipling felt deep compassion for her, and that he believed that such compassion was in some way part of the universe. I also believe—and here I differ from the American critics I have read—that Kipling thought she was right to conceal the truth, even though it added to her unhappiness and loneliness. And, when this story is read with 'Uncovenanted Mercies', 'The Wish House' and 'A Madonna', I am confident he would have said that in her case too the pain did count and would go down in her reckoning on the credit side.

Epilogue

Stranger upon Earth

1. WHO IS KIM?

A visitor to Bateman's once came down into the hall, as the dusk was gathering and before the lamps were lit, and saw the master of the house squatting before the open fire, poking it into life. He remembered the moment always; the short square figure crouched against the glow of smouldering logs left him with an impression of something primeval, very ancient, far back in the consciousness of man; it was as though he had gone back thousands of years in time. He was looking, he felt, at a man from a Long Barrow.

It was the impression of a moment; it was gone as quickly as it came. But there was a truth in it. Today, nearly forty years after Kipling's death, we live in a highly individualist society, and there are those who tell us what we have lost by abandoning the tribe and the family — respect for the ancestors, the rich life of a community in which everyone knew everyone else. Today it is the state that looks after the old, not their children. Brothers and sisters live apart in separate little boxes. Kipling by instinct belonged to that older world, but he was a tribesman without a tribe. He was born in Bombay but his parents spent most of their adult life in Lahore or Simla; one was Yorkshire, one Scottish, and they retired to Wiltshire. Both came of Methodist stock but their Methodism dropped away from them. They were married by the Anglican rite but never became communicants; there was no close-knit community of class or church or place to which they could be said to belong. Rudyard was brought up away from his parents, and indeed with a feeling that he had been deserted by them. He was the odd man out at school and in India; he failed to settle in Vermont. Even when he found a house at Burwash, he was manifestly not at home in Sussex; he was part neither of the gentry nor of the peasantry.

Many an artist or writer has been at least as much the perpetual outsider as Kipling. But few have wanted so desperately to get inside. So far C. S. Lewis was right; a closed circle tightly held together by loyalty was immensely important to him. But this was partly the result of something deeper. He was a highly impressionable artist, recording what he saw, drawing men out to talk, sketching, taking mental notes all the time; he must have had, at least in his early days, 'the woman's trick of taking the tone and colour of whoever he talked to'. Behind this superficial adaptability, behind immense vigour and fluidity, we must suppose a deep need for emotional support. More even than most people, he wanted to be loved. More than most people, he wondered about the tenuous bond of identity. 'Who is Kim—Kim—Kim?' he wrote when he was thirty-five, and he must often as a boy have wondered: 'Who is Rudyard?' And the cracking of identity under intolerable strain was the chief preoccupation of his later years.

It was by just such a strange haphazard trick of fate as so often befell characters in his own stories that he should have been born at the moment and in the class that he was. From about the middle of the nineteenth century till the outbreak of war with Germany in 1914, Britain was an imperial power with interests all over the world and immense responsibilities. Those responsibilities demanded officers, an imperial class, officers for the fighting services but also for duties as magistrates, judges, policemen, collectors of revenue, makers of roads, canals and bridges, conservators of forests. And somehow, without as a rule any formal consultation or recorded decision, there sprang up all over the country schools designed to produce men to meet the need. Kipling's school, of course, was unusual in being deliberately set up to get boys through the army examination, but the spirit of this, as well as of the other public schools, was the result of a more mysterious process. Parents came to picture the kind of son they wanted, schoolmasters the finished product they could deliver; there was general agreement between them but little consultation. 'If only he'll turn out a brave, helpful, truth-telling Englishman, and a gentleman, and a Christian, that's all I want,' mused Squire Brown the night before young Tom went to Rugby. 'Why is he going to school?' he had wondered, and had added: 'I don't care a straw for Greek particles,' firmly putting character before learning. He spoke for most of the parents, and Dr Arnold would not have disagreed with him.

As the century progressed, the kind of training that was needed for the imperial class became more and more clearly seen to involve endurance of some pain and considerable discomfort, strenuous physical effort, the suppression of any display of emotion, an end to dependence on home. Cold baths and cold rooms, plain food, vigorous exercise, were part of it; small boys must wait on big boys and were beaten if they were idle or late or forgetful or tried to avoid football. Boys must first learn to obey and then to command. They must never show fear or cry or tell tales about each other or talk about their mothers. As I have suggested in other books, most imperial peoples have felt that something of the kind was necessary for their ruling class — Spartans, Romans, Aztecs, Incas, and some conquering tribes in Africa. It was a hardening process, meant to produce a man who would set an example to the men he commanded. They would obey him because they recognized in him a quality they had not; he had been through the mill and had learnt to endure hardship, to keep his temper and to keep his head.

It would be hard to exaggerate the importance of this system of training in England during the period from Kipling's birth until the end of the era in 1914. Officers were supposed to be the younger sons of squires, or the sons of parsons who were themselves younger sons, but there were not enough of the landed gentry to go round and the public schools put the stamp on the sons of doctors and lawyers and men who had done well in business. They too were 'licked into shape'. Thus the system brought in new blood and it sifted out those who, whatever their antecedents, were not suitable for the imperial class. But it was not merely a recruiting and selecting device; it also set the tone and defined the nature and structure of the national society, drawing a line between those who on the whole expected to be obeyed and those who on the whole expected to do as they were told.

Of course, the public-school system was not really a system at all; it was much more varied and illogical than has been here suggested. It was shot through with individualism and admiration for the eccentric, and as a by-product it sometimes produced scholars. But the schools did have a great deal in common and, in the broadest general terms, most of them did set more value on character and physical prowess than on intellect. They were designed primarily to produce administrators. And on the whole, with a few failures and a few rebels, they did. A boy who was of average ability and who was, as Stalky had said, 'robust enough', emerged at the end with a gloss of imperturbable confidence that might conceal some inner strain but undoubtedly proved a very useful face to front the world with. A man who cheerfully expects obedience will usually be obeyed. But however good it might be for an administrator or an army officer, no one could suppose this was at all the training for an artist. The one must sometimes harden his heart to take unpalatable decisions; he will almost

certainly have to carry out unpopular measures and it will be a
help if his training has given him some exterior rigidity; the other
needs to be sensitized rather than stiffened.

Kipling, essentially an artist and one who needed affection, was
pitch-forked in among two hundred young administrators who
were being hardened for the business of life in a school which,
because it was young and was specifically designed to produce
candidates for the army, was almost a caricature of the public
school. His parents were not born into the imperial class but were
recruits, and here was a school which was very cheap, which
would set the stamp of the class on Ruddy, and was bound to be
all right because the Headmaster was a friend of the Burne-
Joneses and the Pre-Raphaelite brotherhood. So there he went.

Rudyard had already been through that searing experience at
the House of Desolation, where he had felt himself deserted in a
loveless world. Once again he was deserted, went to cry in the
box-room among the overcoats, wrote letters asking to be taken
away. But this time there was a difference; the Head was on his
side. And because he was at heart a tribesman, he found a great
deal to admire in this strange new tribe. But it was a tribe to
which he could never belong; he could not play games and he was
not going into the army. In any case, a part of him was sure that he
was an artist and a writer and he spent his holidays with the Burne-
Jones family. Because he was a tribesman at heart, and because he
saw the admirable qualities of the public-school type, he could not
be a rebel against the aims of the system—but only against such
minor manifestations as house-matches and housemasters and
prefects. He was too vigorous a personality to drop out or merely
to conform outwardly to a system in which he could play no real
part. He and his friends pretended to be rebels, but inwardly he
admired and envied the tribe he could not enter. He left school
deeply divided.

Nothing that happened in the next seven years did anything to
heal that split. He was reunited to his parents and found that he
liked and admired them both. But they were not really members
of the imperial class; they were tacked on, as it were, to the fringe.
The society in which he found himself was a continuation of
school; men were busy at building bridges and roads, preventing
riots, tracing murderers, struggling with famine or cholera. In
Simla, a few were jockeying for better jobs and to them of course
he had at first to give more attention than they deserved, to show

how knowledgeable he was. But the men he admired went about their work, ignoring him, and he was left out.

Even in the Family Square, the fortress to which he retired for love and companionship, there was—I suggest, but I cannot be dogmatic about this—an unease. Alice Kipling was beautiful and brilliant; everyone is agreed on her wit. But more than one observer has detected a streak of hardness and, even in Rudyard's always devoted references to his mother, there is a hint of it. She looked after him, she applauded—but did she always take him quite seriously enough? Only the silliest of mothers does take her son quite seriously, and Alice Kipling was certainly not silly. Something in him hankered for the kind of devotion Ameera gave to Holden or the girl with the jackal-skins to Valens. And—as I have said earlier—when he gave his fancy full rein, his heroes lose their true parents in infancy and have to find foster-parents. There was that shadow at the back of his mind. Could these really be the people who had deserted him for the long years at the House of Desolation?

No other writer of this period was subjected in quite this way to this moulding experience of being trained as an officer who could never have a regiment, a ruler with no one to rule, an artist who must on no account betray his emotions. James, Conrad, Hardy, Barrie, Shaw, Wells, Bennett—this was not a problem for them. It might have been much less of a problem for Kipling if he had been by nature less dependent on affection, less fluid and intuitive, a man with a hard individual core whose beliefs were tempered by intellectual processes. But his beliefs were reached intuitively and emotionally and then accepted as dogmas.

India left him divided even more deeply and a stranger upon earth. It put an extra coat of polish on the outer surface that reflected the world immediately about him, the Simla drawing-rooms, the talk at the Club and in the mess. But always there was, withinsides, something that stirred obscurely, that sent him out looking for a world in which people did have emotions and revealed them in a variety of undisciplined ways.

On top of this came the events of that short crowded period between the time he left India and his marriage. Into that two years were packed two journeys round the world, the writing of two complete novels and two collections of tales, besides the incidental work involved in republishing in England his Indian stories. At the same time, he met and became half-engaged to

Caroline Taylor and brought that affair to an end; met once more his schoolboy love, Flo Garrard, renewed his proposals to her and was finally rejected; met the Balestiers, fell under Wolcott's spell and collaborated with him, and after some degree of estrangement, left him to go on another journey round the world; came back to find Wolcott dead and — in a mood for the moment almost sacrificial — married his sister. He found in her a mother, a nurse, a manager, a refuge from all minor troubles. But she was the wife emphatically of the surface part of his personality, not of what stirred within. There was a check to his growth as a writer and a personality. The failure to settle in Vermont and the humiliating end to the American adventure were blows to his confidence. The loss of the deeply loved daughter was a wound of which outward signs were repressed but which drove him into forms of activity that were an escape from pain. The split seemed to grow wider; there was the busy posturing figure, raising money for the troops in South Africa, starting rifle clubs, preaching the coming Armageddon — but at the same time there was a beginning of new growth, release of the self in pure fancy, wise and tender memories of the best in India and a new sort of tale, told in a new way, based on a deeper compassion. Then came the War, the loss of his son, personal physical pain, and a rich development of that new vein into the best of the late tales.

So we are faced with a bundle of extraordinary contradictions. There was the man who could speak with callous amusement of a bulldog being prised away from a native 'with his mouth full of the native' and who at the same time could write a deeply compassionate story of the sufferings of an elderly woman, who accepted pain in order to give ease from sickness to a lover who had cast her off. He could sneer, in the last book he wrote, at non-Aryans, meaning Jews, yet he had written in *Puck of Pook's Hill* of Kadmiel with a rare understanding of what it has meant to be a Jew in Christendom, and he had written with affection of the M'Leod family in 'The House Surgeon'. Of the Irish, too, he could say that their 'other creed is hate' and that in the United States the Irish had 'passed out of the market into "politics" which suited their instincts of secrecy, plunder, and anonymous denunciation.' Yet Kim was Irish, and Mulvaney, and it was the same man who wrote 'The Wild Geese' in praise of the Irish Guards.

He could write with passion of the dangers of dictatorship:

All we have of freedom, all we use or know —
This our fathers bought for us long and long ago.

Ancient right unnoticed, as the breath we draw
Leave to live by no man's leave, underneath the Law.

Lance and torch and tumult, steel and grey goose-wing
Wrenched it, inch and ell and all, slowly from the King.

And yet look forward, apparently with approbation, to a world in which all political power had been vested in an Aerial Board of Control of seven bureaucrats. Sometimes blind Chance controls man's fate, sometimes a watchful Purpose seems to be careful that he shall not be tried beyond what he is able to bear. The man who could write about the agony of personal loss with the irony, the restraint and the controlled passion of 'The Gardener' could put into the mouth of a puppy-dog baby-talk of a revolting sentimentality, and publish such schoolboyish immaturity as 'The Tie', both in his last ten years.

The inconsistencies run right through his life and are never resolved. Look for instance at his ideas about heredity. One occurs in 'His Chance in Life' (1888, from *Plain Tales*). In a remote little town in India, there is the beginning of a riot and the police inspector comes for orders to a telegraph signaller, who is Eurasian. This is unlikely, but Kipling explains it by saying that he was 'obeying the old race-instinct which recognizes a drop of white blood as far as it can be diluted'. But there had been white people, in Kipling's sense, in India only a few hundred years, and they had not been regarded with any special admiration for much more than a hundred. It is nonsense to talk about 'old race-instinct'. There is an even more ridiculous idea about heredity in 'Namgay Doola' (1891). There had been recently in Ireland an epidemic of maiming cattle by cutting off their tails. In this story, the descendant of an Irish soldier who has wandered into the Himalayas and settled there as a peasant is supposed to have *inherited* from his grandfather a tendency to cut off the tails of his landlord's cattle! Yet another aspect of Kipling would insist: 'There is neither East nor West, Border nor Breed, nor Birth —', and stress the equality of men within the Masonic Lodge.

A bundle of inconsistencies — but what was the tie that held the twigs together in so strangely mixed a faggot?

2. THE SHADOW AND THE FIRE

It would be a dull writer who displayed no contradictions, and in most writers — perhaps in all men who have achieved any degree of success in life — there must be some discrepancy between the public man, whom the world sees, and the inner man, as he sees himself and may perhaps reveal himself to the person with whom he is more intimate. Browning, so strong an influence on Kipling, wrote about this in 'One Word More', the last poem of *Men and Women*. The poet feels that by using his art so often to please the public, he has staled, indeed profaned, it. Like Moses in the wilderness, he has struck the rock and water has flowed, but the people drank and wiped their lips and sneered and walked away. He must put on the prophet's robes and take the prophet's rod in his hand when he talks to *them* — but now he wants a gift for his wife, and for her he would like to make something quite different, quite fresh, unprofaned by previous professionalism. He would like to paint her a picture — but he can't. 'Other gifts in other worlds, God willing' — but in this world he has only the one gift of verse and so he must, for her, in this one poem, change his style and write in a different key.

But although Browning had this strong sense of another side to himself, which he wanted to show his wife and her only, he could not refrain from *publishing* this different, secret poem — and it is not really so very different from his other work after all. It is still unmistakably his. He could not do without the prophet's robe and, once it was on, he became the prophet. Everything he wrote had the strong stamp of his style — but it was all of a piece in content as well as style. He may try, for a time, to say the things that Bishop Blougram or Fra Lippo Lippi would have said, but there can never be any doubt that it is Browning's voice speaking, and where his sympathies lie. He may sometimes be dull, or hopelessly obscure or involuted, but in all his work there is a unity of feeling. Or, to look at another creative artist of the Victorian period, there is a wide difference between what Dickens thought was the right behaviour to women and the way he did actually behave to particular women, but, once he sat down with a pen in his hand and began to write, you could be confident on which side he would be found. He would find no excuse for Steerforth's treatment of Little Emily. He would never have a good word for the Circumlocution Office. He never suggested that a debtor's prison was an improving place to live in, nor does he spare a tear for the unfortunate creditor who could not get his money back without sending people there.

Kipling's inconsistencies seem to me of an order peculiar to themselves. It was not that his public image was inconsistent with his private, but that within his written work there is tolerance and wisdom and compassion side by side with contemptuous dismissal of people he shut out from his consciousness altogether. He was at least two people in one skin, and surely a good deal of this was because a person naturally sensitive and impressionable had been exposed to a process of desensitization and that — having two sides to his head — he perceived the social value of the process and admired its products.

Thus it is easy to see why Kipling has been hated so intensely at the same time as he has been idolatrously admired. There *was* a side to him that was brutal and insensitive, and those who hate see only that. In the years between the Boer War and the First World War, his public activities were all connected with the outer carapace that reflected the light; he was active in defence of the tribe to which he could never belong and, like all converts, he was noisy in the expression of his beliefs. There were of course plenty of others who did not belong to that tribe, and, if they had decided to repudiate what they could not have, they were all the more indignant with its trumpeter. He was outspoken in his attacks on the 'intellectuals' who rejected the system he admired, and it is not surprising that he acquired a public image that represented only one side of his nature. That obscured the more sensitive and compassionate vein in his earlier work and prevented proper attention being given to his later work. And, of course, his later work was much more difficult. It required far more attention to understand it.

But some, even of those who have taken the trouble to read with care those stories that are not reflections of the class system of the age, and which came from the inner Kipling, will sometimes confess to a distaste that they find hard to define. It arises, surely, from that same uncertainty about his identity. It was this that made him filter his stories through so many interposing layers. He is much happier — such a person will say — when he is writing about Indians or trying to re-create the past or to create a world of fable in the jungle. If he comes into our own times, he must use a veil of Sussex dialect or cockney or sift his tale through so many witnesses, so many layers of conscious irony, that it loses spontaneity. And in this there is a good deal of truth. It is a matter of taste whether you feel that the care that has gone to their construction, the depth of feeling and the flashes of felicity, make up for this.

But what about his idolatrous admirers? Carrington has suggested that he not only described the generation of young officers who were killed in the war of 1914–18 but that he helped to make them what they were. Certainly many identified themselves with Kipling characters, and it is not easy to say how far they were imitating Kipling and how far he was drawing a picture of them. Perhaps no one has had so deep an influence on a whole generation of a certain class as he did. Here was someone who understood the life they were brought up to, their mistrust of politicians and intellectuals, their inarticulate devotion to a cause, the training they had endured, the tenseness that lay beneath the apparently insensitive outer crust, the tenderness they longed to lavish on dogs and children, their nervous respect for those mysterious creatures, women—so fragile compared with themselves and yet so firmly authoritarian as nurses and mothers. They never grew up; as late as 'The Tender Achilles' (1929), we find one eminent consultant surgeon telling another senior doctor that 'even if they were not too old to fight with siphons, the wife would notice the mess on the rugs next morning, and he would catch it.'

They never grew up, or rather there was a side to them that never grew up, just as there was a side to Kipling that never grew up. Kipling, like that kind of Kipling character, had been so drilled in the habit of wary concealment that even to close friends he could not reveal himself but in his letters had to take refuge in facetious schoolboy slang. Fighting with soda-water siphons and tipping people in ponds was another way of turning a difference of opinion into a joke which didn't matter—and above all it was important not to get involved in an intimate discussion that *did* matter and that might reveal the vulnerable inner self.

And surely it was just because his own personality was so divided, so fluid at the centre, that he exerted such an influence on so many who had also been 'licked into shape'—and a shape not quite their own. They had been taught to be brave and hide their fears and doubts, but in the process most of them at one time or another had been made to feel like a little dog that has made a mess on the carpet. So they can be sentimental about little dogs—

who like themselves have an excessive desire for affection and a strong sense of shame—and can talk to them in baby-talk, just as Kipling pictures Dick Heldar in 'The Light that Failed', talking to his 'little dorglums'. And this sentimentality is the counterpart to—and a compensation for—that brutality Heldar shows to a sedentary publisher who has not kept himself physically fit nor been through the mill that makes a man a true man in Kipling's sense.

To be divided is a weakness in a man of the world, but it may be what makes an artist interesting. In Kipling's case, it became a strength; it was just because of that weakness and division in himself that in his old age he concerned himself so deeply with breaking strain and the disintegration of the personality.

But if the English social system, and in particular middle class education, had a good deal to do with this emotional capture of a generation, it cannot explain the affection in which Kipling has been held in America, in France, and lately in the Soviet Union. It is probably true that in these three countries there has been a greater readiness than in England to admire those qualities in Kipling—bright hard colour, violence, vigour—which helped to antagonize his English critics in the middle period. In André Chevrillon's first essay on Kipling, for instance, there is much praise for his understanding of the feelings of men in direct physical combat, when they are trying to kill each other, hand to hand. But there is more to it than that. This wider appreciation is due partly to supreme skill with words and partly to a recognition of that ancient element in parts of his work which come from within and are not surface reflection—the image of the window that you see in the shiny glass as you stand turning the bottle in your hands. They were written by that ancient wizard from the Long Barrow, an Old Thing to whom all races and times were alike. It was he who had planned that meal when 'they ate wild sheep roasted on the hot stones, and flavoured with wild garlic and wild pepper; and wild duck stuffed with wild rice and wild fenugreek and wild coriander; and marrow-bones of wild oxen; and wild cherries, and wild grenadillas.' He had at command a magic of words and vision that breaks through again and again and suddenly brings a scene to life. How, the children asked Parnesius the Roman centurion, had he and his cohort saluted the guard and the Altar of Victory? ' "So!" said he; and he moved slowly through the beautiful movements of the Roman Salute, that ends with a hollow clang of the shield coming into its place between the shoulders.'

And later in the same story, Parnesius's eye was caught by the setting sun:

> It had come down to the top of Cherry Clack Hill and the light poured in between the tree trunks so that you could see red and gold and black deep into the heart of Far Wood; and Parnesius in his armour shone as though he had been afire.
>
> 'Wait,' he said, lifting a hand and the sunlight jinked on his glass bracelet. 'Wait! I pray to Mithras!'
>
> He rose and stretched his arms westward, with deep, splendid-sounding words.

Or again, the fight with the Spanish Armada, seen from the South Coast near Rye: 'Then *they* come sliddering past Fairlight in a great smoky pat vambrished with red gunfire, and our ships flying forth and ducking in again. The smoke-pat sliddered over to the French shore ... '

No one has better understood this ability to link an ancient magic with words than André Maurois. He had said that apart from Swift, whom they read only for Gulliver, and Defoe, whom they read only for Crusoe, French readers who are not specialists read only three English writers, Shakespeare, Dickens and Kipling. Kipling, he wrote, had a 'heroic conception of life, a heroic pessimism', but that was not enough to touch men's hearts. The true secret of his hold on men was his 'natural and permanent contact' with 'the oldest and deepest layers of human consciousness'. Modern men, he continued, are still the men of the most distant epochs. 'Our forests are still sacred groves, our towns temples of the Roman Emperor.' As the embryo goes through every stage in the development of its species, so the human child, in the course of childhood and adolescence, lives again through the magical beliefs of its ancestors. And it was Kipling's secret that he brought this perennial process, which dies for most of us so sadly early, to a perpetual resurrection. In some of his verse, writes Maurois, 'the need for rhythm is so primitive and strong that sometimes whole verses are pure rhythm, metrical onomatopoeia, songs of a savage without one articulate word.'

Consider, in the light of this, one of his creations, Kaa, whom the monkeys fear so much that 'the whisper of his name makes their wicked tails cold.' 'I was singer to my clan in that dim red Dawn of Man', Kipling had written long ago, and who but a tribal bard would have made one of Mowgli's guardians—almost a parent—a serpent thirty feet long?

> Generations of monkeys had been scared into good behaviour by the stories their elders told them of Kaa, the night-thief, who could slip along the branches as quietly as moss grows, and steal away the strongest monkey that ever lived; of old Kaa, who could make himself look so like a dead branch or a rotten stump that the wisest were deceived, till the branch caught them ...

Consider the dance of Kaa:

> The moon was sinking behind the hills, and the lines of trembling monkeys huddled together on the walls and battlements looked like ragged, shaky fringes of things ... Kaa glided out into the centre of the terrace and brought his jaws together with a ringing snap that drew all the monkeys' eyes upon him.
>   'The moon sets,' he said. 'Is there yet light to see?'
>   From the walls came a moan like the wind in the tree-tops: 'We see, O Kaa.'
>   'Good. Begins now the Dance—the Dance of the Hunger of Kaa. Sit still and watch.'
>   He turned twice or thrice in a big circle, weaving his head from right to left. Then he began making loops and figures of eight with his body, and soft oozy triangles that melted into squares and five-sided figures and coiled mounds, never resting and never hurrying and never stopping his low humming song. It grew darker and darker till at last the dragging, shifting coils disappeared, but they could hear the rustle of the scales.

And recall Mowgli's visit to Kaa, to ask for advice about dealing with the Red Dogs. After a little talk, he told Mowgli to be still, while he counted up his years—and he had seen a hundred and a hundred.

> For a long hour Mowgli lay back among the coils, while Kaa, his head motionless on the ground, thought of all that he had

seen and known since the day he came from the egg. The light seemed to go out of his eyes and leave them like stale opals, and now and again he made little stiff passes with his head, right and left, as though he were hunting in his sleep ... Then [Mowgli] felt Kaa's back grow bigger and broader below him as the huge python puffed himself out, hissing with the noise of a sword drawn from a steel scabbard.

'I have seen all the dead seasons,' Kaa said at last, 'and the great trees and the old elephants, and the rocks that were bare and sharp-pointed ere the moss grew. Art *thou* still alive ... ?'

This is magic, and unless you are exempt from it by some stronger magic, it is compelling. It is a part—perhaps more than half—of Kipling's power to bind. The python is sacred for some West African peoples, and all over the world, at many stages of development, there have been nations for whom snakes are holy, possessed of wisdom, to be appeased, symbols of creative energy. I do not think that Kipling had these associations in the forefront of his mind when he wrote of Kaa as he did; rather, he was himself living through those stages of belief. He too for the moment felt that snakes ought to be held in awe as wise and unaccountable creatures. So, too, he absorbed from the Judaism of the Old Testament a sense of the sacredness of the Law, of the necessity for atonement and restoring the balance, of the presence of a righteous anger at the heart of things. And in the same way, never as a creed, never as a formulated philosophy, he took from the New Testament, and accepted as an emotional fact, the redemptive power of suffering on behalf of others. For all these he took what symbols suggested themselves; he was in touch with human needs that existed before the formulations of Judaism or Christianity or Islam. If the symbols were older than the creeds with which they became associated, that did not make them any less relevant to the needs of man or woman.

This consciousness of the oldest and most powerful of human needs would have been no use without the power of words. But the two together made something compelling. All through his life Kipling found moments when he could draw on it, long ago in the days when he had been that 'strangely clever youth who'— you will remember—'has stolen the formidable mask of maturity and rushes about making people jump with the deep sounds, the

sportive exaggerations of tone, that issue from its painted lips' —
and still many years later, when he was an old man in pain, brooding long on perfecting the details of his art, and pondering on the
strange bond that holds a man's discordant elements together
under strains he would have believed intolerable. Now it was the
other way about and sometimes the old man put on the brittle
mask of youth, capering for a moment in stiff unseemly antics.
But in neither case was the true voice that which came from the
painted lips. The true voice came from something within, something obscure, like a shadow and a fire, something he never
understood himself. From whatever hidden source that secret
energy sprang, it was that which grew, above all in a readiness to
comprehend the failures and the forgotten.

1865   Rudyard Kipling born at Bombay.

1871–7   At the House of Desolation in Southsea.

1878–82   At the United Services College, Westward Ho!

1882–7   On the staff of *The Civil and Military Gazette*, Lahore.

1887–9   On the staff of *The Pioneer*, Allahabad.

1889   To London via Japan and the U.S.A., with the Hills.

1890   The *Annus Mirabilis* in London.
Literary success: half engaged to Caroline Taylor;
meets Flo Garrard; meets Wolcott Balestier.

1891   Voyage alone to South Africa, Australia, New Zealand
and last visit to India.
Death of Wolcott Balestier.

1892   Marriage to Caroline Balestier;
Through Canada to Japan;
to Brattleboro, Vermont, U.S.A.

1896   Leaves Vermont; at Torquay.

1897   At Rottingdean.

1899   Last visit to United States; illness in New York; death
of elder daughter Josephine.

1900–8   In South Africa every year from January to March.

1902   Move to Bateman's, Burwash, Sussex.

1915   Only son John missing, believed killed.

1922   Serious illness and operation.

1936   Death of Rudyard Kipling.

1939   Death of Mrs Rudyard Kipling.

PRINCIPAL BOOKS BY RUDYARD KIPLING, WITH CONTENTS
OF SHORT-STORY COLLECTIONS

1886 *Departmental Ditties* (verse)
1888 *Plain Tails from the Hills*
      Lispeth
      Three and—an Extra
      Thrown Away
      Miss Youghal's Sais
      'Yoked with an Unbeliever'
      False Dawn
      The Rescue of Pluffles
      Cupid's Arrows
      The Three Musketeers
      His Chance in Life
      Watches of the Night
      The Other Man
      Consequences
      The Conversion of Aurelian McGoggin
      The Taking of Lungtungpen
      A Germ-Destroyer
      Kidnapped
      The Arrest of Lieutenant Golightly
      In the House of Suddhoo
      His Wedded Wife
      The Broken-link Handicap
      Beyond the Pale
      In Error
      A Bank Fraud
      Tods' Amendment
      The Daughter of the Regiment
      In the Pride of his Youth
      Pig
      The Rout of the White Hussars
      The Bronckhorst Divorce Case
      Venus Annodomini

The Bisara of Pooree
A Friend's Friend
The Gate of a Hundred Sorrows
The Madness of Private Ortheris
The Story of Muhammad Din
On the Strength of a Likeness
Wressley of the Foreign Office
By Word of Mouth
To be Filed for Reference

1890 *Soldiers Three*
This includes three collections previously published in the
Indian Railway Library in 1888.
Soldiers Three
   The God from the Machine
   Private Learoyd's Story
   The Big Drunk Draf
   The Solid Muldoon
   With the Main Guard
   In the Matter of a Private
   Black Jack
The Story of the Gadsbys
(there are nine episodes but they are not separate stories)
In Black and White
   Dray Wara Yow Dee
   The Judgment of Dungara
   At Howli Thana
   Gemini
   At Twenty-Two
   In Flood Time
   The Sending of Dana Da
   On the City Wall

1890 *Wee Willie Winkie*
This also includes three collections first published in India
in 1888.
Under the Deodars
   The Education of Otis Yeere
   At the Pit's Mouth
   A Wayside Comedy
   The Hill of Illusion
   A Second-Rate Woman
   Only a Subaltern

A Conference of the Powers
My Lord the Elephant
One View of the Question
'The Finest Story in the World'
His Private Honour
A Matter of Fact
The Lost Legion
In the Rukh
'Brugglesmith'
'Love-o'-Women'
The Record of Badalia Herodsfoot
Judson and the Empire
The Children of the Zodiac
1894 *The Jungle Book*
1895 *The Second Jungle Book*
1896 *The Seven Seas* (verse)
1897 *Captains Courageous*
1898 *The Day's Work*
The Bridge-Builders
A Walking Delegate
The Ship that Found Herself
The Tomb of his Ancestors
The Devil and the Deep Sea
William the Conqueror—Part I
William the Conqueror—Part II
.007
The Maltese Cat
'Bread upon the Waters'
An Error in the Fourth Dimension
My Sunday at Home
The Brushwood Boy
1899 *Stalky and Co.*
1901 *Kim*
1902 *The Just-So Stories*
1903 *The Five Nations* (verse)
1904 *Traffics and Discoveries*
The Captive
The Bonds of Discipline
A Sahibs' War
'Their Lawful Occasions': Part I
'Their Lawful Occasions': Part II

The Janeites
The Prophet and the Country
The Bull that Thought
A Madonna of the Trenches
The Propagation of Knowledge
A Friend of the Family
On the Gate: a Tale of '16
The Eye of Allah
The Gardener
1932 *Limits and Renewals*
Dayspring Mishandled
The Woman in his Life
The Tie
The Church that was at Antioch
Aunt Ellen
Fairy-Kist
A Naval Mutiny
The Debt
The Manner of Men
Unprofessional
Beauty Spots
The Miracle of St Jubanus
The Tender Achilles
Uncovenanted Mercies
1937 (posthumously) *Something of Myself*

SOME BOOKS ABOUT KIPLING

CHARLES CARRINGTON, *Rudyard Kipling: his Life and Work* (Macmillan, London, 1955)

J. M. S. TOMPKINS, *The Art of Rudyard Kipling* (Methuen, London, 1959)

ANDRÉ MAUROIS, *Magiciens et Logiciens* (Editions Bernard Grasset, Paris, 1935)

ANDRÉ CHEVRILLON, *Rudyard Kipling* (Librairie Plon, Paris, 1936)

L. C. DUNSTERVILLE, *Stalky's Reminiscences* (Cape, London, 1928)

G. C. BERESFORD, *Schooldays with Kipling* (Gollancz, London, 1936)

T. S. ELIOT (ed.) *A Choice of Kipling's Verse*, with an essay on Rudyard Kipling (Faber, London, 1942)

HILTON BROWN, *Rudyard Kipling: a New Appreciation* (Hamish Hamilton, London, 1945)

RUPERT CROFT-COOKE, *Rudyard Kipling* (Home and Van Thal, London, 1948)

J. I. M. STEWART, *Rudyard Kipling* (Gollancz, London, 1966)

ELLIOTT GILBERT, *The Good Kipling* (Manchester University Press, 1972)

ANDREW RUTHERFORD (ed.), *Kipling's Mind and Art* (Oliver and Boyd, Edinburgh and London, 1964)
Essays by:
W. L. Benwick, 'Re-reading Kipling'
Edmund Wilson, 'The Kipling that Nobody Read'
George Orwell, 'Rudyard Kipling'
Lionel Trilling, 'Kipling'
Noel Annan, 'Kipling's Place in the History of Ideas'
George Shepperson, 'The World of Rudyard Kipling'
Alan Sandison, 'Kipling: the Artist and the Empire'
Andrew Rutherford, 'Officers and Gentlemen'
Mark Kinkead-Weekes, 'Vision in Kipling's Novels'
J. H. Fenwick, 'Soldiers Three'

W. W. Robson, 'Kipling's Later Stories'

ELLIOTT GILBERT (ed., with an introduction), *Kipling and the Critics* (Peter Owen, London, 1966)
Essays by:
Andrew Lang, 'Mr Kipling's Stories'
Oscar Wilde, from 'The True Function and Value of Criticism'
Henry James, 'The Young Kipling'
Robert Buchanan, from 'The Voice of the Hooligan'
Max Beerbohm, 'PC X36'
Bonamy Dobrée, 'Rudyard Kipling'
Boris Ford, 'A Case for Kipling?'
George Orwell, 'Rudyard Kipling'
Lionel Trilling, 'Kipling'
C. S. Lewis, 'Kipling's World'
T. S. Eliot, 'The Unfading Genius of Rudyard Kipling'
J. M. S. Tompkins, 'Dayspring Mishandled' (from *The Art of Rudyard Kipling*)
Randall Jarrell, 'On Preparing to Read Kipling'
Steven Marcus, 'Stalky & Co.'
Elliott Gilbert, 'Without Benefit of Clergy: A Farewell to Ritual'

JOHN GROSS (ed.), *Rudyard Kipling: the man, his work and his world* (Weidenfeld and Nicolson, London 1972)
Essays by:
Betty Miller, 'Kipling's First Novel'
Janet Adam Smith, 'Boy of Letters'
A. W. Baldwin, 'John Lockwood Kipling'
Nirad C. Chaudhuri, 'The Finest Story about India—in English'
Michael Edwardes, 'Oh to meet an Army Man'
Philip Mason, 'Kipling and the Civilians'
James Morris, 'Hill Stations'
Colin MacInnes, 'Kipling and the Music Halls'
Leon Edel, 'A Young Man from the Provinces: Rudyard Kipling and Wolcott Balestier'
Louis Cornell, 'The American Venture'
George Shepperson, 'Kipling and the Boer War'
Eric Stokes, 'Kipling's Imperialism'
Robert Conquest, 'A Note on Kipling's Verse'
Gillian Avery, 'The Children's Writer'
Roger Lanedyn Green, 'The Countryman'

Alan Sandison, 'A Matter of Vision: Rudyard Kipling and
    Rider Haggard'
Bernard Bergonzi, 'Kipling and the First World War'
John Raymond, 'The Last Phase'
J. I. M. Stewart, 'Kipling's Reputation'
Philip French, 'Kipling and the Movies'

Index